# TRUE GRIT

www.transworldbooks.co.uk

# TRUE GRIT

The epic true stories of survival and
heroism that have shaped my life

Bear Grylls

BANTAM PRESS

LONDON · TORONTO · SYDNEY · AUCKLAND · JOHANNESBURG

TRANSWORLD PUBLISHERS
61–63 Uxbridge Road, London W5 5SA
A Random House Group Company
www.transworldbooks.co.uk

First published in Great Britain
in 2013 by Bantam Press
an imprint of Transworld Publishers

A CIP catalogue record for this book
is available from the British Library.

ISBNs 9780593071052 (cased)
9780593071069 (tpb)

Addresses for Random House Group Ltd companies outside the UK
can be found at: www.randomhouse.co.uk
The Random House Group Ltd Reg. No. 954009

The Random House Group Limited supports the Forest Stewardship Council®
(FSC®), the leading international forest-certification organisation. Our books
carrying the FSC label are printed on FSC®-certified paper. FSC is the only
forest-certification scheme supported by the leading environmental
organisations, including Greenpeace. Our paper procurement policy
can be found at www.randomhouse.co.uk/environment

Typeset in 11/16 pt Sabon by Falcon Oast Graphic Art Ltd.
Printed and bound in Great Britain by
CPI Group (UK) Ltd, Croydon, CR0 4YY

2 4 6 8 10 9 7 5 3 1

MIX
Paper from
responsible sources
FSC
www.fsc.org    FSC® C016897

To my heroes, past and present.
Forged through hardship, defined by their
actions and remembered for their spirit.
And to the few young who don't yet know they will
be tested and proven into the heroes of tomorrow.

# CONTENTS

Two roads diverged in a wood, and I—
I took the one less traveled by,
And that has made all the difference.

– ROBERT FROST

# INTRODUCTION

One of the questions that I get asked over and over again is: who are my heroes, my influences, my inspirations?

The truth is that it's not an easy question to answer.

For sure, my late father was a hero to me: adventurous, fun, humble – a man of the people – a risk taker, a climber, a commando and a loving, gentle father.

But so much of what has driven me to push myself mentally, physically, emotionally and spiritually, has come from some unlikely sources.

I hope this book will uncover and reveal to you some of the world's most inspiring, moving and mind-blowing feats of human endurance ever undertaken.

There were many to choose from. Some of these stories you will know, many you will not. And for every story of pain and hardship there were often dozens of others to rival it – harrowing and inspiring in equal measure.

But I have put this collection together as it stands, because not only have these stories always moved me, but they also cover such a broad spectrum: from Antarctic hell, to desert disaster; from unparalleled wartime courage to facing the unimaginable horror of hacking your own arm off in order to survive.

But what drives men and women to plumb such depths and to risk it all? Where do those wells of resilience, grit and determination come from? Are we born with them, or are they something we learn?

Again, there are no simple answers, and if I have learned anything it is that there is no mould for a hero – they come in all sorts of unlikely guises. And people often surprise themselves when tested.

At the same time, there is an element of me that sees how certain people are destined for greatness. They develop character and courage, and they cultivate self-belief and vision from a young age. And it stands them well when their time of testing finally comes.

Ultimately, I like to think this quote by the mountaineering author Walt Unsworth sums up the type of character that seeks out adventure:

> There are men for whom the unattainable has a special attraction. Usually they are not experts: their ambitions and fantasies are strong enough to brush aside the doubts which more cautious men might have. Determination and faith are their strongest weapons.

I also believe that we are all capable of great things, as well as having incredible reserves of strength that we might never know we possess. Like with a grape, you don't really know what it is made of until it is squeezed.

One thing all these stories have in common is that, in each case, every one of these individuals was squeezed to within an inch of their life, and they all had to plumb untold reservoirs of courage, tenacity and fortitude.

In the process some died, and some lived. But through their struggles they each touched at the very heart of what it means to be human – they found a fire inside that goes far beyond the physical.

I hope that this book serves as a reminder that this spirit, and glowing ember, lives deep within us all. It just sometimes takes a little coaxing into flame.

I hope that these stories will inspire you to be that little bit braver and that little bit stronger, when your times of testing come around.

And remember, as Winston Churchill once said, 'When you are going through hell, keep going.'

But for now, sit back and let me introduce you to my heroes . . .

# NANDO PARRADO: THE TASTE OF HUMAN FLESH

*'This wasn't heroism or
adventure. This was hell.'*

For 22-year-old Nando Parrado it was only ever meant to be a pleasant family trip.

He played for a Uruguayan rugby team who had chartered a flight to Santiago in Chile for an exhibition match. He'd asked his mother, Eugenia, and his sister, Susy, if they wanted to come along on the journey – one that meant flying over the Andes in a twin-engine turboprop.

Flight 571 took off on Friday 13 October 1972, and a few of the guys joked that this wasn't the best day to be flying over a mountain range that can harbour difficult and dangerous weather for pilots. Hot air rises from the foothills and hits cold air at the snow line. The resulting maelstrom is bad news for aircraft.

But their jokes were just that. Jokes. Because the weather reports looked fine.

Weather, though, has a habit of changing very quickly in the mountains. And especially in these mountains. The plane had been in the air just a couple of hours when the pilot was forced to land in the town of Mendoza in the foothills of the Andes.

They overnighted there. Next day, the pilots were in two minds as to whether they should continue the journey. Their passengers wanted to get to their rugby match. They put pressure on the pilots to fly.

Which turned out to be a very bad move.

The turboprop was flying over the Planchon Pass when the turbulence hit. Four sharp bumps. Some of the guys cheered, like they were riding on a rollercoaster. Nando's mother and sister looked frightened. They were holding hands. Nando himself opened his mouth to reassure them.

But the words didn't come, as the plane suddenly dropped several hundred feet.

Nobody was cheering any more.

The plane was shuddering violently. Some of the passengers started to scream. Nando's neighbour, who was sitting by the window, pointed outside. Less than ten metres from the wing tip, Nando could see the mountainside: a huge wall of rock and snow.

His neighbour asked if they should be so close, his voice trembling with dread.

Nando didn't answer. He was too busy listening to the horrible shrieking of the engines as the pilots desperately tried to gain height. The whole plane was shaking so badly it felt like it was going to break apart.

Nando caught the terrified glances of his mother and sister.

And then it happened.

A violent shudder.

An awful grinding sound as metal twisted against rock. The plane had hit the mountainside. It was being ripped to bits.

Nando looked up. He didn't see the top of the fuselage. He saw open sky.

He felt cold air on his face.

And saw clouds in the gangway.

There was no time to pray. No time even to think. He felt a tremendous force ripping him from his seat. A violent, deafening noise all around.

Nando Parrado must have been sure he was about to die a grisly, painful, terrifying death.

Then he was plunged into darkness.

*

Nando was unconscious for three days after the crash. So he didn't see some of the injuries his companions sustained.

One man had been stabbed in the stomach by a steel tube. When his friend tried to remove it, a length of oozing intestine emerged from his gut.

Another man's calf muscle had torn away from the bone, then twisted about his shin. The leg bone itself was open to the air. His friend had to squash the muscle back in place before bandaging it up.

One woman had been crushed in a pile of seats that nobody could untangle. Her legs were broken and she was yelling in agony. There was nothing that anyone could do, except leave her to die.

Nando's head had swollen to the size of a basketball. He was still breathing, but nobody expected him to live. He defied his companions' expectations, though, and awoke from his coma three days later.

He was lying on the floor of the wrecked fuselage where the survivors were huddled. The dead were piled in the snow outside. The wings had been ripped from the plane. So had the tail. They had crashed into a snowy, stony valley, where they could see nothing but the forbidding peaks of the mountains all around them. But for now, all Nando's attention was on his family.

The news was bad. His mother was dead.

Nando was pierced with grief, but he didn't allow himself to cry. Tears, he knew, would cost his body salt. Without salt, you die. He had been out of his coma for only minutes, but already he was displaying a refusal to give in.

A determination to survive, no matter what.

Fifteen people had died in that horrific air crash, but Nando's next thought was for his sister. Susy was alive, but only just. Her face was smeared in blood, her broken body too painful to move given her massive internal injuries. Her feet were already black with frostbite. Delirious, she was calling out for their mother, begging her to take them home, away from the dreadful cold. Nando hugged her for the rest of the day, and all that night, in the hope that his warmth would keep her alive.

But, gradually, the full extent of the danger they were in hit home.

Night-time temperatures in those mountains could reach –40°C. While he was in a coma, the others had packed holes in the fuselage with snow and suitcases to give them some protection from the deathly cold mountain winds. Even so, Nando awoke to find his clothes stuck to his skin. Everybody's hair and lips were white with frost.

The fuselage – their only shelter – had come to a halt on top of a huge glacier. Even though they were very high up, the mountain peaks that surrounded them were so high they had to crick their necks to see the summits. The air was so thin it burned their lungs. The sun's rays would blister their skin. The glare of the snow dazzled and blinded them.

They would have had a better chance of survival if they were stranded at sea or in the desert. At least those two environments host life. Up here, nothing could live. No animals. No plants. They rationed the small amounts of food they managed to gather from the cabin and the suitcases. But there was very little, and it soon ran out.

Day turned to freezing night, then back into day again. On the fifth day after the crash, the four strongest survivors decided to try to climb out of the valley. They returned hours later: oxygen-starved, exhausted and utterly defeated. It was impossible, they said.

And 'impossible' is a bad word to have in your mind when you're trying to survive.

*

On the eighth day, Nando's sister died in his arms. Once more, though racked with grief, he fought back tears.

Nando buried her in the snow. Everything had been taken from him, except one thing: his father, back in Uruguay. He made a silent promise to him that he would not allow himself to die here in the frozen wastes of the Andes.

There was water everywhere, in the form of snow. It soon became unbearably agonizing to eat it, though, because the dry cold had made their lips bloodied and raw. They started to die of thirst, until one of the survivors invented a snow-melting device from a sheet of aluminium. They would pile snow on to it and leave it in the sun to melt.

But no amount of water would bring them back from the brink of starvation.

Their meagre food supplies ran out after a week. At altitude, and in the cold, the human body needs far more nourishment than at sea level, but now they were getting nothing. Very quickly, their bodies started consuming themselves. They needed protein. If they didn't get it, they'd die. It was as simple as that.

And there was only one source of food available to them now.

The bodies of the dead were lying outside in the snow. Their flesh was perfectly preserved in the sub-zero temperatures. Nando was the first to suggest that they use it to survive. Their only other option was to wait for death to take them, and he wasn't prepared to do that.

They started with the pilot.

Four of the survivors found shards of glass in the fuselage. They used these to hack strips of flesh from the pilot's corpse. Nando took a piece. It was frozen hard, of course, and a curious grey-white in colour.

He stared at it in his palm. Around him, he could see some survivors doing the same. Others had already placed the frozen gobbets of human meat into their mouths and were chewing with difficulty.

It's just meat, he told himself. Nothing more.

He slipped the flesh past his cracked lips and on to his tongue.

It had no taste. Just texture: hard and sinewy. Nando chewed a couple of times, then forced the lump of human meat down his throat.

He didn't feel guilty. Just angry, that their lives had come to this. And although the flesh didn't stop the agonizing pangs of hunger, it gave him hope that he might stave off starvation until rescuers found them.

Because every rescue team in Uruguay would be looking for them. Wouldn't they? They wouldn't have to continue this grue-some diet for long. Surely?

One of the survivors had found a little transistor radio in the wreckage, which he'd managed to get working. The day after they'd first tasted human meat, they managed to tune in to a news programme.

It told them exactly what they didn't want to hear. The search for them had been called off. Conditions were too treacherous. There was simply no chance of finding any survivors.

*

'Breathe,' they would tell themselves when despair started to grip them. 'If you breathe, it means you're alive.'

But now that all hope of rescue was lost, they must have wondered how many more breaths they had in them.

The mountain had more horrors to deliver. The next came in the form of a night-time avalanche. Countless tons of snow slipped over the fuselage in the middle of a winter storm. Large quantities made their way inside the wreckage, covering Nando and many other survivors. Suffocated by their icy blankets, six of them died.

Nando would later compare it to being trapped in a submarine at the bottom of the sea. A furious storm was blowing, so they didn't dare venture out, and they didn't know how much snow had compacted above them. There was every chance that this would be their icy tomb.

The water-melting device no longer worked now they were hidden from the sun. And the only bodies were those of the newly dead.

Before, only those who had cut up the corpses had been forced to watch. Now, all but a few were nearby as the few brave survivors hacked into the dead. The sun had not dried out the flesh of these fresh bodies, so eating their meat was a very different prospect. It was not hard and dry, but squishy and oily.

Raw.

Wet.

It oozed blood, and was full of lumpy gristle. And it was far from tasteless. It took everything Nando and the others had not to gag as they forced wobbling meat down their throats, surrounded by the pungent, sickly stench of festering human fat and tissue.

The blizzard ended. It took eight days for the survivors to dig the avalanched snow out of the fuselage.

In the detached tail of the aircraft the survivors knew that there were some batteries, which might allow them to get the plane's radio working, so they could call for help. Nando and three of his companions journeyed for several painful, exhausting hours across the frozen snow, and eventually found the batteries. In the days that followed they tried to fix the radio, but failed.

In the meantime, the crash site was becoming an increasingly horrific place to be.

To start with, the survivors had limited themselves to small strips of flesh from the bodies of their fallen companions. Some refused to do it, but reports say most came round to the idea when they realized they had no other option. And as time went on, the brutal reality of their diet was there for everyone to see.

Human bones littered the crash site. Amputated arms and legs, the flesh still uneaten, were stacked by an opening to the fuselage – a grisly, but easily accessible, larder. They had stretched large sheets of human fat over the plane to dry in the sun. The survivors had moved on from eating just the flesh, to consuming the offal too. Kidneys. Livers. Hearts. Lungs. They had even cracked open the skulls of the dead in order to scoop out and eat the brain matter inside. The split, empty heads lay discarded in the snow.

Two dead bodies, however, remained untouched. Out of respect for Nando, the others had left the corpses of his mother and his sister unsullied. But Nando knew they couldn't leave perfectly good food there for long. The time would come when survival would win out over respect. He had to try to fetch help, before he was forced to eat his own family. He had to battle against the mountain.

He knew he would probably die trying. But that was better than not trying at all.

They had been stranded for sixty days when Nando and his two companions – Roberto and Tintin – set out to find help. There was no way down from their position. They could only go up. But they did not know that they were about to attempt to scale one of the highest peaks in the Andes – a peak that stretched nearly 17,000 feet above sea level.

Experienced mountaineers would have thought twice about an expedition like this. They certainly wouldn't have attempted it after sixty days of near-starvation, without the equipment crucial to extreme mountaineering.

Nando and his gritty companions had no crampons, no ice picks, no cold-weather gear. No safety ropes or steel anchors. They wore only the clothes they could cobble together from the suitcases in the wreckage, and they were weak with malnutrition, thirst, exhaustion and exposure. This was the first time they had ever tried to climb a mountain. It didn't take long for Nando's inexperience to show.

If you've never suffered altitude sickness, you can't imagine what it's like. Your head splits with pain. You can barely stand with dizziness. You're overcome with tiredness. Go too high and you risk brain damage and death. They say you should climb no more than 1,000 feet in a day when you are at altitude, to allow yourself to acclimatize.

Nando and his friends knew none of this. They climbed 2,000 feet in the first morning. Their blood thickened as it tried to conserve oxygen. They hyperventilated. They dehydrated.

They also kept going.

Their only sustenance was scraps of human meat that they had stripped from the bodies of their dead friends and stuffed into an old sock to transport it. But by now, cannibalism was the least of their worries. The biggest problem they had was the sheer magnitude of the task ahead of them.

In their inexperience, they chose the most difficult routes up into the mountains. Nando led the way, and he had to learn advanced mountaineering skills on the job. He had to find his way up impossibly steep gradients covered with sheet ice. He had to avoid deadly couloirs and traverse razor-thin, slippery ledges. When they came across an absolute sheer rock face, hundreds of feet high and covered with compacted snow and ice, Nando didn't retreat. He used a sharp-tipped stick to carve a stairway up it.

At night, the temperature dropped so low that their water bottle cracked and shattered. Even during the day, the men couldn't stop shivering from the inhuman cold and their utter exhaustion. They reached the peak of the mountain against all the odds, but the cruel Andes still had another blow to deal. Nando had expected to see beyond the mountain range. Looking around from that incredible vantage point, he saw nothing but other peaks as far as the eye could see.

No green.

No civilization.

No help.

Nothing but snow, ice and rock.

When you're fighting to survive, morale is everything. Despite the disappointment, Nando didn't allow himself to be downhearted.

He could make out two smaller peaks whose tips were not covered in ice. Was this a good sign? Perhaps they indicated the edge of the mountain range? But they were, he estimated, 50 miles away. They didn't have enough human meat for all three of them to continue the journey. And so Tintin, the weakest of the three, was sent back to the crash site so that Nando and Roberto could continue. It took him only an hour to slide back to his friends in the fuselage.

They were descending now, towards the clouds, putting themselves at the mercy of not only the mountain, but also gravity.

Nando fell, and tumbled into walls of ice. His thin, weakened body was bruised and battered. Still he and Roberto went on, forcing themselves to put one step in front of another, even though they were in exhausted agony.

As they lost height and the temperature increased, the human meat they had stashed in the sock started to thaw and putrefy. The stench of the rotting flesh was bad enough, but it was also becoming apparent the meat was inedible. If they didn't find help soon, they would simply waste away.

On the ninth day of their trek, however, their luck changed. They saw a man.

On the tenth day, the man brought help.

He also brought supplies. Nando and Roberto ate their first hot, non-human food for seventy-two days. More importantly, they gave the local police the message they had crossed the Andes to deliver. 'I come from a plane that fell into the mountains . . . In the plane there are still fourteen injured people.'

And on 22 and 23 December, thanks to Nando and Roberto's stubborn refusal to be beaten, and just in time for Christmas, a helicopter airlifted the remaining survivors to safety.

Of the forty-five people on that dreadful flight, sixteen survived. The greatest wonder is that there were not more deaths.

Many people, when they hear the story of Nando Parrado and his desperate companions, take away nothing but a grisly tale of human cannibalism. Some people even criticize them for the decision they took.

They're wrong, of course.

In one of their darkest moments, the survivors made a pact with each other. If any of them died, they gave permission for the others to eat their bodies. Because they knew that, in eating the meat of their dead companions, they weren't showing a disregard for human life. They were showing just how precious it is. So precious that they were willing to do anything to cling to it as an unimaginably harsh environment did its best to rip it from them.

The survivors of Flight 571 showed remarkable courage, ingenuity and, I think, dignity. They demonstrated a fact as old as life itself: that when death seems almost certain, one of the most human reactions is a refusal to lie down and let it win.

# JULIANE KOEPCKE: CAULDRON OF HELL

*'I'm falling, slicing through the sky ...
about two miles above the earth.'*

JULIANE KOEPCKE

Christmas Eve, 1971. A 17-year-old student born in Peru to German parents is firmly strapped into her aircraft seat next to her mother. It's a short hop, from Lima to Pucallpa, and should only take an hour.

But Juliane Koepcke's journey is going to take a lot longer than that.

The aircraft is a Lockheed Electra turboprop, cruising at 10,000 feet. When she'd first seen it back on the ground, Juliane had thought it looked awesome. She didn't know that it was designed principally for flying over desert landscapes. Or that it was totally unsuited for taking on the turbulent mountain air above the Andes.

And little did she know that the aircraft was about to fly into the eye of a storm.

Minutes ago, it was daylight outside. Now it is as dark as night. Out of the windows Juliane can see violent strobes of lightning splitting the skies all around her.

The aircraft starts to shudder. It feels as if some external power is shaking it, like a child shaking a toy. The aircraft might have looked mighty and formidable on the ground, but up here, surrounded by such massive forces of nature, it is as insignificant as a humble fly.

The overhead lockers suddenly drop open. Luggage tumbles out. Food scatters everywhere. Everybody's screaming.

Juliane Koepcke tries to stay calm. So does her mother. She tries to reassure Juliane, to tell her everything will be all right.

But it won't be all right.

A searing white light blinds Juliane. Something's happened to the right-hand wing. A lightning strike? It's impossible to say. There's a sickening jerk. The front of the plane tips downwards. The screaming gets worse, but it's dwarfed by the deafening roar of the engines as the stricken aircraft plummets, faster and faster, towards the ground.

Juliane hears her mother speak among the screaming of both engines and humans. It is a quiet acknowledgement that death is approaching.

The plane is breaking up around her. And suddenly, Juliane Koepcke realizes that she is not surrounded by the other passengers any more. Or even by the plane itself. She can no longer hear either the screams or the engines.

All she can hear is the immense roar of the wind in her ears.

She is still strapped into her seat, which has broken away from the body of the airliner. She is still 10,000 feet in the air.

She's falling back to earth. Fast.

But, amazingly, her epic story of survival is only just beginning.

Juliane Koepcke would later recall how the seatbelt strapping her to the seat, dug tightly into her guts, pushing the air from her lungs as she fell. There was no time to feel scared. She slipped in and out of reality. During a moment of consciousness, she sensed that she was upside down and spinning fast, drilling her way through the empty air as the jungle canopy below spun up to meet her.

Then darkness, as she blacked out again.

She awoke to find herself lying on the rainforest floor. The plane seat was on top of her, but she was no longer strapped in.

She looked at her watch. Nine in the morning.

She tried to stand. Sudden dizziness. She collapsed to the jungle floor again.

Her collarbone felt strange. She touched it. Broken: the two ends of the break were pushing upwards, but mercifully they hadn't punctured the skin. There was a deep cut on her left leg, but strangely it wasn't bleeding. She felt lethargic with concussion, and had lost her glasses, so it was difficult for her to see clearly for more than a few metres.

Only then did it strike her what had happened. And that now, she was utterly alone. She called out to her mother, but nobody called back. The only sounds she could hear were those of the rainforest.

She had survived the unsurvivable. Now she would have to survive in one of the most unforgiving environments on earth.

Dense, uninhabited, primary jungle.

If you want to get out of your comfort zone, go to the jungle.

A mixture of constant high temperatures and humidity, plenty of water and plenty of sunlight mean that rainforests are homes to the most complex ecosystems on the planet. Life is everywhere: crawling, clawing, biting through the undergrowth, crouched in the trees, slithering along the branches. It can take your breath away with its beauty; but it can also kill you in an instant.

Juliane Koepcke knew this. The jungle was not, to her, totally unfamiliar. Her parents had been zoologists, and had taken her to the jungle when she was a child.

Consequently, she also knew that the worst thing she could do, alone and injured, was panic. She needed a clear head and a calm mind. She needed to be alert, and to consider her every move carefully. If she allowed herself to freak out, she'd probably never make it through a day.

She realized that she was only wearing one shoe. The other must have come off as she fell from the sky. In her previous visits to the jungle, she'd always worn rubber boots to protect herself from snake bites. Venomous snakes or spiders could be lying anywhere, camouflaged to invisibility, but guaranteed to strike if disturbed. One covered foot was better than none, she figured.

Other than the shoe, she was wearing nothing but a thin summer dress. Ripped to shreds already. Hardly the ideal gear for jungle survival.

Then the thirst hit her: sudden and overpowering. Juliane looked around to see broad green leaves covered with moisture. She sucked the water off the leaves.

Moving and navigating in the jungle is an art form. And it is also bloody hard work – even with all the right gear and footwear. One section of jungle can appear almost indistinguishable from another. To the untrained eye, it can be just a blur of noisy, steamy, filthy, stinking green.

In her previous experiences, Juliane had used a machete to hack markers into the trees to ensure she wasn't walking around in circles. But now she had nothing. So she examined her surroundings carefully and remembered an especially imposing tree. A fixed landmark to help her orientate herself. Then she started to stagger around the area, looking for survivors.

And, especially, for her mother.

She found nothing but a tin of boiled sweets that had landed in the vicinity with her. Hardly what she was hoping for, but it was sustenance of a sort.

Far above, through the thick jungle canopy, she heard an aircraft circling. She knew what that meant: rescue teams were searching for survivors. But there was no way they'd ever be able to see her. Her spirits sank.

If she was going to get out of there, she would have to do it alone.

The hard way.

Above all the strange noises of the jungle she caught another sound. Running water.

She remembered a piece of survival advice her father had once given her: if you're lost in the jungle, find running water and follow it. It doesn't matter how feeble it is: chances are it will meet another tributary and become a stream. Then that stream will meet another stream and become a small river. And where you find a river, you've a good chance of finding people . . .

She located the source: a tiny, weak stream, blocked continuously by fallen trees. As she trekked, the stream grew a little wider – twenty inches. Exhausted and disorientated, she continued to follow it. She would make it her path to safety.

At about 6 p.m., night fell swiftly, as it always does in the jungle. Utter blackness surrounded her, as did the strange, eerie sounds of the rainforest at night. She had been shown how to light a fire by the friction of rubbing sticks together. A fire would give her some warmth, and ward away dangerous animals. But the process of lighting a fire was impossible: it was the rainy season, and everything was soaked through – not to mention that she had no tools to cut into the wood in the first place.

Night-time can be very intimidating in the jungle, but Juliane was too burned out to be afraid. She slumped against a tree, exhausted.

*

Her first night had done little to relieve her exhaustion. Her fatigue was the result of both shock and concussion. But Juliane knew she had to press on.

She followed the same stream, taking care to step with her sandalled foot first. The trickle of water twisted and turned its way through the undergrowth, adding distances she couldn't even measure to her path through the jungle. The further she walked, the more she felt the energy draining from her body. But she couldn't risk taking any shortcuts. Without her glasses she couldn't see very far into the distance. She dared not stray from the stream. And so she continued to struggle, her strength continually ebbing away.

Lost in a jungle, humans need to be aware that they are not the only ones searching for water and food. Every other animal and plant is doing the same. So while a stream can be a tool for survival, it can also be a magnet for danger.

She passed a bird-eating spider – the second biggest spider in the world with venomous fangs that can easily puncture human skin. She eased her way gingerly past it, but it wasn't the worst jungle creature she was going to encounter by a long shot. She later heard the ominous, slow flapping of wings. Longer and louder than any other bird. With a sick feeling in her gut she knew that she was listening to a king vulture.

And she knew exactly what the king vulture feeds on.

Carrion. Rotting flesh.

She turned a bend in the river, and there she saw it: a row of three seats from her aircraft. And strapped in to the three seats were two men and one woman.

They were upside down, their heads stuck into the floor of the jungle. Their legs were broken, pointing awkwardly up into the air.

She saw the vultures next. They were perched in the trees,

watching and waiting. The flesh was still too fresh for their liking. But soon they would descend and rip the rotting meat from the corpses.

She looked around to see if there were any more bodies. Nothing. Just a few scraps of metal littering the jungle floor. And so she hurried on her way, leaving the dead and the beady eyes of the hungry vultures.

She wasn't carrion. Not quite yet, anyway.

*

Juliane dared not eat anything.

The rainy season is not the best time to be foraging for food in the jungle, as most of the fruits flourish during the dry season. That's not to say the jungle can't be an abundant source of food at any time, but you have to know what you're eating. There are many plants that look delicious but are in fact deadly poisonous.

Juliane had no knife to hack out palm hearts or roots that she knew would give her sustenance, nor any means to catch fish or animals. When her last boiled sweet ran out, she had nothing to eat.

She did, at least, have water, but the stream along which she was walking had brown scum floating along the top. In previous visits to the jungle, she had always boiled water before she drank it. That's the sensible thing to do – the only way to be sure of killing the myriad bugs that can infest unknown water sources. But Juliane had no means of making fire.

So she drank the dirty water in huge quantities – both to keep hydrated and to stave off hunger by keeping her belly full. It is always a risk drinking water like this, but desperate times call for desperate measures.

She tried to keep track of the days, but it wasn't easy. At six in the morning it grew light. At six in the evening, night fell fast. After the deep, concussed slumber of her first night, sleep seldom came again. During the long nights she found herself surrounded by mosquitoes which seemed intent on eating her alive. Her skin was covered with burning welts, and the only relief came when it rained.

Only that was no relief at all. It is cold at night during the rainy season, and the freezing rain soaked her thin cotton dress, leaching all the warmth from her body. It was during those unbearably long, painful nights that she felt herself steadily abandoning all hope . . .

Little wonder then that, starving, partially concussed, her bones broken, her clothes soaked, her skin burning with sores and bites, that any sense of time became jumbled. So, she wasn't sure if it was on the fifth day or the sixth that she heard the call of a hoatzin – a bird which she remembered makes its nest on wide rivers under open skies. She scrambled through the thick brush, which continuously ripped at her skin, and eventually found herself by a broad river.

There was zero sign of human habitation.

The river bank was too overgrown to walk along. So, she waded along the shallow edge of the water, wisely feeling her way with a stick so that she could scare off any stingrays that might be lurking in the mud.

She kept sinking into the deep oozing mud. And so she soon decided to swim instead. Which took a lot of guts. She knew there were piranhas in that water. Then there were the caimans – South American relatives of the alligator, that can grow up to four metres long.

She had little choice but to brave them both.

And pray.

She drifted slowly downstream with the current. Then, as

darkness fell, she pulled herself up on to the bank for another of those agonizingly long jungle nights.

*

Juliane had a cut on the back of her right arm. It was difficult to see but felt uncomfortable so she twisted her arm around to take a better look.

Maggots.

Flies had laid their eggs in the open wound. The eggs had now hatched and the larvae were a good centimetre long. The gash was infested as they fed off the rotten skin.

Juliane tried to pick them out. But without success.

She knew that these parasites would not harm their host – indeed, maggots can help keep a wound clean because they only feed on dead tissue. But while the wound was open it could become infected – and an infected, open wound in the jungle could kill her very fast.

There was little she could do, so she left the crawling maggots where they were and lowered herself once more into the piranha and alligator river and continued her dangerous swim.

As the day wore on, she knew that her body was steadily falling apart around her. She could soon feel a sharp pain between her shoulders. She touched it gingerly. Blood. As she'd been drifting downstream, the sun had been beating down on her back, scorching the skin. She had bleeding, second-degree burns just from the sunlight.

Soon, too exhausted to continue, she collapsed on the river bank. She awoke to find several baby caimans just inches from her body.

And, nearby, the mother, preparing to attack: hissing, mouth open.

She fled into the river, hoping the caiman would stay with its young.

But soon she had an even worse enemy to deal with: her hunger. She'd been struggling through the jungle for more than a week, and she was severely weakened. She found herself on all fours, frantically trying to catch one of the frogs she saw jumping around her, but without success . . .

\*

On the tenth day of her jungle nightmare Juliane was drifting like a corpse through the water, in a daze of confusion and pain, when she saw it.

At first, she thought her eyes were deceiving her. A hallucination, brought on by exhaustion on the brink of death.

But then she realized it was real. There was a small boat on the river bank.

She dragged her broken, bleeding body towards it. There were footsteps leading from the boat up the bank. She crawled after them. It took her hours just to cover a hundred yards. But she finally found a simple shelter. There was a canister of petrol there, for the outboard motor of the boat. She poured some on to her maggot-infested wound. It was agony, but it had the desired effect: the maggots – most of them, at least – came worming their way to the surface and she was able to wipe them away.

Then she discovered a tarpaulin and wrapped it round her to protect her skin from the mosquitoes. That night she slept like a baby in that little shelter. She would later say it felt like a five-star hotel.

The following day, three men found her.

She explained who she was, that she had fallen from the skies and survived for ten days in the jungle. They stared at her in amazement, not knowing how any human could have survived such an ordeal.

And they also stared at her in horror. It was not her bleeding back that horrified them the most, nor the maggot-infested wound, nor the broken skin, blistered with angry, suppurating insect bites.

It was her eyes. The blood vessels had burst all across her eyeballs from her extreme fall at terminal velocity. They were oozing blood – sockets of weeping red.

Juliane Koepcke had fallen two miles from the sky and survived through sheer good luck. But after that, luck had very little to do with it.

She survived the horrific ordeal of the next ten days by using the little knowledge she had to very good effect. Despite the terrifying situation she found herself in, she stayed calm and adapted her mindset to survive the jungle terrain around her. She trusted her instinct and refused to give in, despite the often hopeless outlook of her situation.

How many people in Juliane's situation would have panicked? But Juliane knew that to panic was to die. She kept her cool and she kept moving. She ignored the pain, and she stuck to her plan. And, ultimately, it was that indomitable survivor spirit that saved her life.

Now there's a girl with some real grit.

# JOHN MCDOUALL STUART: THE MADDEST EXPLORER EVER?

*'The explorations of Mr John McDouall Stuart may truly be said, without disparaging his brother explorers, to be amongst the most important in the history of Australian discovery.'*

WILLIAM HARDMAN, EDITOR OF THE JOURNALS OF JOHN MCDOUALL STUART

JOHN M'DOUALL STUART, THE AUSTRALIAN EXPLORER.

It's a long way from Fife in Scotland to the Australian outback. And I'm not just talking about physical distance.

In summer, temperatures in the arid zone of the outback can top 45°C. In winter, they can drop below freezing. The desert lands are so vast you can travel for days without meeting anyone or anything. And while nowadays it's possible to take tourist trips into the outback, or go on bushcraft tours, in the mid-nineteenth century very few people had dared to venture far into the Australian heartland. They preferred to keep to the exterior, where it was fertile. Where there was water. Where the temperatures were less extreme.

All of which makes it intriguing that the outback's most persistent explorer was a Scot. His refusal to let the stark, grim, unrelentingly severe conditions of the Australian interior beat him, means that now many national monuments are named after him.

And with good reason.

The man in question was John McDouall Stuart, and he was one of the toughest – and some might say most eccentric – explorers in history.

*

Stuart left Scotland for Australia at the age of 23.

He was five foot six inches tall and weighed less than nine stone. On the voyage out, he was found on deck clutching a blood-soaked handkerchief to his mouth. Ordinarily that was a sign of tuberculosis. In this case it was a symptom of the stomach ulcers that would plague him all his life.

You wouldn't think, to look at him, that he would turn out to be one of the toughest men in the fifty-year-old colony. But tough explorers aren't ever made in a mould. They become tough by displaying spirit and determination against overwhelming odds. Stuart was made from that stock.

When he arrived in Australia, he started work as a surveyor, marking out blocks of land for new settlers in the semi-arid bush. There he learned to love the remote areas of the Australian inland.

Stuart also developed a reputation for excellent bushcraft skills. As a result, he was approached by the British explorer, Captain Charles Sturt, to join him on his 1844 expedition inland.

The plan was to explore north-western New South Wales and then head on further into Central Australia. They managed this with a small team, but the expedition had a brutal effect on their health. Captain Sturt suffered acute scurvy in the desert interior; as the expedition wore on he became almost blind. Good job he had Stuart with him, who was able to use his excellent surveying skills to map the areas they travelled.

But Stuart also grew very seriously ill with scurvy, not to mention persistent ulcers and beriberi – a horrific illness that can cause paralysis, vomiting and mental impairment. When Stuart returned he was so thin you could see his bones, his gums were bleeding profusely, his teeth were loose and his muscles wasted. He was bedridden for months, and his doctor didn't think he'd survive.

You'd think an experience like that might put him off exploring this forbidding landscape for ever. It didn't.

Stuart liked it in the bush. Where other people saw an empty wasteland, he saw much more. He saw how watching flocks of birds, or following cracks of rocks, could lead you to precious water. He learned to make shelters from stringybark. He could employ his surveying skills to navigate accurately, using compass bearings and landmarks. He became sensitive to subtle changes in the landscape.

It was as if he was at one, naturally, with this harsh environment.

As the months and years passed, Stuart spent more time in the bush than in the towns. And, in May 1858, when he was 42 years old, he set off on his first major expedition.

The plan was to explore the area beyond the Oratunga mine in the Flinders mountains of South Australia, where no white person had set foot. Ever.

Around the same time, an explorer named Benjamin Herschel Babbage was preparing for a similar, but much better-funded, expedition. Babbage and his men were to take with them such luxuries as 20 kilos of chocolate, 38 kilos of German sausage, 150 sheep and two 22-litre water condensers.

The tough, weather-beaten Stuart and his two companions took, in total, just six horses, a compass, and four weeks' worth of the most basic rations.

Stuart and his men headed into the bush. They came to the vast salt lake – now known as Lake Torrens – 200 kilometres wide and 30 kilometres long. The temperatures were burning hot. The land gave them nothing to drink.

They found a member of Babbage's team. That expedition had not been a great success, and one of their number had been left behind by the others.

He was dead. His skin had shrunk tight against his skeleton and browned 'like the top of the drum'. Driven wild by thirst, he had cut the throats of three pack horses so he could drink their blood. The true horror of his final moments, though, was scratched in a few words on his metal water bottle as he lay there dying:

'My eyes dazzle. My tongue burns. I can see no way. God help, I can't get up . . .'

It was the kind of place that sucked the very life out of those not hardy enough to endure it.

Stuart spent four months in this harsh environment. He travelled 2,400 kilometres. No wonder that he returned to civilization with a growing reputation as the toughest explorer of the age.

But the truth was, he'd barely even started.

Stuart was as weather-beaten and rugged as his surroundings. He was certainly no gentleman, and had a taste for strong rum. He was, according to one report, 'not only the beastliest drunkard but the dirtiest man I ever had to deal with'. Or to use the words of a 14-year-old boy who once met him: 'He is such a funny little man, he is always drunk . . . on coming off one of his long journeys, he shut himself up in a room, and was drunk for three days.'

He must have come across as a pretty crazy guy – and getting crazier – but he obviously didn't much care what other people thought of him. He avoided company. He avoided crowds. This was a man who lived to explore.

At the time, South Australia was completely cut off from the northern coast. There was no road cutting across the continent, and there was no telegraph wire.

If somebody could find a route from coast to coast – say, from Adelaide in the south to Darwin in the north – both roads and wire could be built. It would mean that South Australia would have a link with the north and, by extension, to the rest of the world.

Stuart made the discovery of such a route his driving goal in life.

Most explorers give themselves plenty of time to recuperate after expeditions such as Stuart's punishing trek of 1858 into the outback. The body needs time to heal. So, sometimes, does the mind.

But Stuart didn't have the time or the inclination for anything as comforting as rest and recuperation. He wanted to get back in the saddle.

And so, a few months later, in 1859, he launched another assault on the harsh interior of Australia. He found himself a second-in-command called William Kekwick.

Stuart had learned a great deal about how to be a leader when he had been part of Captain Sturt's team – or, rather, how not to be a leader. Remarkably, by the end of that expedition, Sturt hadn't even known Stuart's Christian name.

When Stuart and Kekwick found undiscovered springs near Mount Eyre, on the other hand, Stuart named them after his second-in-command. He may have been the beastliest drunkard and the grubbiest man in town, but he knew how to look after his men. And it would be a source of personal pride to him that, in all the gruelling journeys he ever made to the Australian interior, no men ever died on any of his expeditions.

Although he very nearly lost his own life. Many times.

Stuart completed a total of three such expeditions in 1859, with barely time to catch his breath between them. Come 1860, he allowed himself only two months' rest before hurling himself back at the arid wastelands. He instructed Kekwick to gather ten good men. His second-in-command came back with only one – an unfit and unimpressive young man called Ben Head.

Nobody else would dare to brave such a crazy endeavour.

Stuart wasn't put off by the lack of a great team. His unconventional method of exploring was to travel light and fast. So, the three of them set out to discover the very centre of Australia.

It was a punishing expedition by anyone's standards. Unexpected rain spoiled their supplies, meaning they had to carry on with half-rations. Ben Head – a big lad to start off with – lost half his body weight. Water became horribly scarce. Stuart went down with scurvy, and he started to go blind in his right eye. Despite all this, they found – roughly speaking – the centre of Australia, but they knew they couldn't go any further north and survive. They had to head back.

This was easier said than done.

They were in a terrible state. Lack of water meant they had to go miles out of their way to track down springs. From sheer exhaustion, Stuart fell from his horse and badly injured his shoulder. The scurvy, which was affecting all of them, made their tanned skin turn yellow, then green, then black.

And if that wasn't enough, they had to deal with some Aboriginals who didn't take kindly to trespassing on what they saw as their land.

Ordinarily, Stuart got on well with the indigenous Australians he encountered on his travels. Not this time.

In their badly weakened state, they came across the Warumungu tribe. These Aboriginals set about them aggressively, raiding their camp and stealing their supplies. They hurled weapons at the explorers' horses and set fire to the dry grass around their encampment.

The three men had no choice but to run – while they still could.

Starving, scurvy-ridden and with no supplies, they struggled on through the arid wasteland. But they never gave up, and refused to let the desert beat them. They eventually reached civilization, barely alive.

True to form, less than three months later, Stuart was off – again.

*

By now, the fame of this crazed, wild explorer was such that the South Australian government was willing to fund him in his attempt to find the vital route from the south coast to the north coast. Kekwick struggled to keep his drunken boss sober before their departure, but Stuart eventually led eleven men, plus horses and a dog called Toby, north. This was his largest expedition yet.

It was scorching hot. Unseasonably so. They soon lost some horses and the dog to the heat, and the uncompromising Stuart sent a couple of his men back south when it was clear they weren't up to this extreme undertaking.

The rest of them pushed north, past the centre of the country and within 500 kilometres of the north coast. Over a period of nine weeks, Stuart personally led eleven attempts to break through the arid plains that would lead them north. Eleven times he was forced to retreat in order to stay alive.

Eventually, he had to concede defeat. He returned to the south coast full of anger and humiliation. The terrain had beaten him – badly.

But he wasn't going to stay beaten for long.

The search for a route across Australia was dominating his life. Nothing was going to get in his way. Neither money, nor even his own dramatically deteriorating health.

He was a man on a mission. I know that feeling. Obstacles don't matter. Nor does the prospect of pain and hardship. The goal is all-consuming.

He allowed himself just a month to recuperate, before having another go.

This time, in October 1861, he led ten men and seventy-one horses into the outback. Most of them were drunk as they set out, and onlookers had the enjoyment of watching them falling off their mounts. Were these really the individuals that would find a route all the way across Australia?

To do what no man had ever done before?

It didn't seem likely at first, especially not when their leader also fell off his horse, only to have another horse stamp on his hand. The impact and weight of the horse mangled the tendons and dislocated the joint. Infection set in, and for a while it looked as if Stuart would need the hand amputated.

But it healed – enough, at least, for the team to press on. They crossed through the centre of Australia, but each time they tried to break through to the northern coast the brutal climate and a lack of water sent them back. This happened five times until, finally, on the sixth attempt, Stuart located a series of watering holes where his men could rehydrate.

Refreshed, the men pressed onwards. They soon reached a tributary of the Adelaide River. Stuart knew his journey was almost at an end. This was terrain that had been previously mapped by other explorers. If they could cross it, so could he.

And so, after six months of arduous trekking through the outback, they finally broke through to the northern sea. Stuart was the first to stagger across the beach and wash his hands and face in the Indian Ocean.

Victory, at last. But Stuart didn't stick around to rest, or to lap up praise.

Twenty-four hours later he turned round and started the return journey. A mere 3,100 kilometres.

And it was now that his problems really started.

*

You can't expose yourself to those sort of brutal extremes without it putting unimaginable stress on your body. And, despite his incredible resilience, Stuart's battles with the outback were beginning to show.

It wasn't just that the men were short of rations, or that, as they headed south, their horses started dying. It was Stuart's right shoulder which succumbed first. A burning pain developed and spread across his body – so much so that he had trouble breathing.

His eyes, already damaged by the searing sunlight he'd exposed them to over the previous few years, became next to useless. The master navigator became reliant on others to find his way. (At least they had the detailed maps he had already prepared during his wanderings.)

Their water supplies dried up, and they frequently went for three days without a drink. Three days without food is bad enough; three days without water, in that kind of heat, and your body starts poisoning itself – never mind the all-consuming pain that a parched throat and swollen tongue brings on, you really have reached the limit of a human's ability to survive.

In their desperation, the riders would pack lumps of clay into their handkerchiefs and squeeze them in an attempt to try to get some moisture out.

Stuart's legs turned black. His shivering, sweating body was overcome with fever.

Scurvy had wormed its way into his gums, which were covered in festering sores and bleeding profusely. Everything he ate tasted of his own blood.

With their rations running perilously low, they found a nest full of wild puppies. Survival is rarely pretty. They boiled the puppies and ate them.

On the brink of death and unable to speak, Stuart finally indicated his permission to slaughter one of the horses – something he'd never normally do. His men made a nourishing soup out of the horse's lips. It gave Stuart just enough strength to continue until, finally, after forty-four weeks of crippling exploration, he and his men made it back down to the south coast. A miracle in itself. A testament of courage, grit and endurance.

Stuart was so ill he was ordered to rest, or die. That didn't stop the rest of Adelaide turning out to have a massive street party in his honour.

Stuart's heroic persistence and skill had allowed him to succeed where almost anyone else would have failed. But his days of exploration were over. He'd given it his all, achieved his ultimate aim, and now his body couldn't take any more.

Eighteen months later he left Australia for good.

Tragically, he died at the age of 50, lonely and penniless in London, where he lived with his sister. His body was totally worn out. Burnt out.

His funeral was attended by just seven people.

Now he lies buried in Kensal Green cemetery – half a world away from the continent where his greatest feats of exploration were conceived and executed. His epic accomplishments didn't earn him great wealth, or even great fame in his own country. But those fickle masters never really mattered to him. He'd done what he set out to do. And he'd done it well.

Now his name remains immortalized, from the south coast of Australia to the north. The Stuart Highway, linking Adelaide to Darwin, bears his name, as does Mount Stuart, which he discovered in the interior. And there are many other statues and memorials in his name throughout Australia.

In short, his achievements have now, finally, and rightly, been recognized. Goals of that scale demand sacrifice, and they also demand that we ignore the suffering that so often accompanies ambitious callings.

And a little dose of eccentricity so often goes hand in hand with such endeavours.

I embrace that. And I salute Stuart's quirks, his foibles, and his refusal to conform.

Huge goals require big character. And John McDouall Stuart was as big as they get.

I like to think he'd raise a dirty mug of rum to that.

# CAPTAIN JAMES RILEY:
# SLAVES IN THE SAHARA

*'My God! Suffer us not to live
longer in such tortures!'*

FROM THE JOURNAL OF
CAPTAIN JAMES RILEY

The date: 28 August 1815. The place: the west coast of Africa. The American ship the *Commerce* had already been at sea for the best part of three months. It had set sail from Connecticut before stopping off at New Orleans. It had then travelled across the Atlantic to Gibraltar, and now it was heading south. Its intended route: west of the Canary Islands and on to Cape Verde, where it would load up with precious salt to take back to America.

And under no circumstances was it to drift close to the wild desert land now known as Western Sahara – where, so the stories went, Christian sailors were captured by Muslim nomads and treated much, much worse than dogs.

In command of the *Commerce* was Captain James Riley: husband, father and career sailor, who took the welfare of his men as seriously as his own. In later years, he would become an outspoken critic of the miserable worldwide trade in slaves. There was a very good reason for this.

Captain Riley was about to become one.

And so were all of his men.

★

The two things most likely to scupper a nineteenth-century sailing ship were poor navigation and storms. At the end of August 1815, as it sailed south from Gibraltar along the African coastline, the *Commerce* suffered from both.

High winds and perilous currents had pushed the ship off course. The sails were full, the masts were creaking and the decks were a salty blizzard of blinding spray.

It was night – pitch black. Not realizing how close to the shore they were, Captain Riley ordered that they turn to the south-east. Then the unthinkable happened. With a horrific, gut-wrenching jolt, the *Commerce* ran aground.

Vicious waves pounded against the hull and broke it on the rocks. The sailors had no choice but to abandon ship. Riley ordered his men to gather as much water and food as they could, and stash it into their escape boats. Then they braved the wild ocean and prayed they would make it to shore.

Somehow they did, but they were still in very grave danger. They were shipwrecked on the western shores of the Sahara, one of the hottest, most brutal deserts on earth.

But worse than the desert were the nomad slave traders.

The sailors were in a fearful region where infidel white men were seen not as fellow humans, but as slaves to be traded – and treated worse than animals.

The ferocious desert people of the Sahara were unlikely to give them a warm welcome. But they were very likely to find them.

Sure enough, as dawn came, a figure appeared on the beach walking towards them. He had dark skin, a deeply lined, leathery face and a knotted beard stretching down to his torso.

Riley tried to make friends with the stranger. He even offered him some of their shipwrecked supplies. The man simply took what he wanted, then strode off out of sight.

The sailors feared he had gone to get reinforcements.

They were right.

More tribesmen and women arrived. They carried sharp knives, axes and spears. They plundered everything the sailors had.

Riley attempted to negotiate with them. But they didn't want to negotiate. Their leader grabbed the captain's hair and yanked his head back. Then he rested a wickedly sharp scimitar against his throat. Riley was sure that this man was about to behead him. Instead, he simply sliced the captain's clothes from him.

Riley and his men were no good to the locals if they were dead.

Thinking quickly, the captain told his captors where they had buried some coins in the sand. When the Saharans ran to fetch the plunder, he and his men escaped. They swam through the rough Atlantic seas back to the wrecked *Commerce*.

But one of their number, an older sailor called Antonio Michel, was left behind. They watched from the ship, sickened, as the tribesmen beat him to a bloodied pulp.

They then saw the nomads pile their plunder on to Michel's back as though he was a pack horse, then beat him savagely again – like the slave he now was – and watched as they drove him on, over the dunes and out of sight.

They now had two options. Return to land and submit themselves to the barbarous tribesmen who would surely capture and enslave them. Or, they could patch up a badly damaged longboat and take their chances on the open sea.

They chose the sea.

Riley and his crew crowded into the longboat: eleven men, one keg of water, twelve bottles of wine and a pig who had survived the wreck.

They were crammed in like sardines. The longboat leaked water and they had no rudder. They spent their days either rowing against the strong sea currents, or bailing water out to stop themselves sinking.

Rations were scarce. Each day they shared between them a bottle of water. It was a little more than a mouthful each. For food, they had a scrap of salt-pork each day.

They rowed east, hoping to hit the Canary Islands, but the wind and the current were against them. They made very little headway.

On the third day they slaughtered the pig. As they cut its throat, the blood spilled out. The sailors carefully collected it, then drank it down to slake their thirst. Then they devoured the moist, oozing liver.

But still, the heat and the strenuous work dehydrated them dramatically. As they emptied the water bottles, they refilled them with their own urine to keep and then drink.

As the days passed, their tongues grew thick and furry with dehydration. Their hearing deteriorated as the moisture in their inner ears dried up. They were cramped, feverish and dying of thirst.

Their skin, unprotected from the sun, was burned raw and covered in weeping sores where it rubbed against the wooden oars and the salt. Each day, the crew shared out pitiful quantities of raw pig flesh, which was already turning rancid. And as the water supplies dwindled, they allowed themselves only enough urine to moisten their parched mouths.

As the urine passed through their body, only to find its way back into the sailors' bottles, it became more and more concentrated. Undiluted, it was now a thick, stinking poison. Riley described it as a 'wretched and disgusting relief'.

But it was all they had.

The sea and the sun were beating them. No question.

The sailors' condition was so monstrous that, when land came into view again, it was almost a relief. They headed straight for it. They knew full well how cruel the local people could be, but they decided that nothing could be worse than this remorseless torture at sea.

They were wrong about that.

*

They washed up on a tiny, barren stretch of sand. They had no idea where they were (in fact they had drifted 200 miles south). They chose to head east, into the harsh terrain of the Sahara.

The next morning they started their march.

There aren't many places on earth where it's harder to survive than this. The Sahara stretches for 3,000 miles in one direction, 1,200 in the other. Humidity levels can drop as low as 5 per cent. The men found no plants, no animals and no water. They started hallucinating through thirst as they staggered, close to death, through this hostile wasteland. Their mouths were cracked and bleeding, and they would gladly have given their own lives for just a sip of water.

When they saw the light of a fire in the distance, they had no choice but to stagger towards it. They knew they would get a hostile welcome, but it was that or die on the burning Saharan dunes.

They prayed together. Then they crawled towards the light.

They found one man, two women and some children gathered around a well. The man instantly brandished his scimitar and forced Riley and two of his crew – George Williams and Aaron Savage – to remove their clothes. Then he stalked towards a fourth sailor called Deslisle. He forced Deslisle to carry his companions' clothes.

The implication was clear. The four sailors belonged to him now.

The women forced the rest of the men to strip naked. Suddenly, though, a cloud of dust kicked up and a crowd of tribesmen – some on foot, some mounted on camels – thundered towards them. A huge fight ensued among the natives. Scimitars flashed and blood flowed as they fought over possession of the eleven slaves.

After an hour, the fight subsided. The slaves had been divided up. Riley and Deslisle were now the property of the nomad they had first seen. His name was Mohammed, and the women were his sisters. Mohammed dragged his slaves to the well, where the sisters beat their meagre, dehydrated bodies with thick sturdy sticks.

Other women, though, brought them bowls of foul, stale water. It was a stinking, putrid liquid, but it was nectar to these men dying of thirst.

When you're chronically dehydrated, you have to resist drinking too quickly. Your body can't handle the sudden intake of liquid. Riley knew this, but he couldn't stop himself. He and Deslisle drank deeply and without stopping. Almost immediately, their stomachs cramped in on themselves and explosive spurts of diarrhoea gushed down their naked legs.

The other men – all of them now slaves – joined them. As they drank they suffered the same symptoms. Their sweat sizzled on their scorched skin.

The nomads prepared to leave the well with their camels and their new slaves. One by one, the sailors were taken away from their companions. Finally only Riley and four of his men were left.

The nomads instantly put them to work hauling water up out of the well for their camels, then forced the wretched sailors to follow them out into the desert. Riley and his four companions were so weak that they simply fell to their knees. At first, the nomads laughed at them. Then they whacked their scalding backs with thick sticks once again, until the burnt skin peeled off and the flesh underneath oozed blood.

The nomads treated their new slaves like the lowest forms of life. But when it was clear that they simply couldn't walk through the desert, they forced them to sit on the camels, just behind the hump. The camels' rough skin ground against the slaves' naked flesh. Blood slathered down the inside of Riley's legs, dripping constantly on to the sand below.

He found himself looking around for a stone with which to beat himself to death. He found none. He had no choice but to keep going.

The following day, they were forced to walk again. The soles of their feet wept with blood.

The nomads didn't care. The sailors were just possessions now. They could treat them however they wanted.

It was the habit of the desert dwellers to wander in small groups, but now and then they joined other caravans of nomads. So it was that Riley saw some others of his fellow sailors in the days and weeks that followed. They were in a similarly bad state. George Williams had huge folds of skin hanging off him. Underneath, Riley could see the new skin already plastered with angry red sores.

But the next time he saw the wretched man, he was even worse.

The outer layer of his skin had completely burned away in the sun. One of the nomads had smeared camel fat all over his raw flesh in an attempt to save him. It was clearly not working. The fat simply sizzled in the sun, cooking the sailor-slave from the outside in.

Riley could do nothing to help the dying man. Williams's master just led him away into the desert – never to be seen again.

*

Riley was bought and sold among the nomadic tribe. Each master was as cruel as the last. They poked at their slaves' raw skin, and laughed when they howled. And, of course, the slaves were kept on the brink of starvation and thirst. Whenever Riley saw a camel urinating he would rush to cup his hands under the stream. The urine tasted foul, but at least it was fresh (and therefore sterile) and wet.

It kept them alive, but the symptoms of dehydration were getting worse. Their joints ached as the fluid in them dried up. Their bodies became incapable of producing either saliva or tears.

The slaves had all heard rumours that cannibals lived in the Sahara. But as the weeks passed, the sailors became cannibals themselves. As their burned skin flaked from their arms and legs, they gobbled it up hungrily. They were literally eating themselves alive.

And, on one occasion, Riley learned that some of the slaves travelling with him had abducted an Arab child. Driven mad for want of something to eat, the slaves were preparing to slaughter the child.

Riley stopped them just in time, and tried to reassure them: as slaves, they were no good to their masters dead. The nomads would keep them alive so that they could eventually be sold.

In theory, he was right. But there was another problem. The nomads themselves seemed to be wandering aimlessly around the pitiful desert. They, too, were running dangerously low on water and food.

When push came to shove, the nomads would let the animals die before themselves.

And they'd let the slaves die before the animals.

It seemed to Riley that, out here in the forgotten wastelands of the Sahara, they needed a miracle.

Sometimes, miracles come in strange disguises.

\*

It was midday. Riley's masters were sheltering in their tents from the extreme sun. Two men approached out of the desert. Their skin was scarred and they carried muskets.

Riley's master invited the strangers to join them, as was the desert custom. One of the men was called Sidi Hamet. He was accompanied by his brother.

Sidi Hamet appeared a little kinder than Riley's current master. He even gave him some fresh water.

Riley spotted an opportunity. These desert wanderers were traders. Everything had a price. Riley had only one thing to trade: his own life, and that of the sailors who remained with him.

He approached Sidi Hamet. In a mixture of pigeon Arabic, French and Spanish, he explained what had happened to him and his shipmates, adding that he had a wife and children waiting for him back home. To his astonishment, Sidi Hamet shed a tear. He too had a family. He understood.

Had Riley found a small stream of goodness in this desert of horror?

So far, he had told Sidi Hamet the truth. Now he told a lie. He said that he had a friend in the nearest city, Swearah. If Sidi Hamet would purchase Riley and as many shipmates as they could locate from their cruel masters, his friend would buy them back for fifty times what he'd paid.

'What is the name of this friend?' Sidi Hamet asked.

'Consul,' said Riley.

Sidi Hamet accepted the deal, with one proviso: 'If you are lying to me,' he said, 'I will cut your throat and recoup my losses by selling the rest of your men.'

The deal was done. Sidi Hamet bought Riley and three others.

But they weren't safe yet. Not by a long shot.

★

It was several hundred miles to Swearah. They needed food, so Sidi Hamet bought an old camel for slaughter.

He killed it at midnight, pulling its neck back as far as its hump and cutting its throat. He siphoned the blood into a big pot, which he placed on the fire. The blood congealed, and Hamet allowed Riley and his men to scoop out great handfuls and feed.

Later, when they were crazed with thirst from trying to digest the congealed blood, he allowed them to drink a foul green fluid straight from the gaping stomach wound of the slaughtered camel.

This was real desert survival.

The journey to Swearah continued to be grim beyond belief. Unlike Sidi Hamet, Riley and his men were not used to these conditions. Their bodies continued to deteriorate. Riley wrote in his journal: 'The remaining flesh on our posteriors, and inside of our thighs and legs, was so beat and literally pounded to pieces, that barely any remained.'

Occasionally they found water. When they did, they drank their fill. Otherwise, they had to make do with handfuls of camel urine. And when the camels stopped urinating through thirst, they had nothing.

Occasionally they came across other nomads who shared their food, or sold them animals for slaughter. The slaves happily feasted on raw goat entrails, uncleaned and still warm from the slaughter, or on camel blood. But then, for hundreds of miles, they saw nothing but the hard, stony desert floor or the sand dunes, where barely anything could live. Their hunger soon returned.

The desert contained other threats, in the form of bandits. Despite the dreadful state their bodies were in, Riley and his enslaved companions were a valuable cargo. Sidi Hamet had to defend himself from evil cut-throats who would gladly kill him and his brother, before stealing the slaves and condemning them to a life of utter hopelessness.

But, for now, hope was the one thing they had. And amazingly, after a trek across the desert that almost took as much out of the nomads as it did out of their slaves, they reached Swearah.

A very strange thing had happened. Sidi Hamet and Riley, master and slave, had become friends. But only after a fashion. Hamet still insisted that if it turned out Riley was lying about having a friend in Swearah who would buy their freedom, he would still cut the captain's throat.

Riley knew he meant it.

And so, knowing that if he played this wrong he would surely die, Riley wrote a letter to the consul, a man named William Willshire.

Willshire came good. He arranged the money, and their freedom. After all their sufferings, they were free.

At Riley's urging, William Willshire was able to locate and free one more of the enslaved sailors, a man named Archibald Robbins, whose experiences had been at least as harsh as those of Riley and his companions.

But of the remaining sailors, nothing was ever heard again. We don't know how long they lived or what indignities and suffering they endured. All we know was that they must have lived out their lives in an almost unendurable state of misery, degradation and slavery, before death came as a bitter relief.

*

When Captain Riley returned to America he published his memoirs, which he called *Sufferings in Africa*. It became a bestseller, even in a land where slavery was commonplace, as it was in the Southern states of America at the time. The story of a white man condemned to slavery was a sickening irony. Could some good finally come from Riley's horrific ordeal? Certainly the young Abraham Lincoln read *Sufferings in Africa*, and later said that Riley's story had a great influence on him.

Sometimes we have to see things back to front in order to understand their purpose. Riley had experienced the servitude that was being inflicted on untold men and women in the Deep South at the time. And as he later said, 'Men, though covered with a black skin, are not brutes.'

It was a controversial opinion in those less enlightened times.

Had Riley not been so determined to survive, he could never have told this tale.

Robbins, one of the crew members who endured this ordeal, later wrote that 'the crew of the *Commerce* seem to have been designed to suffer themselves, that the world, through them, may learn'.

And there is little doubt that Riley's story of survival, at the very edge of what the human spirit can endure, has been a continuing inspiration to many people ever since.

Myself included.

# STEVEN CALLAHAN: 'MY BODY IS ROTTING BEFORE MY EYES'

'It is beauty surrounded by ugly fear.
I write in my log that it is a view
of heaven from a seat in hell.'

STEVE CALLAHAN

Why does a man, or a woman, dream of crossing an ocean in a tiny boat that could easily be crushed by the tremendous forces at work in the waves?

Why would they wish to endure the kind of relentless solitude that human beings are simply not used to?

It's a question worth asking, because so many have done it.

The seven seas have been crossed single-handed by all manner of sailors, and almost any of them would warrant a place in this book. Take Mick Dawson and Chris Martin, for example, who rowed 4,500 miles across the Pacific in 189 days. Or Laura Dekker who, at the tender age of 14, had to battle not only the oceans but also the courts that took her into shared care with her parents to stop her becoming the youngest person to circumnavigate the globe single-handed.

Those both took true grit.

Ask any of these people the same question and you'll probably get a different answer. But perhaps the most poetic comes from the awesome Steve Callahan. He said that to go to sea was a way of reminding himself how insignificant all humans are in the face of the natural world. That it is a way of glimpsing the face of God.

But in 1981, when 29-year-old Steve Callahan's tiny boat

suffered the worst that the sea could throw at it, he got a chance to glimpse not the face of God, but the face of hell itself.

*

Steve's boat was called *Napoleon Solo* and he'd built it himself. It was 20 feet long and well made. Steve had built a number of watertight containers into the hull to help its buoyancy in bad weather, but it was light enough to travel fast when the winds were right.

There is a special kind of bond between a sailor and his boat. That was definitely the case with Steve and *Napoleon Solo*. He knew it intimately, and it was all he had. With a mate, he used it to cross the Atlantic from west to east, and it held together well.

But he'd always had a dream: a solo transatlantic crossing from east to west. He wouldn't be the first to do it, and although not many vessels the size of *Napoleon Solo* had completed such a journey, some had managed to do it. That wasn't the point for Steve. He wasn't out to break records. He was just out to test himself, his abilities and the boat he had designed and built. So he signed up for a transatlantic race called the Mini-Transat. It would take him from England to Antigua.

At least that was the plan.

Three days into the race, the weather grew alarmingly bad. The boat found itself riding to the top of ten-foot waves before crashing violently back down on the other side. The wind was screaming all around. The crash of the sea lashing against the boat was deafening.

And the water was coming in.

The hull had cracked. And Steve knew it wouldn't be long before the force of the ocean exploited that weakness and ripped the boat apart. He had no option but to head for the Spanish coast. His race was over.

It took four weeks to repair the boat, after which time Steve headed down to the Canary Islands. He considered mooring in Tenerife for the winter, but the ocean was still calling to him. He had set out to cross the Atlantic. He was out of the race, but that didn't mean he couldn't do it off his own back. And so, on a clear night – 29 January 1982 – he took to the water once again. His destination: the Caribbean.

For a week he had calm seas and favourable winds. He ate well, rowed and generally enjoyed his solitude surrounded by the boundless sea and sky. But then, on 4 February, things changed. The wind got up. Boiling clouds rolled in. The sea became stormy, rising and falling.

The weather was bad, but not impossible. Steve prepared to sit it out.

Night fell. The wind and the waves grew stronger. He tried not to think about how many tons of water each massive wave contained, as he hunkered below decks, consoling himself with the thought that he had weathered storms like this before, and survived.

But then, suddenly, came a massive, ear-splitting noise. Something had hit the boat. Steve had no idea what, but he later decided that it must have been a whale, so immense was the impact.

He heard the sound of the hull ripping apart. Then, suddenly, water was crashing over him.

The boat was going down. And if Steve didn't get off it quickly, he'd be going down with it.

*

There was a life raft on board. Steve burst through the hatch that led to the deck where it was kept. He was supposed to get the raft into the water before inflating it, but that wasn't an option: it was like a bucking bronco on the boat. So he yanked the cord and the raft inflated just as a wave hit. Steve jumped into the raft and the wave carried him off the deck and on to the tempestuous ocean.

A halyard connected the raft to the *Solo*. But Steve wasn't going to break it yet. It wasn't just that he loved that boat – it also still contained the emergency supplies. Somehow he needed to get his hands on them before the boat sank completely or was broken up by the waves. He wouldn't survive long without them.

But that meant re-boarding a sinking boat.

He was cold, drenched and his eyes stung from the driving salt spray. But the survival instinct in him was strong. He pulled himself up towards the side of the sinking boat and climbed aboard again.

Ignoring the huge waves looming and crashing above him, he lowered himself once more down the hatch and into the cabin.

With a bang, the hatch shut fast behind him.

It was strangely quiet in the cabin as he gasped for air, submerged himself and then felt blindly for his emergency bag. Once he had it, he struggled back through the hatch and hurled it back on to the raft. Then he returned to the cabin again, braving the dangers of the waterlogged vessel, to grab his sleeping bag.

Back on the raft, he grabbed anything he saw floating out of the boat: a cabbage, a box of eggs, a tin of peanuts. There were more vital supplies still on the boat – ten gallons of water, survival rations to last up to eighty days, a thick, neoprene survival suit. Should he return again?

But by now he was too exhausted to do any more. If he was going to brave the *Solo* again, it would have to wait till morning.

For now he was abandoned on his circular inflatable raft, huddled under the tent-like structure that was supposed to protect him from the elements but which was being battered continually by huge, curling waves.

And then, well before dawn, it happened. The rope attaching the raft to the *Solo* broke in the roaring storm. Boat and raft drifted away from each other.

Steve's limbs hurt with exhaustion and cold. His body ached with a plethora of wounds he hadn't noticed himself sustaining as he escaped the boat.

The storm was still raging, filling the life raft with cold, salty water. Steve engaged his sea anchor – a kind of underwater parachute to slow you down – so that he wouldn't capsize as he tumbled down the slopes of the massive waves. Even so, it was touch and go. Steve knew that a single capsize could catapult him free and kill him.

Night turned to day.

The gale raged on.

Steve had an EPIRB – emergency position-indicating radio beacon. It had a range of 250 miles and enough battery life for seventy-two hours. He turned it on, but deep down he knew it was useless. He was 450 miles from the nearest shipping channels, and no planes passed this way. He was lost and alone, and nobody could hear him scream.

At night he protected himself from hypothermia by wrapping up in his drenched sleeping bag. Almost instantly, his sore, salty skin erupted with hundreds of putrid boils. His back, knees and bum were covered with cuts and bruises. The salt stung continually as it wormed its way into his flesh.

By day, he took notes of his equipment and tried to work out how long he would last with the supplies he had. Fourteen days max, he estimated, till he died of dehydration. He had some solar stills in his survival pack. These work by using the heat of the sun to evaporate salt water, then allowing the fresh water to condense and be collected. But they're useless when the sea is rough.

As long as the weather remained bad, he would have to rely on the eight pints of emergency water rations he had in the raft, and whatever rainwater he managed to collect.

He rationed himself to a mouthful of water every six hours as he sat out the storm. He certainly couldn't drink sea water. The high levels of salt would poison his kidneys.

There was water everywhere, but he might as well have been adrift in a desert.

The storm finally subsided after three days. But when you're at sea there are other kinds of weather you have to worry about. Invisible weather, under the sea. The currents form massive underwater highways. If your raft gets caught in one of these you have no choice but to submit to its mercy.

Without sails or a motor there's no way of getting out of these currents. And Steve found himself in one of them. He hoped that, eventually, it might take him to land. The question was: could he survive long enough to make the journey?

On his fourth day at sea, Steve spotted a fin approaching. At first he worried that it was a shark, but then he realized he was being followed by a school of dorados. Big, strong, lithe fish – and a potential source of food. He had a spear gun in his emergency kit, and as a dorado came close to the boat, he tried to shoot it.

If you've ever tried to use a spear gun, you'll know how difficult it is. Not only are the fish fast and cunning, but the water also refracts the light coming off them, so they're never quite where they appear to be.

He missed. And he kept missing. The voracious hunger, now his constant companion, continued to gnaw away at his insides.

Scabs started to form over the sores on his legs, but they were washed away again whenever a wave broke over the raft and his legs got wet. As he drifted west the daytime temperature increased, up into the nineties. The solar stills returned nothing but salty water. He cooled himself down by pouring sea water over his body, all the while trying to ignore the agonies of his sores, thirst and hunger.

He tried again and again to spear a fish. On the eleventh day he managed it but, agonizingly, the fish escaped his weakening arms as he fought to pull it aboard.

His water supplies were dwindling. He was beginning to starve. His movements were slow and ponderous. His muscles were beginning to atrophy.

Things were looking bad.

True grit isn't just about endurance. It's about ingenuity too.

Steve had a Tupperware box and some empty water cans. He managed to cobble these together into a solar still that actually produced fresh water, not salt. And, finally, he managed to spear a fish – not a dorado, but a much smaller triggerfish. They can be poisonous to humans, and taste so bad that even sharks avoid them. But he was past caring about that.

He ripped his teeth into the tough flesh and sucked down the bitter blood. It was disgusting, and made him want to be sick. He squished the eyes between his teeth. He gobbled down the liver and the other organs, then hung one fillet up to dry for later.

He had water. He had a little food. Things were looking up.

But not for long.

The shark arrived when the waters were calm. Steve was asleep on the raft when he felt its thick, grey skin rub against the bottom of the vessel. If it punctured the raft with its teeth, that would be the end.

Steve tried to spear it, but the point of the spear rebounded off the shark's tough skin. The beast swam lazily away, but that night, as Steve was trying to sleep, another one arrived. It almost capsized the raft, but Steve managed to chase it away. It was a reminder, though, that at sea calm waters can be as dangerous as rough ones.

In the weeks that followed, Steve would have to fight off many more of these sharks as they tried to attack either his raft or the schools of dorado that had started to follow him.

When he managed, finally, to spear a dorado, and bring it on board, he divided up the meat and dried it in the sun: rations for the days to follow. Then he discarded the inedible parts by throwing them as far as possible from the raft. If sharks were to detect the blood – and they probably would – he wanted them as far from the raft as possible.

On his fourteenth day at sea, he saw a ship in the distance. He fired some emergency flares. They went unnoticed. It would happen several times during his voyage of endurance, as he crossed two major shipping lanes. Each time, they faded uselessly into the sky.

The mental anguish must have been desperate. When you see salvation slip away under your nose, it messes with you – big time.

The raft started to disintegrate. He had to keep it pumped up with an emergency hand pump, but the salt, the sun and the battering of the aggressive dorados caused punctures, releasing the air and letting water in. He had a little repair kit – but just try repairing a puncture when the surfaces are wet. He was forced to improvise, plugging holes with pieces of sponge, or tying cord tightly around punctures to keep the air from hissing out.

But it was clear that the raft had a finite life. It was supposed to last for forty days at sea. But forty days had passed and still there was no sign of land.

Steve's body was disintegrating too. He had no meat on his legs or behind – just bones sticking through the sore skin. He was covered with unhealed cuts and boils which had grown bigger, become infected, burst and turned into agonizing ulcers that grew wider and deeper with each passing day.

He sustained himself with lumps of dried dorado. He worried that he'd had no urge to move his bowels, despite the large, puffy haemorrhoid bulging from his backside. Was his gut shutting down?

He looked like a wild man. Matted hair, bony body, skin covered in sores and fish scales. Days and nights and weeks passed. How long could he survive like this?

He scraped rust from empty food cans into his drinking water to get some iron into his body. If he caught a dorado with undigested fish in its stomach, he gorged on it – as if it were the greatest treat of all. Two for the price of one.

The saltwater boils grew worse still, suppurating around his crotch and pocking his skin. Patches of skin rotted away, giving off a foul, malodorous stench.

His spear gun broke, and he had to improvise by tying a small blade to the spear's shaft. But each time he struck a fish, the shaft buckled slightly. It wasn't going to last for ever . . .

And neither was he . . .

The sores on his body bit into the nerve endings, and oozed a foul discharge. Horrific, fiery pain licked up his dying body. The raft sustained more and more punctures. A high wave crashed on to the improvised solar still and broke it.

Steve was now half submerged, starving and rotting away.

But he wanted to live. And, sometimes, that urge is stronger than even the forces of nature herself. I know that feeling. It is powerful. It comes from deep inside and it is hard to explain. Some see it as the hand of the Almighty, reaching out, touching us to keep us going.

Steve kept working. He never gave up. He used a folded canopy to catch rainwater. He managed to snare a couple of sea birds that landed on his disintegrating rubber boat, and he gorged on their meat, innards and semi-digested silver fish in their guts. He continued to catch triggerfish and dorado to keep in the fight.

Because that's what it was: a war of attrition between him, the vast ocean and the brutal forces of nature.

A war he was determined to win, even though the odds were vastly stacked against him.

By now, his body and mind were closing down. He later spoke of feeling the ghosts of all those who had ever been lost at sea surrounding him.

Waiting for him to become one of their number.

But they would have to carry on waiting. Steve wasn't quite beaten yet.

After seventy-six days adrift, alone at sea, Steve Callahan saw a lighthouse twinkling in the distance. It was the Caribbean island of Guadeloupe.

He knew his ordeal wasn't over yet, though – the currents and waves could easily smash him against the rocks, and he would be too weak to defend himself from the elements. But, for once, luck was with him.

He had been throwing inedible fish guts overboard, so a crowd of sea birds were following him.

By chance some fishermen saw the birds. Knowing that birds at sea normally mean fish nearby, they set out for some sport.

But they found a very different quarry, floating helplessly and close to death among the waves.

They helped Steve aboard. He had lost a third of his body weight, and it would take another six weeks before he could walk again. But after nearly eleven weeks railing against death, Steve Callahan was finally safe.

The ocean is vast. Far bigger than anyone can really imagine when they haven't taken it on single-handed. And, of all the terrains the natural world has to offer, it is one of the most inhospitable. Humans are not meant to survive at sea. There's plenty of life under the water, of course, but we are poorly adapted to join it. At sea, we're no longer king of the hill.

All of which makes Steve Callahan's seventy-six days at sea one of the most amazing stories of survival. A reminder of what humans are capable of when their bodies, minds and souls are pushed to their extremes.

But Steve Callahan makes this book not only because of his achievements during those long weeks of hell. It is also because of the lessons he learned from it. Before the sinking of the *Napoleon Solo* he admits that, like most of us, he was preoccupied with insignificant complaints. He mistook, as we all do, the difference between what we need and what we want.

We humans like to surround ourselves with material possessions and convince ourselves that they're necessary to our happy existence. But happiness can sometimes be masked in adversity, and it sometimes isn't until we lose every comfort we have ever known that we truly appreciate the simple truth: that the best things in life are never bought.

Pride, joy, calm, simplicity of existence, and our relationships with those around us, are the greatest wealth we ever own.

# THOR HEYERDAHL: THE *KON-TIKI* EXPEDITION

*'Progress is man's ability
to complicate simplicity.'*

THOR HEYERDAHL

Thor. The Norse god of thunder.

Any Norwegian man given that name has large boots to fill. Enter Thor Heyerdahl.

Some men and women show true grit by enduring hardships that would break most people. Some show it by conquering fear. Some by pushing themselves to do things that appear, to ordinary mortals, impossible.

Thor Heyerdahl did all of these. But he did something else, too. It didn't involve pain, or endurance or survival. In fact it was relatively simple. And yet, in its own way, it was so gutsy that most of us, if we're honest with ourselves, would find it almost insurmountably difficult.

By the time you've read the story of Thor Heyerdahl and his remarkable seafaring expeditions, I think you'll understand what I'm talking about.

*

As a kid, Thor Heyerdahl already had the heart and soul of an adventurer. And also the guts. Encouraged by his mother, he set up a little zoological museum in his father's brewery. The main attraction was a deadly poisonous snake which he'd caught himself.

His love of nature was compounded when he befriended a grizzled old hermit called Ola. Ola lived a solitary life in a nearby valley. His house was an old sheep pen. There was no real furniture – just logs and stones to sit on. He cooked his simple meals on a small fire.

By spending time with Ola, Thor learned a very important lesson. Life is, in its essence, very simple. Humans make it more complicated, but the things we really need to survive are few.

Heyerdahl also learned something of the dangers of the sea at a young age. He would later tell a story about a time when, aged only five, he watched some older boys playing on the ice in his native Norway. He decided he wanted a go, but his game went very wrong and he found himself under the ice.

Surrounded by freezing water, he struggled to make it back to the surface; he became disorientated, and the hole through which he'd fallen had disappeared. He whacked his head against the ice. His lungs burned. Everything was spinning . . .

And then, suddenly, he was back on the surface, screaming. One of the older boys had managed to grab his ankle and pull him out. He was safe.

You might think that such an event would have scared the young Thor Heyerdahl away from water for the rest of his life. But he wasn't the kind to give in to fear.

As a young man, Thor studied biology and geography at the University of Oslo. In 1936 he married his wife, Liv, and together they embarked upon a journey to the Polynesian Islands. There, they spent a year on the jungle island of Fatu Hiva. It's the most remote and isolated of the islands of French Polynesia, almost bang in the middle of the South Pacific, with Asia and Australia to the west and South America to the east.

At first it seemed like paradise. They stripped off their clothes, built a simple home from bamboo and palm leaves, and pulled crayfish from cool, clear streams. But as the months passed, they started to understand the harsh realities of jungle living.

It wasn't the snakes that got to them, or even the huge, poisonous millipedes. It was the mosquitoes. As the rainy season arrived the insects swarmed around the couple in great, thick clouds. Their skin was crawling with them, and covered in huge, angry welts where the mosquitoes had sucked thirstily on their blood. Massive boils developed on Liv's legs. When they burst, the boils mutated into agonizing open sores.

They then learned that they were almost certain to become infected with a worm called filaria, which causes elephantiasis.

Leprosy was also rife.

Paradise was turning into hell.

They decided to leave that part of the island, and headed to where the mosquitoes were less numerous, and where simple, tribal people led simple, tribal lives. Thor befriended one tribesman in particular, and through their conversations he learned something profound. So-called 'civilized' people think themselves far more advanced than those who still follow the tribal ways. But we dismiss other cultures at our own risk. Perhaps by understanding them, we learn to understand ourselves a little better.

The tough, rugged naturalist was also becoming a dedicated anthropologist. Slowly, the pieces were slotting into place for the expeditions that would make Thor Heyerdahl's name.

And it all came together when Thor found his way to the neighbouring island of Hiva Oa. It was here that he uncovered a most perplexing mystery.

*

Nestled in the tropical rainforest of Hiva Oa was a collection of very ancient statues. Nobody knew much about them – neither precisely how old they were, nor who had made them. However, Thor did learn something curious: similar statues had been discovered 8,000 kilometres away to the east – across the sea in Colombia, South America.

This was strange. Most people believed that the indigenous Polynesians had originally travelled to that remote part of the South Pacific – by canoe – from Asia. From the west.

Could it be that all the experts were wrong?

The young explorer thought it could.

Thor's studies were interrupted by the arrival of the Second World War. When the enemy occupied his homeland, he joined a parachute infantry regiment of the Free Norwegian Forces to battle against the evil of the Axis powers. But at the end of the war Heyerdahl resumed his life as a scientist and explorer – and he continued to tout his controversial ideas about the original settlers of Polynesia.

Almost everybody laughed at his theories, but that didn't put him off. Just because lots of people thought differently, it didn't mean they were right.

So Thor tried to work out how the early inhabitants of South America would have made the epic journey. The sea vessel favoured by those native South Americans was, anthropologists all agreed, the balsa raft. Have you ever handled a piece of balsa wood? It's very light, but it's also incredibly brittle. You could snap a small piece in your hands without any trouble. Surely a material like that would make a terrible boat?

Also, the experts said, balsa wood is absorbent. It might have been all right for pottering round the coastlines of South America, but for a journey of 8,000 kilometres across the South Pacific? No way, they said. It would break up before it even got a quarter of the way there.

Thor Heyerdahl begged to differ. He argued that humans – even primitive ones – were capable of remarkable things. Of great endurance and incredible ingenuity.

Unfortunately, he was young, unknown and unimportant. The experts scoffed at his ridiculous idea that anyone could survive for so long on such a ridiculously unseaworthy vessel.

And so he decided to prove to them that it was possible.

The idea for the *Kon-Tiki* expedition had been born.

In 1947, Thor Heyerdahl travelled to Peru. There, he started building his raft.

To prove his point, he was determined to use only materials that would have been available to those early settlers, five hundred years previously. Thor's raft was to be constructed solely out of balsa-wood beams lashed together with lengths of hemp rope, a bamboo deck and cabin, and a 29-foot mast made of mangrove wood.

First, though, he had to find the balsa wood. Balsa trees were harvested in the high rainforests of the Ecuadorian Andes, and everyone – everyone – told him that it was impossible to get to the balsa plantations during the rainy season.

Thor didn't like the word impossible. He set out with one buddy to reach the interior of this rainforest.

Having hooked up with some locals, they had to battle against rain storms so heavy that they turned the dirt tracks leading down from the plateaus of the Andes into torrential flowing rivers.

Then there were the bandits who, in that part of the world, would rob and kill them without a second thought. And, of course, the venomous snakes that seemed to lurk everywhere, along with the scorpions – one of which stung his buddy in the leg.

They finally found the trees they were looking for and, with the help of some locals, cut them down. But how were they going to get them back all the way to Peru?

With the help of their horses, they dragged the trunks (which being freshly cut were still heavy with sap) through the thick, unforgiving jungle towards a great river. Here, they bound the trunks together using the tough stems of climbing plants, and made them into a makeshift raft. They boarded it, and braved the fast flowing waters to head downriver.

The river itself was rife with alligators. When they stopped by the bank for the night, they could hear the screeches of wild cats all around them. Simply sourcing the wood for the *Kon-Tiki* was turning into an epic adventure all on its own.

Eventually they drifted on the fast current, through the heavy rainfalls and jungle dangers, to civilization, where Thor set about building his raft.

He refused to use any of the technology that had been developed in the construction of the great ocean liners of the twentieth century, or even the wooden-hulled battleships that went before. No wire, no modern rope and no nails.

And if he found himself in trouble in the middle of the Pacific, thousands of miles from help – thousands of miles from anywhere – that was his own lookout.

Five other men made up his crew. Each of them as rugged and courageous as Thor himself. They needed to be. Over the next three months they would be forced to survive with scant supplies on the unforgiving ocean – a place where humans were never meant to live.

The *Kon-Tiki* set sail on 28 April 1947, blown westwards by the currents and the prevailing winds. So far, so good. But the real test would come when it hit stormy waters.

Storms at sea are terrifying. Not to mention deadly. The crashing waves and high winds of the Pacific had crushed many sturdier vessels than *Kon-Tiki*. Imagine what they could do to this lightweight, ramshackle raft constructed by a crazy Norwegian who wouldn't take no for an answer.

Thor and his men hit two major storms over the next three months. No doubt the naysaying academics, sitting safely behind their desks, fully expected the elements to send Thor, his crew and his boat down into the depths.

It didn't happen.

Thor and his men faced up to the storms – one of them lasted for a solid five days – and battled against them. When great walls of white water crashed over their craft, they clung for dear life to the bamboo mast before returning to the Herculean task of steering the *Kon-Tiki* through the treacherous peaks and troughs, all the time rallying against the howling winds.

And despite the predictions of Thor's opponents, the *Kon-Tiki* and its crew proved to be a match for the brutal elements. When the waves crashed over it, the water simply ran down the gaps between the balsa planks. Thor's theory was proving right.

Of course, it wasn't just a question of whether the boat would survive. The men on it had to survive too. One of the greatest dangers they faced was the possibility of losing a man overboard. This was just a raft, after all. Amazingly, all six crew members managed to cling to the raft – and to life – during these terrifying storms.

But even when the sea was calm, danger could rear its head at any time. There's a whole world under the ocean that few of us ever get to see – a home to all manner of deadly creatures, including whales and sharks. As the *Kon-Tiki* drifted west it passed through shoals of these beasts, that could rear up from the water at any moment and attack the men on the raft, or simply upturn it with a nudge of their massive bodies.

Neither happened. Luck was with the *Kon-Tiki* expedition – the kind of luck that has a habit of accompanying real backbone.

The men had taken with them a supply of water. But they knew it was never going to be enough.

Throughout their voyage, Thor and his crew had to collect rainwater whenever they could to supplement their rations. And when they managed to catch fish, they used them to get much needed liquid into their parched bodies.

Raw fish is a good source of fluid. You can rehydrate yourself by swallowing fish eyeballs (try to gulp them down whole, if you want to avoid the taste!), and you can also squeeze liquid – as the *Kon-Tiki* crew did – from their spines and lymph nodes. Sometimes the crew removed the liquid from fish by squeezing lumps of flesh wrapped in a piece of cloth.

When it was searingly hot, they would jump into the water, then lie, draped in damp clothes, under the canopy of the raft to limit their sweating. And then they would slowly dry off to avoid getting wet sores.

But the explorers also learned that sometimes water isn't enough to quench your thirst. If you've been sweating a lot, your body requires salt. So, by mixing a little sea water into their fresh water rations, the dreadful burning in the back of their throats could be eased.

They also learned how to catch sharks.

These sharks were their constant companions, visiting daily and swimming in the wake of the raft. At first, Thor and his men tried to capture them using their harpoons. But these barely pierced the sharks' tough skins. If they were going to hunt shark, they needed to think a bit smarter.

They had dolphin carcasses on board, which they decided to use as bait. They filled the dolphin's belly with a load of their biggest fish hooks attached to good, strong line. Then they set the carcass free in the water to tempt the passing sharks.

It worked first time. A shark swallowed the dolphin carcass whole. The dolphin was stuck in the shark, and the hooks were stuck in the dolphin. Thor and his men hauled the shark on to the raft and stayed well clear while it writhed and flapped its immense, sinewy body in a final death dance, suffocating now it was out of the water. When it finally died, they soaked the meat in salt water to make it edible, then ate it.

Using just their guile and the few tools they had to hand, Thor and his men had learned how to conquer the kings of the sea.

Sometimes, alone and with boredom setting in, they developed a more dangerous way of catching sharks, just to keep themselves entertained. If you can grab a shark's tail fin and lift it out of the water, it becomes paralysed. (If you get it wrong, of course, then the game gets a little edgy!)

The men would sit at the edge of the raft, and wait for one of these powerful beasts to slide past. They'd plunge their hands into the water, grab its tail fin, and yank it above the water line. When the beast froze, they'd haul it on board.

That's the kind of survival that requires some real grit to practise.

Finally, after 101 days at sea, the raft washed up on the shores of the Polynesian island of Raroia where, after a week, natives from the other side of the island found and welcomed the crew.

Thor Heyerdahl hadn't proved that the indigenous Polynesians had originally come from South America. He'd simply proved that it was possible. But he'd also proved something else. Something just as important. When it comes to surviving what other people swear blind you can't survive, then determination and self-belief go a very long way.

Thor Heyerdahl's ballsy seafaring expeditions didn't end with the *Kon-Tiki*.

It was known that the ancient Egyptians built very large boats, principally out of papyrus. The accepted – and supposedly unassailable – belief was that such boats could never have travelled very long distances. Certainly, they wouldn't be up to crossing the Atlantic. The papyrus, surely, would simply dissolve long before the vessel hit land again.

And yet . . . anthropologists had long known that there were certain similarities between ancient civilizations in Mexico and Peru, and those around the Mediterranean and North Africa. Had they developed independently of each other? Or was it, as Thor Heyerdahl presumed, possible that these papyrus boats were a lot sturdier than all these modern, self-styled 'experts' proclaimed?

Would those wily ancient Egyptians really have built these great big ships if they were barely seaworthy?

No prizes for guessing what he did next.

Thor Heyerdahl's first papyrus ship was called the *Ra*. Like the *Kon-Tiki*, it was built using only the materials and techniques that would have been available to ancient civilizations, including highly buoyant reed bundles. It set sail in the spring of 1969 from Safi in Morocco. Its destination: Barbados.

And it nearly made it.

*Ra* travelled 5,000 kilometres across the Atlantic before the ship started to lose the elasticity it needed to ride over the rolling ocean waves, and the reed bundles on the starboard side of the boat started to disintegrate. They had to abandon ship and were saved by a passing yacht. The *Ra* had been at sea for fifty-four days. Another seven and they would have arrived in Barbados.

Was Thor disheartened? Absolutely not. Whenever you try something new, or difficult, or heroic, there are going to be setbacks. The trick is to redouble your efforts and throw yourself back into the endeavour with everything you've got.

Which is what Thor Heyerdahl did. A year later, a new, improved papyrus boat called the *Ra II* set sail. It was just 12 metres long and was once again built using primitive materials and methods.

Fifty-seven days later it landed in Barbados.

Admittedly it was covered in barnacles and so waterlogged that, in Thor's own words, 'sharks could virtually swim aboard'; and they had spent their last few days at sea sitting on the roof of the bamboo cabin.

But they'd done it.

Thor Heyerdahl had refused to be beaten. And he had refused to give up after his first failed attempt.

Once again, he had proved the naysayers wrong, and shown just what humans can do when they put their minds to it.

Cast adrift on tiny rafts in the middle of the boundless oceans, Thor Heyerdahl's expeditions were both epic and dangerous. Like all great adventurers, he pitted himself against the natural world in the full knowledge that it could chew him up and spit him out at any moment. His only weapons were human ingenuity and his indomitable spirit and determination.

But for me those heroic journeys, amazing though they were, were not his most impressive achievement. I said at the beginning that Thor Heyerdahl managed something many of us find almost impossibly difficult, and it's this. So often in life, we find people telling us that our ideas are stupid, or that our dreams are impossible. And it's easy, in the face of that kind of negativity, simply to give up.

Thor Heyerdahl didn't give up. Nor should you.

Don't let anyone ever tell you that something can't be done. What they're normally saying is that they can't do it.

That doesn't mean you can't.

# JAN BAALSRUD: THE GREATEST ESCAPE

*'A man who refused to die under circumstances that would have killed ninety-nine men out of a hundred.'*

NEW YORK TIMES

Jan Baalsrud was a young Norwegian soldier with a taste for adventure. So the Linge Company, which trained up commandos to be inserted undercover into Nazi-occupied Norway, was the perfect place for him.

In March 1943, when he was just 25, he found himself on a fishing boat approaching one of the many tiny islands along the Norwegian coastline. At least, it *looked* like a fishing boat. In fact, it was a very heavily armed Allied vessel containing eight crew, several machine guns, eight tons of high explosive, plus Jan himself and his unit's three other commandos.

They had all been highly trained in covert espionage at secret Special Operations Executive (SOE) training camps in Scotland – and now they were to be operating for real. The mission: to destroy an important air-traffic-control tower, and recruit as many locals as they could into the Norwegian resistance.

The mission was highly dangerous. If the Nazis caught them, they'd be horrifically tortured for information, then shot.

The men were well prepared and confident in their ability. They all knew the dangers involved, yet their nervousness must have been palpable.

On the night of 29 March, as the small craft approached the tiny island, the unit leader, Sigurd Eskeland, climbed into a small dinghy and headed to shore. The unit had been given the name of a local shop. The shopkeeper, they'd been told, would help them on their mission.

But out-of-date intelligence can kill an op – and this intelligence was as bad as it gets.

Having made contact with the shopkeeper, Eskeland revealed the existence of the commando unit and its boat, only to find out there and then that the shopkeeper he was supposed to be talking to had died a few months previously.

The new owner had the same name. But not the same loyalties.

The shopkeeper was terrified of the Nazis. He knew that the crime of helping the enemy would be death. And so he reported what he had learned.

Eskeland returned to the craft, and the following day the worst happened: a German warship slipped into view and opened fire on them.

The men quickly destroyed their top-secret ciphers before abandoning ship, hurling themselves into some small dinghies to get ashore – but not before setting a delayed-fuse detonator on the explosives in their fishing vessel.

From his dinghy Jan Baalsrud laid down rounds on the German vessel from his sub-machine gun, but it only halted the warship for a moment before it continued to bear down on them.

The Germans had the dinghies in their sights. They blasted the commandos with rounds, blowing massive holes in the sides of the little boats, which started to sink.

The men had only one choice. Stay where they were and wait for the German rounds to rip them to shreds. Or swim.

It was about 60 metres to the shore, and the freezing water was riddled with ice.

They went for it.

The Germans thundered all their guns at them. Still the men

crashed through the water, fully dressed, expecting at each moment to feel the terminal thud of a bullet in the back of their skull.

Amazingly, they made it to shore. But as Jan ran out on to the beach, one of his comrades took a round to the head. A flash of red burst from his skull and he fell on to the beach.

Jan knew he couldn't stop. He sprinted towards the cover of some rocks, and only then did he turn back. All the remaining commandos were lying face down on the shore.

He looked around and realized that he was surrounded at a distance by Gestapo soldiers. And they were closing in.

Jan barely had time to think. He ran towards a snow-covered gully and fought his way up it. But the Gestapo were catching up. A round from one of their revolvers pinged past him. Jan pulled out his own automatic pistol and, when the first Nazi came into view, shot him dead.

He fired off another round, wounding a second Gestapo soldier. And then he continued his frenzied struggle up the snow-covered gully.

He came into view of the warship back down below. It opened up on him as he reached the top of the gully where he was able, for a few moments, to seek refuge.

Jan looked back down to the beach. It was crowded with Germans. He looked at his own body. He had lost one boot as he swam to shore, and a German round had hit him in the foot, blasting off his big toe. Blood oozed from the wound, staining the snow red all around him. The foot itself was almost frozen solid. His uniform was black against the white snow, and he was leaving a red blood trail behind him.

He was easy prey, and he knew that Germans would be swarming round him any moment.

So he did the only thing he could. He ran for his life.

*

With a frozen, bleeding foot and a head crazed with fear, Jan crossed the island. He saw another island to the east, and wondered if he could swim there. In truth, he didn't have much choice – he couldn't hide from the Germans for long. He decided to pit his exhausted, frozen body against the frozen Arctic sea.

It was a cripplingly savage swim. The night was dark, the waters freezing and his body almost gave up. But, eventually, he washed up on the far shore, where two little girls found him and took him to their mother.

The mother had heard about what had happened, and knew that the Germans would be scouring the surrounding islands looking for Jan. Just having him in her house could mean death for her and her family. He was at their mercy.

But she was made of sterner stuff than the shopkeeper. She bandaged the bloody stump on his foot and gave him dry clothes and shoes, as well as food and hot drinks. But both she and Jan knew that her house would only be safe for a few hours. The Nazis would come calling in the morning.

Those small islands were not good for hiding. Jan had to get to the Norwegian mainland. Maybe then he could trek south into neutral Sweden. When the woman's son came home, he offered to row Jan to a neighbour who was planning a trip to Tromsø, and might be able to take him.

The pair set out in the bleak darkness of the following dawn. But when they reached their destination, the son found that the neighbour had already gone. His wife gave him some food, but Jan was now left with no option but to head for the south of the island in the hope that from there he could somehow make it to the mainland.

But he had no idea of the terrain that was waiting for him.

The interior of the island was mountainous and covered with snow. Jan was wearing inadequate rubber boots, and his mashed-up toe left him in agony. Surrounded by frozen clouds of snow and mist, his clothes were soon, once more, soaked through.

The snow lay thick over the rocks, but still he limped through it, avoiding avalanche-prone couloirs and all the very real dangers of these ice-bound mountains, determined not to let the elements beat him. Every step was a massive effort, but he kept on going, knowing that this was his only chance to evade the Nazis.

Through sheer grit and determination Jan reached the south of the island. There, sympathetic locals gave him shelter and directed him to the house of the man who ran the local telephone exchange. He would help Jan get to the mainland, he said.

And so he did – along with his 78-year-old father, a tough old sailor who thought nothing of rowing ten miles at midnight across open seas in the middle of a snow-filled gale, nor of risking the Nazi firing squads if their actions were discovered. These hardy islanders deposited Jan on the mainland and gave him a set of skis before turning back to brave the stormy waters again to get home.

Once more, a sympathetic local man gave Jan shelter for the night. Jan explained to him his only plan: to head south, for Sweden. The man told him that the only way he could do this and avoid the Nazis was to head over the Lyngen Alps – a huge, treacherous mountain range of icy, snow-covered peaks. But only a madman would try a journey like that at this time of year. It was suicide.

But staying put was also suicide.

So Jan clipped on his skis and expertly headed towards the mountains.

He had to pass through a German garrison on the way. Germans were milling around on either side of the road. It was impossible to skirt around them. A master of the skis, he simply burst through an entire German platoon. The Germans were caught off duty and off guard, and they had hardly expected their bullet-fast enemy to speed through their ranks. They made chase. But Jan was Norwegian, and he was tough. He left the Germans far behind as he skied up into the mountains.

Things were going OK. He covered 20 miles at speed. But then the weather changed abruptly. Jan was suddenly surrounded by freezing fog. Visibility: 15 feet. He was forced to remove his skis and continue on foot. The wind kicked up the powdery snow. He had to close his eyes and mouth to stop it blinding him and freezing his throat. Ice formed on his body and in his beard. He couldn't tell which way he was going, but he knew he couldn't stop because to fall asleep in the brutal cold would mean he would be unlikely ever to wake up.

He wandered blindly among the frozen, treacherous peaks for four long, gruelling days and nights.

Then he got caught by an avalanche.

Jan was falling. Faster and faster. He was totally immersed in tons of suffocating, tumbling snow, crushing him from all sides.

To survive an avalanche like that is almost unheard of.

Jan did.

But he was in a bad way.

His hands and feet were frozen solid. He was now almost completely blind. His skis had broken into pieces. He had lost his small backpack of food.

But he kept going, stumbling blindly with no idea of his position or bearing. He was hallucinating: horrible visions of being chased appeared in front of his unseeing eyes. But something in him was sane enough not to stop and fall asleep.

It was entirely by good fortune that he stumbled across a small log cabin.

He burst through the door and collapsed, incoherent, right in front of a family in the middle of eating their dinner.

Again, luck was with him. He had fallen into the cabin of a local resistance leader named Marius. Here, in a tiny Arctic village which was riddled with Germans, he had found a man willing to risk his own life to save Jan's.

The family treated his encroaching frostbite by gently massaging his feet while he slept. A little bit of life returned to the frozen limbs, but they were still in a very bad way. The family gave him food and hid him in a corner of their barn. He lay there, semi-conscious, for a week, suffering agonizing pain in his hands and feet, and also in his eyes that were now beginning to regain their sight. But his presence was very dangerous for Marius's family, surrounded as they were by Germans. They had to get him out of there.

Trouble was, Jan couldn't walk.

And so Marius entrusted the knowledge of his secret patient to two friends. Together they loaded Jan on to a stretcher and carried him through the village, in the dead of night, to a small boat on a nearby lake. Then they rowed him to a deserted log cabin, four miles from any other habitation. Here, they hoped, he would be safe, for a while.

Marius and his friends left Jan alone in the cabin, promising to come back a couple of days later to check on him. Once he was alone, Jan did nothing but sleep and eat, hoping that his body would regain enough strength, and that his limbs would recover sufficiently for him to continue his escape. He was only 25 miles from Sweden, but in his current state he might as well have been on the other side of the world.

He could tell, just by looking at them, that his feet were deteriorating. His toes had turned black. He couldn't move them or feel them. When he touched them, skin peeled away easily, and stinking, black effluent wept out of them.

Two days passed. Marius didn't return.

Three days.

Four.

Jan grew delirious again. But through the delirium he was aware of one thing: utter, all-encompassing pain. It started in his feet and spread up his legs. He could only think that the blood in his dying toes had turned poisonous and was now spreading to the rest of the body.

If that was the case, he reasoned, then he needed to draw the blood.

He had no surgical implements with him, of course. Just a small penknife. Using the sharp point of the blade, he pierced the rotting skin on each of his putrefying feet and allowed the foul mixture of pus and blood to ooze out of his damaged limbs, and spill all over the small bed in which he was lying.

Lying agonized and on the brink of death, Jan felt sure Marius had been captured and killed by the Germans.

But Marius hadn't been captured. He'd been busy trying to sort out another escape route for Jan – a route that involved climbing up into the mountains again. When Marius finally returned, however, he found a man whose feet were clearly in no state to do that.

Jan's skin was white, his eyes dull. The blankets keeping his legs warm were saturated with blood. Marius cleaned the suppurating, bloodied feet as best he could. He revived Jan with hot drinks and food. But then he had to leave him once more.

He needed to think of another way to get him out of there.

A plan came to Marius before long. It was bold, incredibly risky and more than a little bit mad. But it was the best they had. Marius started to put it into action.

The first challenge was to get Jan and a large sledge to a frozen plateau 3,000 feet up the mountain. Here, another party of men would meet them and drag Jan on the sledge downhill and across the Swedish border.

To carry an injured man down a mountain is one thing. To carry him up a mountain is quite another. Jan was in such a poor state of health that Marius and his three friends believed the journey would kill him. But he would also die if they left him in the cabin. This was their only option.

They wrapped Jan in blankets then crammed him into a sleeping bag. Then they tied him to their sledge and, at midnight, started dragging him up the foothills of the mountain using short ropes and brute strength. As the mountain grew steeper, they devised a complex system of belaying up, but their progress was frighteningly slow.

Lying at an angle, with his head lower than his feet, Jan was mostly unconscious. Now and then Marius and the others turned him round to get his circulation going, but when the blood ran to his feet, it spurted out of the dreadful wounds on his pus-ridden toes.

Jan's face was racked with agony, but he endured, and his rescuers persisted. They traversed treacherous faces and deathly chasms that they would have barely dared to tackle even without a heavy sledge in tow. They pushed their bodies to the very limits, while Jan held on through a cocktail of pain, exhaustion and fear.

And somehow they managed it.

It was a measure of just how desperate their endeavour was that they should have felt relief at reaching the plateau 3,000 feet up in the mountains. This was a howlingly desolate place. Forbidding mountain peaks stretched away to the east as far as the eye could see. There was no sign of life, human or otherwise. Just rock, snow, ice and wind that would suck the life out of anybody foolhardy enough to stay there too long.

But their relief soon turned to despair. There was no sign at all of the men they had been expecting to meet on the plateau.

They left Jan tied to his sledge as they searched the plateau. But without success. Something had gone very wrong.

Marius and his men had been away from home too long already. If they didn't return soon, the Germans would notice their absence. And not only did the rescuers have insufficient time to carry Jan back down to the bottom of the mountain, they had insufficient energy too.

Jan knew this as well as Marius and his men. He listened while Marius promised to get a message through to ensure someone came to pick him up the following night.

But no one really believed this would happen.

For now, Jan knew that his brave rescuers had no choice but to leave him, with nothing but a little food and the dregs of a bottle of brandy.

Here, far from civilization, he would undoubtedly freeze to death.

Once more, Jan was alone in the mountains. Unable to walk. Barely clinging to life.

Nobody came to his rescue the following night.

Or the night after that.

Marius and his men had lowered him into a snow hole with a few scant provisions. It was more like an open grave, but it would at least give him a little protection from the elements. It was too cold to sleep. His wet sleeping bag and blankets froze solid. As fresh snow fell, it drifted over his motionless body. He managed to keep his head free, but the rest of him was totally covered.

It carried on snowing. Soon, even his face was completely covered. He could breathe for now, but was entombed in snow. Waiting to die while the wind howled menacingly above him.

Another day and night passed. Then a week.

Ten days.

When Marius reappeared, he had no expectation of finding Jan alive. But, incredibly, he was. Marius dug Jan out of his icy tomb, gave him some food, and explained that the guys from the other side of the mountain had been waylaid by the bad weather. They would try again just as soon as the weather cleared. But nobody knew when that would be.

Until then, Jan would just have to wait.

And so he did, his commando spirit still dimly shining through.

For another forty-eight hours he endured the cold and the pain. Only then did the rescue party find him. They pulled him and his sledge out of the snow hole and started dragging Jan's half-dead corpse across the icy plateau.

Yet again, the weather hit them with everything it had. A massive blizzard stopped them in their tracks. It was obvious that moving Jan any further would be impossible. For now, he was safer on the plateau than trying to descend the mountain. They dragged him to a rock that would shelter him from the wind, left him some food and promised to come back when they could.

He was alone yet again.

And he would remain like that for the next three weeks.

In many ways his new position was worse than the snow hole: more exposed, and therefore even colder. But he did have more room. That meant he could wriggle his legs out of the sleeping bag and examine his feet. The sight of them – gnarled, blackened and pus-filled – was so disgusting it made him want to vomit.

He was resigned to losing his feet if he ever got to safety. But he worried that gangrene would spread from his toes further up his legs. Simply draining the pus from them as he had done before wasn't enough to stop this. He needed to do something more drastic.

Jan pulled out his penknife. He used brandy as an anaesthetic. And over a period of three days, he carved slowly through the flesh, bone and tendons that joined his remaining nine toes to his feet, amputating each one of them. He smeared the raw wounds with cod-liver oil and bandaged them with strips torn from one of his blankets.

All in all, Jan Baalsrud remained on that icy plateau for twenty-seven days and nights.

He was eventually rescued by a hardy Laplander and his team of reindeer, who dragged him off the plateau and back down into Sweden. But even that final part of his epic journey was fraught with danger. A German patrol saw them as they approached the border. They chased them, unleashing a torrent of rounds in their direction. Feeble and shaken, Jan was forced to try to unload his automatic pistol in their direction.

But against all the odds, they made it to Sweden, where Jan recuperated in a hospital under the care of the Swedish Red Cross.

He may have lost his toes and almost lost his life, but the most amazing part of Jan's story is that he never lost his spirit. Back in England, he learned to walk again. His greatest wish was not a quiet life after the horrors of his war. Jan still retained his thirst for adventure. He returned to active service and was back in Norway working as an undercover agent yet again when the war came to an end in 1945.

In terms of his ability to endure hell and survive at all costs, Jan Baalsrud has to be one of the great heroes of the war, and his never-say-die attitude is an embodiment of quiet courage and true grit.

# LOUIS ZAMPERINI: WRECKED, SURVIVED, TORTURED, REVIVED

'*Where there's still life, there's still hope.*'

LOUIS ZAMPERINI

There are different types of courage. There's the courage to endure the hardships that fate throws your way. There's the courage to face your demons, and confront your fears. There's the courage to fight.

But there's another, quieter kind of courage. It's perhaps more difficult than the others. It's certainly rarer. By the time you've finished reading the story of Louis Zamperini, I think you'll understand what I mean.

The Second World War was a time when ordinary people were called upon to do extraordinary things. The young Zamperini was far from extraordinary, unless you count his ability to get into trouble. He was a tough, unruly little kid. He was drinking and smoking by the time he was eight. He also became an adept thief and scam artist. The name Louis Zamperini was well known to the local police of Torrance, California.

All in all, he was not the kind of youngster who seemed destined for great things.

As a teenager, however, he turned his life around. He became a champion long-distance runner, and qualified for the 1936 Berlin Olympics. He finished eighth in the 5,000 metres, thanks to a final spurt of speed. Not fast enough for a medal, but he was still the fastest American, and his performance caught the interest of Adolf Hitler, who asked to meet him.

'Ah,' Hitler said, as they shook hands. 'The boy with the fast finish.'

Zamperini didn't think much of the Führer, and his success on the track hadn't entirely killed off the cheeky kid inside. To make his feelings clear, he climbed a 50-foot flagpole outside the Reich Chancellery one night and stole a Nazi swastika – a souvenir of the Games that he would keep for the rest of his life.

Zamperini had challenged Hitler once. Like many of his fellow Americans, he would soon be called upon to do it a second time . . .

Zamperini's intention was to take part in the 1940 Tokyo Olympics, but they never happened. War got in the way. The young Zamperini found his career heading in a very different direction. He trained as a bombardier in the American Air Force, before becoming part of a B-24 crew stationed in Hawaii.

On 27 May 1943, his life changed.

An American aircraft had crashed near Palmyra in the northern Pacific. The call came in for Zamperini and his B-24 crew to mount a search-and-rescue mission. But about 800 miles south of Hawaii, things went very wrong. One of the B-24's engines failed. In a moment of panic, another crew member accidentally switched off a second engine. Bad move. The plane fell from the sky. Like a stone.

From a height of 1,000 metres the aircraft entered freefall. Imagine the violence as it hit the water. It did a half-cartwheel in the air, then exploded and broke up as if it had crashed into solid rock. Zamperini would later compare it to being hit on the head with a sledgehammer. It was a miracle that anyone survived the impact.

As the remains of the aircraft sank below the waves, Zamperini lost consciousness. He woke up moments later to find himself stuck in the sinking, twisted remnants of the B-24's fuselage. Somehow he managed to squeeze himself out of the wreckage and into the water, ripping all the skin from his back as he did so.

When he emerged above the surface he saw smoke, blood and twisted chunks of deformed metal. Of the eleven members of the B-24's crew, he saw only two other survivors.

Russell Phillips was the pilot, Francis McNamara the tail-gunner. Phillips was in a very bad way. Blood was pouring from his carotid artery and Zamperini used all his strength to pull him aboard a life raft. McNamara joined them. After the horror of the plane crash, the three survivors must have been thanking God that they were alive and safe.

They were alive, but they weren't safe. Not by a long chalk. In fact, their problems were only just beginning.

It didn't take long for the sharks to find them, attracted by the human blood in the water. Zamperini later recorded feeling them rub the underside of their raft. As the raft deteriorated, the creatures started thrusting themselves over the sides, forcing the castaways to beat them back with their oars. They were under constant threat of shark attack. But terrifying though that was, far more dangerous was the threat of thirst, starvation and exposure.

The lifeboat had a few provisions: a handful of chocolate bars, some tins of water, a flare, some pliers, a few fish hooks and line. The chocolate was fortified with the vitamins and minerals they needed to survive. They were supposed to eat one square a day. During the first night, McNamara gorged the whole lot. Leaving them with nothing to eat.

The water lasted less than a week. It must have been agony, to be surrounded by seawater, knowing that to drink it would be suicide. They managed to catch a little water in their tins when it rained, but they were forced to hydrate themselves by other means. They were able to catch the occasional sea bird that landed on their raft – including albatrosses. They would devour the meat raw – the feet, the eyeballs, the lot – and drink the blood to stave off their thirst.

On one occasion, Zamperini ripped off the head of an albatross and held the neck over the open mouth of the ailing McNamara, squeezing the bird's body so every last drop of thick, warm blood trickled down his parched throat.

But even with the occasional fish or bird, food was horribly scarce. The trio grew painfully thin as their bodies used up their fat reserves and started to waste away.

They had to be inventive. On one occasion Zamperini grabbed the tail of a four-foot shark. It reared up, mouth wide open, ready to attack them. Phillips shoved a flare canister in its mouth to stop it biting them, and Zamperini gouged the pair of pliers through its eye and into its brain, killing it.

They couldn't eat the whole beast: thankfully Zamperini knew that raw shark meat would make them very ill. The only bit you can eat raw is the liver, which is full of essential vitamins. Ravenous, they ripped it from the shark's carcass and devoured it, shovelling lumps of raw, warm, quivering liver down their throats in a blood-soaked, frenzied feast.

The days and nights passed. The raft drifted. The men clung to life and sanity. And then things grew even worse.

After twenty-seven days, a bomber appeared in the sky. It must have spotted the raft. They soon discovered the aircraft was Japanese. For the next forty-five minutes it strafed overhead, firing on them mercilessly. They were like sitting ducks in a pond.

Zamperini jumped into the water, and dived down as deep as he could to avoid the machine-gun bullets that ripped through the raft and water. As he surfaced, he beat off the sharks that were attacking him by thumping them with all his might on the nose and gills.

Phillips and McNamara had no strength left and could only lie in the raft awaiting death. Astonishingly, none of the Japanese bullets hit them, though many punctured the already sinking raft. This only encouraged the sharks to try their luck at the stricken craft, now semi-submerged beneath the waves.

As the aircraft disappeared over the horizon, Zamperini found himself praying for the first time.

He made a pact with God: if you save me, he promised, I'll be yours for ever. It was the desperate prayer of a desperate man.

Painstakingly Louis began to patch the raft, one puncture at a time. If he failed in this task, he knew that they would eventually be taken by the sharks.

McNamara passed away on the thirty-third day. By this point he looked like no more than a skeleton with a thin covering of skin. His remaining companions spoke a few solemn words, then tipped him overboard. Now they were two.

Phillips had astonishingly survived the awful injuries he sustained in the crash. Now he and Zamperini clung to life as they continued to drift, not knowing where they were or what would become of them. Two more weeks passed. They must have felt like months. But on the forty-seventh day, they spotted land. The raft had drifted south-west more than 2,000 miles. By sheer courage and endurance, they had survived the longest known journey ever in a life raft.

They were now approaching the Marshall Islands. The relief they felt at seeing land must have been incalculable.

But if they hoped their hardship was over they were sorely mistaken. Instead, they were about to enter hell itself.

The Marshall Islands were controlled by the Japanese. Zamperini and Phillips were immediately picked up by the Japanese Navy. These two men on the brink of death were tied to a mast and whiplashed with a pistol until they were unconscious.

They were alive – just – but now they were in the hands of the enemy and about to be delivered bound and broken to the infamous 'Execution Island'.

Its real name is Kwajalein. It's part of the Marshall Islands, 4,000 kilometres south-west of Hawaii. It was not a good place for Zamperini and Phillips to end up. Nine American Marines had previously found their way there. They'd all been tortured then beheaded with a samurai sword. Zamperini's Japanese captors beat him and tortured him daily. For the following six weeks, he expected every day to be his last. Part of him must have wished it was.

He was kept in a cell six feet long, six feet high and thirty inches wide. At one end was a small hole that served as a toilet. It was infested with maggots. When he wasn't being tortured or beaten, his captors made him lie with his head in the hole. His guards pushed whatever leftovers hadn't been served to the pigs into his cell, so he had to scramble around among the faeces on the floor to pick it up.

He had persistent diarrhoea. Mucus dripped constantly from his backside. The cell was full of flies that laid their eggs in the mucus. He was infested from top to toe. All the while, the guards pierced his broken body with sharp sticks and, between the beatings, conducted perverse medical experiments on him, injecting him with agonizing unknown substances. They were stripping him of all dignity. All hope.

After six weeks of this, Zamperini and Phillips were put on a boat to the Japanese mainland. Over the next twenty-five months Zamperini would see the inside of three of the most brutal Japanese POW camps. The conditions were truly horrendous. Intentionally so. Prisoners, to the Japanese, were beneath scum, they were a scourge to their own dignity.

The prisoners were forced to sleep on wooden planks infested with huge lice and bugs that would emerge at night and crawl all over their bodies, biting them incessantly. This alone was enough to drive any normal man insane. But this was before – at the second of the POW camps, Omori, in Tokyo Bay – Zamperini met 'the Bird'.

The Bird's real name was Mutsuhiro Watanabe. He later appeared high in General MacArthur's list of the forty most wanted war criminals in Japan. The Bird saw to it that Zamperini endured tortures and indignities that no man should ever have to suffer.

It started off with the beatings. Mostly, the Bird used his fists or a stick. Sometimes he used a kendo stick – a sturdy cudgel the size of a long baseball bat. If he thought Zamperini had failed to stand to attention, he would remove his belt, which had a heavy steel buckle weighing more than a pound, and, with all his strength, the Bird would whack Zamperini across the head. Each time Zamperini struggled to his feet, the Bird hit him again. Harder.

During one spell, the Bird personally beat Zamperini all day every day for a period of ten days.

The Bird pushed men to the limits of their endurance, attacking their minds as well as their bodies with continued mock executions.

The prisoners' days were filled with brutal forced labour. And there were no exceptions, even for the very ill. If you had a temperature of 103 or less, you worked until you dropped. Then you were beaten and forced to work some more. The men were forced to walk the two miles to the steel mills every day, twice a day. Even when there was snow and ice on the ground, they went barefoot. Why? Because if the Bird saw that they had dirty shoes, not only would he beat them, he'd also make them lick the shoes clean.

The latrines were disgusting and when they were full, the prisoners had to scoop out the faeces with their hands and spread it as fertilizer on the fields. When it rained, the latrines overflowed. All over the concrete floor where men had to step. And when the Bird saw that their boots were filthy he made them lick the soles of them clean too.

'Or die,' he told them.

It started out being a day like any other. One of Zamperini's guards ordered the prisoners to line up. They all assumed they would have to endure some new brutality.

But they didn't.

'The war is over,' they were told.

At first, Zamperini didn't believe him. But they were told to paint the letters POW on the roof of their barracks. Then they were told to wash themselves in the river.

Surely that meant something.

It did.

An American plane flew overhead. Its lights were flashing in Morse code. The flashes spelled out: 'The war is over.'

Zamperini and his fellow POWs – those who had survived, like his crew mate Phillips – had just received their ticket out of hell.

Back in America, Zamperini married a beautiful young girl he had fallen in love with before he had left for war. But his years of incarceration and degradation had taken a terrifying toll on his mind.

Although the world might have seen a war hero who had finally made it home, there was much more going on below the surface. It's so common, even today, for soldiers to come home suffering terribly from the effects of what they have survived. These days we have a name for it: post-traumatic stress disorder (PTSO). Back then, they didn't. There is little doubt, after everything Zamperini had endured, that he was suffering badly from this condition.

He started to drink heavily, and every night his dreams were haunted by the horrors he'd experienced and the people who had inflicted them upon him.

Especially the Bird.

His sadistic captor came to him every night, filling Zamperini with feelings of hate and revenge.

Hate and revenge are not good companions. They can poison our lives. Nobody, I think, would have blamed Zamperini for succumbing to this. It would take a power greater than himself to open his eyes.

In 1949, Louis Zamperini was taken by his then desperate wife, to a talk by the young Christian evangelist Billy Graham. He sat there filled with anger at the words of forgiveness he heard being preached. Then something happened. Like a lightning bolt. In his rage he remembered the prayer he'd offered up on that lonely life raft six years previously as the Japanese bomber had disappeared into the distance.

If you save me, I'll be yours for ever.

That night he knelt and prayed for God's help and mercy to heal him. And God answered. He found himself being given the courage to confront his past, and to embrace the one quality that would help him regain his life.

That quality was forgiveness.

He knew he had to forgive his tormentors. And he didn't just pay lip service to the idea. He really forgave them. Face to face.

In 1950, Zamperini travelled back to Japan. There, he met many of the guards who had terrorized him in the Japanese POW camps. He told them that he bore them no ill will. And he meant it. So far as he was concerned, the slate was wiped clean. As he wrote in his autobiography: 'The one who forgives never brings up the past to that person's face. When you forgive, it's like it never happened. True forgiveness is complete and total.'

But what of the Bird? Did Zamperini ever come face to face with his arch-torturer? Did he ever manage to look him in the eye and tell him that he forgave the indignities that man had inflicted upon him? He wanted to, and he tried to do so on several occasions. But the Bird would never meet with him. He couldn't face Zamperini's forgiveness. To confront such mercy was too overwhelming.

As for Zamperini, his life's journey was complete.

Louis Zamperini's life had been one of unimaginable challenges that required almost superhuman feats of courage and endurance to overcome. The courage to remain alive when cast adrift on that ocean. The spirit to endure the pain, suffering and dehumanizing indignities inflicted upon him by a war criminal and his ruthless fellow guards.

But the courage Louis showed during time of war is only surpassed by the courage he showed in time of peace.

It takes far more guts to forgive than to fight. To maintain peace requires more grit than to perpetuate war. But how many of us could imagine finding the strength and spirit to shake the hand of those who might have brutalized us in such a fashion, and act as if the past had never happened?

Louis Zamperini did. And for me, that was the bravest thing he ever did.

# ALISTAIR URQUHART: THEY DON'T MAKE 'EM LIKE THIS NO MORE

*'I remember that life is worth living and no matter what it throws at you, it is important to keep your eyes on the prize of the happiness that is to come.'*

ALISTAIR URQUHART

If you travel to the town of Broughty Ferry, near Dundee in Scotland, you might be lucky enough to meet Alistair Urquhart. I doubt you'd notice anything remarkable about him. You'd think he was an ordinary pensioner. He lives in sheltered accommodation. He helps other retired people learn how to use their computers. He goes to tea dances.

And for more than sixty years Urquhart was happy to be just that. A man peacefully getting on with his life. Even his wife knew nothing about the hellish events he endured during the Second World War. Events that would surely have broken a lesser man.

Alistair Urquhart was one of many thousands conscripted into the British Army in 1939. He joined the 2nd Gordon Highlanders when he was 19 years old, and was sent to Fort Canning in Singapore.

If there was ever thought to be a cushy posting during the war, Singapore was probably it. This strategically important port was a place where British ex-pats lived a life of ease, surrounded by servants who ran their households and poured their drinks. Nobody seriously thought it was vulnerable to attack. It was one of the greatest bastions of British colonialism, where enormous guns pointed out across the sea to defend it from attack. It was impregnable.

Except, of course, it wasn't.

If you know your history, you'll realize that things turned out a bit differently to how the British expected. In December 1941 the Japanese invaded.

Big time.

The fall of Singapore has been called the biggest British military disaster of the modern era. It was certainly one of the most brutal. Captured by the enemy, Urquhart and his men were sent to Changi POW camp. At once, they were surrounded by the brutality and ravages of the Japanese conquest: Chinese heads impaled on spikes, machine-gunned bodies lining the streets, and the overpowering stench of putrefying bodies.

At Changi, 50,000 men were kept in an area originally designed to house only 4,000. Urquhart was set to stay there for eight months, until one day he and some of his other Gordon Highlanders were moved. They were crammed into a railway carriage so full that the occupants could barely breathe under the weight of bodies heaped upon bodies.

On the 900-mile, five-day journey that followed, those that hung on to life had no choice but to lie in their own excrement, crammed inside their steel carriages. In the stench and heat and misery many died, as others rode on towards their fate.

It was only when they reached a featureless clearing in the middle of the jungle that they learned why they were there: to cut a railway through the harsh and mountainous Burmese jungle. An endeavour that has gone down in history as one of the most torturous, slave-labour brutalities of the Second World War.

It became known as: the Death Railway.

*

When the British were in control of Burma in the early twentieth century, they had proposed building a railway from Thailand to

Burma. In the end they decided it was just too difficult. The jungle terrain was not only mountainous, the line would also have to cross a large number of rivers. They scrapped the idea.

But when Japanese forces took Burma from the British in 1942 they needed a railway to transport troops and supplies. If they used the sea routes they risked their ships being downed by Allied submarines. All the Japanese required was a workforce, but that was no problem. They had one to hand. It consisted of more than 300,000 prisoners of war. Alistair Urquhart was one of these.

After the war, the story of the Burma Railway was given the Hollywood treatment in the film *The Bridge on the River Kwai*. To watch that movie you'd imagine the British workers whistling 'Colonel Bogey' as a gesture of defiance against their Japanese captors. The reality was very different.

The suffering of the workers on the Burma Railway was almost unimaginable. Suicides were daily occurrences. Crazed by the conditions, men would kill themselves by diving head first into the latrines.

If you want to know what would make a man do that, read on.

The prisoners were kept on the brink of starvation, being fed only a few handfuls of putrid rice slop, which crawled with lice and other bugs, a day. Their body weight routinely dropped by half. Disease was everywhere. Potentially fatal illnesses such as beriberi, malaria, dengue fever and dysentery afflicted almost everyone.

When Urquhart developed horrible weeping ulcers on his legs, the only cure was to go to the disgusting latrines and find colonies of maggots that were crawling over the festering tubs of warm diarrhoea. He grabbed a handful of the squirming white maggots from the putrid waste and dropped them on to his rotting leg. The maggots immediately started eating up the ulcers. Like I've said before, survival is rarely pretty.

Cholera was rife. It was in the water, and carried around by the massive rats that were so common the men didn't even bother trying to scare them away. When Urquhart succumbed to cholera, with explosive diarrhoea, projectile vomiting, agonizing cramps and paralysing dehydration, he was unable to move – let alone work. He was put into one of the foul-smelling 'death tents', where most sufferers died within hours, before their bodies were burned on huge funeral pyres. Yet still he clung to life.

But malnutrition and pestilence were not the worst things Urquhart and his comrades had to put up with. The guards on the Burma Railway subjected them to brutal inhuman beatings, torture and humiliations. Urquhart remembers how the guards would regularly, repeatedly and violently, beat the ulcerated sores that covered his body.

A common punishment was to tie wet rattan – a material made from palm leaves – around the ankles and wrists of a prisoner, then tie him to a stake. As the rattan dried, it would contract, cut into the flesh and bone, and literally pull the limbs from their sockets.

When an angry guard smashed Urquhart in the mouth with the butt of his rifle, one of his front teeth snapped in two, agonizingly exposing the nerves. There were no dentists on the Death Railway. Just a bunch of orderlies in the medical hut. When – and only when – Urquhart had finished his day's work, one of these orderlies held Urquhart's head while the other went at the tooth with a pair of pliers, tugging hard until the root worked free of the jaw.

And then, of course, there were the executions.

Urquhart recalls a man who tried to escape. The guards caught him, and brought him to two of the most brutal of their commanders: Lieutenant Usuki and Sergeant Okada, whom the Brits referred to simply as the Black Prince and Dr Death.

One of Okada's favourite pastimes was to pour water down a

prisoner's throat and nose until his abdomen was fully swollen. He'd then wrap barbed wire round his victim's naked belly and jump on him. Invariably, his victims died.

On one occasion his boss, Usuki, approached a wretched prisoner with a viciously sharp samurai sword. The prisoner made no attempt to beg for his life. He knew what was coming. The other POWs were forced to watch as Usuki swiped the samurai sword against his victim's neck. Urquhart closed his eyes, but he couldn't close his ears. He heard the sound of the blade slashing through the air. Then he heard the sound of the prisoner's head thumping on the ground.

Urquhart did what he could to stay out of the way of his guards – something that wasn't always possible. One night, suffering from dysentery, he ran to the latrines. On the way back, a Korean guard stopped Urquhart and made it clear he had sexual intentions towards him. The prisoner refused, but the Korean guard was persistent. And so Urquhart attacked the guard. Before long he found himself, beaten and bloodied, up in front of the terrifying Black Prince.

Urquhart was told to stand to attention and not to move. His toes were already broken from a previous beating, but each time he slumped, he received a series of rifle blows to the kidneys.

Sunrise came. As his fellow prisoners passed, they avoided looking at him for fear of getting a reprisal beating for any show of defiance.

The day wore on. The burning heat eventually rendered him unconscious, but each time he passed out he was kicked back to consciousness and back to attention. Blood oozed from his swollen face, hands and feet. The sun scorched his skin. Insects crawled all over him, gnawing at his flesh.

That night he started hallucinating, but still the guards beat his mashed-up body if he failed to stand rigid.

The following morning the Black Prince decreed that Urquhart should be sent to the black hole.

This was a pit into which men were lowered, encased in a bamboo cage so small that it was impossible to stand up or lie down. The cage itself was littered with the faeces of previous prisoners, and very few men ever emerged from it alive.

Urquhart spent six days in the pit. It was covered by a sheet of corrugated iron that turned it into an oven. He shivered uncontrollably with malaria. Ulcers and kidney stones racked his broken body with unspeakable pain. His filthy body was covered with lice.

For six days he drifted in and out of consciousness, the solitary confinement made even worse by the dreadful conditions. He didn't expect to survive.

But he did.

When he emerged from the black hole, a British Army doctor nursed him back to health using the scant resources at his command. Days later, Urquhart was working – almost naked, barefoot, brutalized and humiliated – back on the railway. There was no respite.

Yet Urquhart kept on hanging in there, kept on surviving. He held on where so many had died, whether from starvation, disease, torture, execution or exhaustion. Of the 330,000 POWs set to work on the Burma Railway, over 100,000 perished.

Despite everything he'd experienced, Urquhart's war was far from over.

Towards the end of 1943, when his time on the railway was up, he was returned to Singapore, where he was set to work unloading supplies from Japanese ships. The bags he had to carry were heavier than him, which wasn't hard: he now weighed less than seven stone. In September 1944, however, he was moved again, this time into the rusting hull of a cargo ship. He didn't know it at the time, but this was one of a fleet of ships that would become dubbed the 'hell-ships'.

The name was well earned. There were so many men packed into the holds that it was impossible to move. You couldn't sit, or crouch, or lie down – not that you'd want to, because to fall meant you would get trampled to death. The holds stank of human waste and death. Most of the men were suffering from the same diseases that were rife on the Burma Railway: dysentery, malaria and beriberi. Once the prisoners were plunged into this claustrophobic blackness, the hell-ship set sail.

There was no water down there in the hold, and the temperature could reach 100°F. Thirst started to overpower every single one of the captives.

You think you've been thirsty in your time? You haven't. Not truly thirsty. So thirsty that your tongue swells to three times its normal size and you start to hallucinate. So thirsty that you forget what it is to be human. Soon more and more men died of dehydration down there, adding the stench of rotting flesh to the foul odour of faeces, urine, vomit and sweat.

They were forced to drink their own urine, and some resorted to murder in order to drink the blood and eat the flesh of their victims.

When men died, their bodies were not removed. They just remained there, festering, bloated and rotting.

Urquhart expected to die. But, once more, fate had other plans for him.

*

There were fifty-six hell-ships in the Japanese fleet. Of these, American submarines sunk nineteen, causing the deaths of 22,000 Allied POWs.

Urquhart's floating prison had been six days at sea when a torpedo ripped through the hold. The ship started to sink. The Japanese started shooting men in the hold at random. But, astonishingly, as the water started to flood in, Urquhart found himself being washed out into open sea.

In his youth, Urquhart had been a Boy Scout, where he had learned certain survival techniques. One of them was this: if you're in the vicinity of a sinking ship, swim as hard as you can away from it. Otherwise the currents caused by the submerging wreckage will pull you down. And so, despite his weakened state, he swam for all he was worth.

The surrounding sea was a huge slick of burning oil. Like boiling treacle. Urquhart swam through it. Hot oil poured down his throat and scorched his skin, but still he kept going. When he finally found the courage to look back, he saw a flaming sea, and the outlines of the hell-ships sinking below the surface, taking hundreds of men to their graves.

He saw many of the surviving men succumb to the hopelessness of their situation, allowing the sea to take them as they cried out the names of their loved ones.

Urquhart started vomiting violently, a gruesome mixture of crude oil and salt water. But when a small life raft drifted past, he grabbed it and collapsed. Not a moment too soon. There were sharks in those waters that soon began to feast on those who were still afloat in the sea.

He remained on that raft for five days. In a state of near death.

By day he had to rotate his body, like a kebab on a spit, hiding different parts of him from the sun as the burning became too much to bear. The sun had seared his retinas so he was almost totally blind. All the hair on his head had fallen out. His tongue was so swollen he couldn't talk or swallow. He was chronically dehydrated and hallucinating. His body was covered in sores, made ever worse by the agonizing mixture of salt water and crude oil.

He was on the brink, but still he refused to die.

You'd think by now that Urquhart deserved a break. Just a little good fortune.

No such luck. On the sixth day, his tiny raft crossed the path of a Japanese whaling ship. The crew picked him up and deposited him on the Japanese mainland. Once more, he was a prisoner. And he was about to find himself caught up in the worst killing device the world had ever seen.

The POW camp in which he was being held was in the vicinity of a Japanese town called Nagasaki.

Alistair Urquhart couldn't have known that the war was almost at an end. Nor could he have known that the devastating event that would bring hostilities to a close would occur almost under his nose.

On 9 August 1945, Urquhart was emptying the prison latrines with his bare hands, when he heard the massive roar of an explosion from the direction of that unfortunate city, Nagasaki. Seconds later, a tremendous, burning wind – like a hot hairdryer – knocked him sideways.

Nobody in the camp knew what had happened. They could never have guessed the awful truth. That gust of hot air was caused by the bomb known as 'Fat Man'. Where it had fallen in Nagasaki, temperatures had reached 4,000°C. At least 40,000 people were vaporized in an instant. Urquhart had been on the fringes of that. The Japanese realized they had no chance against an enemy with such awesome weapons, and surrendered.

Nearly fifty years later, Urquhart would develop an aggressive cancer, which may well have been down to his exposure to the radiation emitted by the Nagasaki atomic bomb. But, in a perverse kind of way, that awful explosion saved his life.

Because now, the war was over.

US marines soon arrived to liberate the prisoners, and Alistair Urquhart was going home.

For a soldier, homecomings can be the hardest battle of all. How can you expect anyone to understand the things you've seen and endured? How can you pretend to be interested in the minutiae of civilian life when you've witnessed the true visceral horrors of death and suffering for so many years?

The story of Alistair Urquhart's attempts to reintegrate himself into civilian life, in a time when PTSD was unheard of, and returning soldiers were expected simply 'to get on with their lives', is a humbling one, and required much of the same mental toughness he had shown throughout his years as a POW.

But when I remember Urquhart's astonishing story, I'm struck by his insistence that, despite everything, he was one of the 'lucky' ones. Yes, he experienced inhuman and dehumanizing horrors beyond description, but he did survive. He made it through hell, by a cruel combination of raw courage, unending determination, and moments of sheer luck.

And still to this day, the unassuming man from Broughty Ferry, Scotland, bows his head to those many poor, wretched souls who paid the ultimate price of war alongside him.

# NANCY WAKE: THE WHITE MOUSE SPY

*'I hate wars and violence, but if they come I don't see why we women should just wave our men a proud goodbye and then knit them balaclavas.'*

NANCY WAKE

In 1944, just after the liberation of France from the Nazis, a very beautiful young woman was dining at the British Officers' Club in Paris. Weeks previously, it had been called the German Officers' Club. Not any more.

A waiter, as he was serving her, muttered something under his breath in French. 'I prefer the Germans any day, to you rotten English.'

Unfortunately for the waiter, he didn't realize that the young woman spoke perfect French.

Even more unfortunately, he didn't realize that she was Nancy Wake. One of the toughest, bravest, most ruthless Allied operatives of the Second World War.

Nancy followed him out of the dining room and gave him a piece of her mind. Followed by a piece of her pretty fist. He crumpled, unconscious, to the floor.

Nancy Wake later stated that she was never brought up to be a violent person. Determined? Certainly. Rebellious? Without question. But violent? Not until the war started. It changed her, like it changed so many people.

Few of them, though, had a story to tell that was quite so remarkable as Nancy Wake's.

*

Nancy had an unhappy childhood. After moving the family to Australia when Nancy was 20 months old, her father walked out on them. Her mother showed her very little affection, and Nancy became a rebellious kid. The rebellion that flowed through her veins would prove to be a major asset to the Allied war effort.

She ran away from home when she was 16 to work as a nurse, but she clearly had a wanderlust. When her aunt sent her the substantial sum of £200, she was off. She travelled to London, and then across Europe, working as a journalist. She lived life to the full, and in 1937, at the age of 25, she found herself in Vienna.

There, in a picturesque Viennese square, she was about to see something that would change her view of the world – and perhaps the course of the coming war – for ever.

A group of Nazi stormtroopers had gathered together some of the local Jewish population. The stormtroopers had chained their prisoners to enormous metal wheels. As they rolled these wheels round the square, the Nazis were whipping the captives violently, inflicting great, bleeding welts on their already crumpled bodies as the desperate prisoners screamed and clung to each other in agony.

Nancy was witnessing, first hand, how the Nazis would ulti-mately brutalize, torture, degrade and attempt to destroy an entire race of men, women and children – for nothing more than the peaceful faith they professed, the community values they lived by and the heritage that ran through their veins.

This cruel and sickening scene had an immediate effect on Nancy. She decided there and then that she would do whatever it took to make life more difficult for the loathsome Nazi party.

Over the coming years, she certainly did that. And some.

*

Nancy was a very beautiful woman – she looked more like a film star than a war hero. In 1939 she married a wealthy French businessman called Henri Fiocca and settled down to live a life of glamour in Marseilles.

Except, of course, things didn't turn out like that. When war was declared, her husband received his call-up papers. It would have been assumed that Nancy would stay at home and wait for him.

But Nancy Wake wasn't made that way.

Henri used some of his wealth to provide an ambulance, and Nancy joined a voluntary ambulance unit. She drove to northern France to help the Belgian refugees who were pouring over the border. Her hatred for the Nazi regime only increased when she saw German bombers strafing bullets down on elderly women and young children as they fled south.

Nancy didn't have to see the wounded, dying bodies of many kids to make her decide to do something about it.

Her time was coming.

In 1940 Paris fell to the Germans. Nancy wept for her adopted homeland. But she knew that crying wouldn't achieve anything. And she hadn't forgotten her vow.

She became a courier for the embryonic French Resistance. Because of her status as the wife of a wealthy businessman, she could travel around France with more freedom than most women, at least at first. She used that freedom to smuggle messages and food to members of the Resistance in southern France.

This was highly dangerous work. The Gestapo – Hitler's secret police – punished with brutal severity any members of the Resistance and anyone suspected of helping them. Resistance members were routinely and horrifically tortured, and then coldly executed.

Gestapo methods of torture included almost drowning their victims in bathtubs full of ice water, fixing wires to their bodies and blasting them with electrical charges, burning flesh, beating the prisoners with whips, tying their hands behind their backs and hanging them by their wrists in order to dislocate their shoulders . . .

Very soon, the Gestapo started to suspect Nancy. They started tapping her phone. Opening her mail.

It didn't put her off. Far from it.

It simply meant she had to start fighting a little smarter.

In order to continue her work with the Resistance it was important that Nancy could move around France. She acquired several fake identities to enable her to do this. But she had something more important than false papers. She had nerve.

She would flirt outrageously with German guards to get past their checkpoints and road-blocks. She would keep a couple of old turnips in the basket of her bicycle, so she could pretend she was on her way to or from the market if she was questioned.

France was full of prisoners of war and downed British airmen. They needed to escape if they were to avoid brutal incarceration by the Nazis. But it wasn't easy. To the north: German forces. To the east: Mussolini. To the west: the Atlantic. To the south: the Pyrenees.

Those mountains, which formed a natural barrier between France and the safety of neutral Spain, are formidable and not passed easily even today. But between 1940 and 1943 Nancy helped more than 1,000 POWs and downed British airmen cross them. In total, she traversed the Pyrenees on foot seventeen times. Just goes to show that pretty and gritty can go hand in hand.

Nancy became supremely adept at whisking Allied servicemen

out from under the Nazis' noses. And try though they might, they simply couldn't catch her. The Gestapo gave her a nickname – the White Mouse. They put a price on her head.

Five million francs.

But still the Nazis couldn't catch her.

And all the time she spent dodging the agents of the Gestapo, was time spent using up their resources.

By 1943 Nancy was number one on their most wanted list.

A bad place to be.

But Nancy Wake wasn't scared.

She would later say that she'd never felt a moment's fear in her life.

The Resistance, however, knew that France was becoming too hot, even for Nancy. So did her husband. They persuaded her that the time had come to make her own escape across the Pyrenees.

Reluctantly, she agreed.

She never said a proper farewell to Henri. She just walked out the door, saying she had some shopping to do.

In fact, she had a lot more than groceries on her mind.

Nancy attempted to cross the Pyrenees six times. Now that she was trying to make her own escape, the elements got the better of her. On one occasion the terrifying, pro-Nazi Vichy police captured her. They subjected her to four days of brutal interrogation.

They beat her continually – heavy blows across her head. But then, in a feat of extraordinary daring, the Belgian Resistance fighter Albert Guérisse – better known by his pseudonym Patrick O'Leary – walked straight into the police commissioner's office. He announced that he was a member of the Vichy police, and that Nancy was his mistress. He then showed them false papers to support his claim.

Astonishingly, Nancy and O'Leary pulled it off and she was released.

Goes to show what a bit of nerve can do.

On her final march over the Pyrenees, Nancy climbed for forty-seven hours solid. Temperatures were freezing. On her feet, she wore only espadrilles and two pairs of socks. The wet pair she wore for climbing; the dry pair was for the brief minutes of rest she took every few hours, so that she could avoid frostbite.

She had a few companions with her and, when a young girl called Jean said she couldn't go on any further, Nancy had a direct way of dealing with it. She pushed the girl into a freezing stream then gave her two options: stay here and freeze to death, or keep going.

She kept going.

Nancy's seeming brutality probably saved the young girl's life.

A blizzard raged around them for hour after hour. Biting ice blasted against their numb faces, soaking their sub-par clothing. Halfway through the climb they realized they were also suffering from food poisoning from some lamb they'd eaten beforehand.

It never rains but it pours, eh?

It didn't stop Nancy Wake.

She drove herself and her companions on and up, over those unforgiving mountains with relentless courage and determination.

They eventually made it to Spain. Just.

From there, she continued to England, where she was finally safe and secure.

But safe and secure wasn't the way Nancy liked it.

The Special Operations Executive: Churchill's 'Secret Army'. Its brief: espionage, sabotage and reconnaissance in occupied Europe. Top secret. Highly dangerous. You get caught, you die.

It was tailor-made for someone like Nancy Wake. Given her

exploits with the French Resistance, it's hardly surprising that the SOE got their hands on her.

Only thirty-nine women joined the French section of the SOE. Like the others, Nancy did so under the auspices of the First Aid Nursing Yeomanry, nicknamed the FANYs.

She was taken to a training camp in Scotland. It would have suited her. She might have been beautiful, but she was also hard-drinking, foul-mouthed and ruthless. She could more than hold her own in the male environment of the SOE.

In Scotland she was trained in the use of weapons and munitions.

They taught her survival skills.

Codes and ciphers.

Communications.

Parachuting.

And they taught her how to kill silently.

All the essential skills of an undercover special forces operative.

She was also an excellent shot. Her fieldcraft was second to none, and she could move across country without anyone detecting her. In just a few months, she had been turned from a brave Resistance fighter into a lethal weapon.

In April 1944, still determined to wreak havoc with the Nazis, she parachuted back into France.

Nancy Wake landed in a tree in central France. It was an inauspicious start.

Her Resistance contact found her dangling from the tree branches. He turned on the charm. 'I hope all the trees in France bear such beautiful fruit this year.'

'Don't give me that French sh*t,' Nancy replied.

And then she got to work.

There were many local bands of rural Resistance fighters. They were called the *maquisards*. Nancy's objective was to locate and organize them. That way they could become a much more effective threat to the occupying Germans. She helped bump their numbers up to 7,000. And she helped arm them.

It was dangerous and tough work. She moved, night by night, from rebel group to rebel group. Her fieldcraft was put to the test continually, as she had to spend many nights hiding in the forests of the Auvergne while the Nazis tried to track, hunt and kill her.

Three or four times a week, the Allies would perform parachute drops of weapons and ammo. It was Nancy's job to organize them, and to keep finding new drop points.

Her work ensured that the Auvergne caused the Nazis more trouble than any other part of France.

This, in turn, meant they planned to do something about it.

The Germans bolstered their forces in the region. They armed themselves with heavy artillery and aircraft. They surrounded the stronghold of the *maquisards*. And they prepared to wipe out the rebels. Ruthlessly.

There were 22,000 German troops. There were 7,000 *maquisards*.

Nancy and her fighters didn't stand a chance, right?

Wrong.

Between April 1944 and the liberation of Paris in August of that year, the battle raged. The Germans lost 1,400 men. The *maquisards*, 100. And at the centre of the fighting was Nancy Wake.

She wasn't afraid to kill Nazis by the dozen. In fact, she seemed to revel in it. On one occasion, she led an incredibly audacious attack on the Gestapo headquarters itself in Montluçon.

They knew the German commanders would be congregating for their pre-lunch drink around noon. Nancy screamed up in a Resistance car and sprinted into the headquarters from the rear of the building. She bolted up the stairs and opened the door to the room where the Germans had congregated.

Then she threw in several grenades.

Thirty-eight key Gestapo officers were killed.

On another occasion, she crept up behind an SS guard, intending only to knock him unconscious. But then the guard turned and saw her. Her SOE silent-kill reflex kicked in. The guard opened his mouth to shout out. But before he could get any noise out, Nancy whacked her forearm up under his chin. There was a sickening crunch as the guard's neck broke.

He slid, dead, to the floor. Nancy Wake had just killed a man with her bare hands.

Courageous action by anyone's standards.

And she wasn't afraid to make difficult decisions. When it transpired that some of her *maquisards* had been sheltering a young girl who turned out to be a German spy, Nancy was the only one with the guts to execute her.

You hesitate, you die. She knew that all too well.

Perhaps her finest moment came just before D-Day. A German raid had forced one of her radio operators to burn his top-secret code books. But these codes were essential. Without them, the *maquisards* could expect no fresh supplies or weapon dumps.

Unthinkable. The codes needed replacing. The only way to do this was to make contact with another Resistance cell in Châteauroux, 500 kilometres away.

And so Nancy Wake got on her bike.

It was an incredible and ambitious plan. She not only had to cycle her way through occupied territory, but she completed the epic journey in a staggering seventy-two hours. Talk about a Tour de France, and, believe me, Nancy Wake wasn't riding a carbon-fibre bike. She was riding an old boneshaker, with turnips in the basket.

When she finally arrived in Châteauroux, Nancy couldn't stand up. Or walk. In fact she couldn't even speak. She could only cry quietly in pain. But she'd done what she set out to do. Against the odds. And it enabled the Resistance to continue with their vital mission.

Looking back on the war, she would recall that bike ride as being among her proudest moments.

There's no doubt that the French Resistance played a massive role in the defeat of Hitler. And in the middle of the *maquisards*, calling the shots and leading them with unbelievable courage, was Nancy Wake.

And yet, for her, the liberation of France was bittersweet. She revelled in the sudden excitement in the streets, and enjoyed the sight of the Nazi occupiers fleeing the scenes of their crimes. But there was sadness too. She learned that her husband, Henri, had been captured by the Germans after her escape from France in 1943. They demanded information about Nancy.

He refused to give it to them.

They tortured him.

He still refused to give it to them.

And so they tortured him until he was dead.

Nancy Wake would always blame herself for his death. But from the end of the war until she died, in 2011, she never once regretted her ruthless actions against the Germans.

She knew that if she was caught, she could expect the same treatment as twelve of her fellow female SOE agents in France finally received: torture and execution.

She later recalled, 'There had been nothing violent about my nature before the war, yet the years would see a great change. The enemy made me tough. I had no pity for them, nor did I expect any in return.'

Once the war ended, Nancy continued to work for the SOE

until 1960. She was honoured with many medals and awards, including the George Medal from Britain, the Légion d'Honneur from France and the Medal of Freedom from America. But, as always, medals only tell half the story.

For me, Nancy Wake's wartime contribution is best summed up in the words of one of her Resistance comrades.

'She is the most feminine woman I have ever known, until the fighting starts. Then, she is like five men.'

# TOMMY MACPHERSON:
# THE MAN WHO TOOK
# ON 23,000 NAZIS

*'I like a man who grins when he fights.'*

WINSTON CHURCHILL

June 1944.

An Allied aircraft – a Halifax bomber – flies low over the skies of occupied France. Two commandos parachute out, attached to the plane by a static line that will engage their chutes almost immediately.

Their target is a remote field where, they hope, they will rendezvous with their hosts: a small group of French Resistance fighters. They make an accurate landing, but their arrival causes a commotion among the Resistance. 'Boss!' one of them is heard saying about the new arrivals from the sky. 'There's a French officer and he's brought his wife!'

Right on one count: one of the new arrivals was indeed French – a soldier named Michel, who had escaped his homeland before the Nazis arrived.

But he hadn't brought his wife, although it's easy to see why the confusion arose. Because the second guy was Tommy Macpherson of the Queen's Own Cameron Highlanders, and he'd parachuted into occupied France in full ceremonial battle gear.

Which included his kilt.

Maybe the Resistance fighters took him less seriously for that. They'd have been wrong to do so. Because this guy had already waged a private war that would have broken most people.

And, by the time he parachuted into France in 1944, he was only just getting started.

\*

Tommy Macpherson's first acts of bravery took place a long way from his native Scotland. At the start of the Second World War he fought against Vichy forces in Lebanon, and saw action in Crete and Cyprus. He was shot at, shelled and stabbed – in short, he had been given a brutal introduction to the harsh realities of war. A hero before he was even 21 years of age.

In 1941 he was part of a four-man unit. Their mission: a covert reconnaissance mission into North Africa. They were to insert by submarine, then row to the beach in two-man canoes known as folbots. Once they'd made land, they needed to recce the area and ensure it was suitable for a larger force to land. It was an important mission: the Allies were sending in troops to kill Rommel. Once the four-man unit had completed their initial beach task, they were to return to the sub.

But it didn't happen like that.

They had no problem inserting into North Africa. The problems came when they tried to leave. As they paddled out to sea in their folbots they headed on a bearing directly towards where the submarine was supposed to break the surface to meet them.

But when they got to the RV point, there was no sub. Just a German transport ship, full of troops.

They evaded the ship, but now they were alone at sea. Their only option was to return to the coast.

The unit split up into two groups. One headed inland and was quickly captured. Tommy and his mate lasted a little longer. When they came across a German encampment Tommy had the courage to break inside and steal some food. Then they trekked further on into the Libyan desert – stopping only to blow up an enemy communications centre on the way.

They moved further into the desert in their attempt to evade capture, ignoring their cracked toenails and septic feet. Their thinking was good: in the desert they'd be able to hear any German trucks approaching and find somewhere to hide.

Unfortunately, they didn't take into account the possibility of a troop of Italian soldiers on bicycles.

The enemy silently surrounded them.

They were captured.

Tommy didn't panic. Unseen by his captors, he removed the magazine from his Colt automatic pistol and slipped it into his pocket.

They were whisked away for a long, gruelling interrogation. Tommy found himself faced with four interrogators and six armed police. He wasn't fazed. When one of his interrogators produced his Colt and, somewhat naively asked him to explain how it worked, Tommy slipped the magazine back in and held all ten men at gunpoint.

His plan was to escape the interrogation room, steal the Italians' car and get out of there. But his trek through the desert had wreaked havoc with his legs. When he tried to make his move, he was suddenly crippled with cramp. He collapsed. The Italians pounced on him.

His first ever escape attempt had ended in failure. But he'd marked himself as one to watch. The enemy duly dispatched him to the grim POW camp at Montalbo in Italy.

The camp was overcrowded and there was never enough to eat. As a non-smoker, Tommy was able to swap his cigarette rations with another prisoner for a few potato peelings, but he still developed jaundice.

He endured the winter there before being moved to a new POW

camp – one for particularly dangerous prisoners – in the town of Gavi, outside Genoa. There he spent his days trying to keep fit and learning Italian, which he knew he would need if he ever managed to escape. But when the Italian armistice occurred in 1943, things changed. These category A prisoners were transferred to yet another POW camp.

But, as ever, Tommy was on the lookout for a way to escape.

He managed it when they were at a transit camp near the Austrian border – by the gutsy method of joining a group of French prisoners who were being sent out to work in the surrounding fields, donning a French uniform and simply walking out of the camp with them.

Together with two other escapees, Tommy broke free and made a brave trek across Europe, through snow and biting wind, up and over treacherous mountain ranges – only to be captured once again and delivered straight into the hands of the Gestapo.

They were lucky not to be shot on the spot. The Gestapo imprisoned Tommy in a tiny, cramped cell too small for him to stand up or lie down. Then they delivered him directly to a new POW camp on the Polish border: Stalag 20A.

He escaped from Stalag 20A on his 23rd birthday, part of a daring night-time escape party that cut through the wire and made a brazen run north for the Baltic coast, where Tommy stowed away in the dirty coal bunker of a goods ship heading for neutral Sweden. From Sweden he boarded a flight back to Scotland, where he arrived precisely two years after his initial capture on the North African coast.

Was Tommy Macpherson ready for a long period of R & R? Um, no. He was a fighter, and a good thing too, because the British had earmarked him for greater things.

He was about to join Operation Jedburgh.

\*

Operation Jedburgh was a highly secretive unit of small patrols who were to parachute into France, fire up the French Resistance and conduct sabotage missions against the occupying Germans.

And the Resistance needed firing up, especially in the south. When a few plucky guerrillas had destroyed a railway line between Toulouse and Bordeaux, the Germans had retaliated by taking twenty hostages and hanging them on meathooks along the railway, where they left them to die. Having witnessed atrocities like that, many ordinary French people no longer had the stomach for resistance.

The Jedburghs needed to turn that situation around.

Unlike other members of the Special Operations Executive, who tried to work under the radar, the Jedburghs were instructed to carry out highly visible attacks – proof that the Allies were coming, and that they weren't afraid for the Germans to know it. They were made up of people who had demonstrated that they had grit in adversity. As Tommy Macpherson had.

Tommy had a three-month period of intensive training to supplement his commando skills. He became proficient in demolitions, coding and firing enemy weapons – not to mention man-to-man combat. And then he was parachuted in to France to start winding the Germans up, right under their noses.

Not for the faint hearted. But, then again: nothing ventured, nothing gained. And Tommy knew that if you are going to make a difference in a war you have to go all in – no holds barred. Total commitment, total courage.

It was 1944. The war was not going Germany's way and everybody knew it.

But a wild animal is at its most dangerous when it's backed into a corner.

The Jedburghs were guerrillas. Spies. They didn't have the protection of POW status. If they were caught, they'd be tortured. And when they'd been forced to give up every last bit of information they'd be shot.

Make no mistake: kilt or no kilt, when Tommy Macpherson jumped out of that Halifax bomber in June 1944, he was parachuting straight into the lion's den.

Tommy and his comrades had parachuted in very heavily armed: they had Sten guns, mortars, a light machine gun, grenades and a massive amount of plastic explosive.

Unfortunately, the eight-man Resistance unit they joined was less impressive. Four of them were just boys, and they had never actually hit back in any way against the Germans.

That was about to change.

Tommy got to work immediately. Their first targets were bridges, which they destroyed under cover of night, resulting in logistical chaos and mass confusion for the Germans. But, within days, this tiny guerrilla unit would have a much bigger task on its hands.

The D-Day landings of 6 June 1944 were a turning point in the war. Tens of thousands of Allied troops spilled on to the Normandy beaches.

The shockwaves reverberated throughout Europe, including south-central France, where word reached Tommy Macpherson that a massive German tank division was about to crush its way through his patch, on its way to reinforce the German troops in Normandy and take on the Allies.

And this was not just any German tank corps. This was the 2nd SS Panzer Division. Also known as Das Reich.

The Das Reich Division were justly feared. They were battle hardened from the Eastern Front, where they'd learned a thing or two about how to deal with civilians who dared to resist them.

As they made their way up through France in June 1944 they left in their wake a trail of horrific war crimes. In one village they rounded up nearly two hundred men, machine-gunned the men's legs so they were unable to walk, then, when their bones were splintered and the blood was oozing out of them, the Panzer division poured petrol over their shrieking, wounded victims and burned them to death.

On another occasion they imprisoned nearly 500 women and children in a church. Then they set it alight. If anyone tried to escape, they mowed them down with machine guns. Only three survived.

This was the kind of force Tommy Macpherson and his band of inexperienced Resistance fighters were up against. If they were caught, they would be brutally killed. But Das Reich had to be stopped. By any means necessary. The war effort depended on somebody having the sheer guts and ingenuity, somehow, to stop them.

Tommy Macpherson was that man. He hardly had the resources to take on an entire Panzer division.

His methods, though, were simple but effective.

Overnight, Tommy and his tiny band of men cut down thick tree trunks and used them to make several blockades along the roads which the Panzer division would need to pass on their way north. At each of these blockades they planted a different booby trap.

At one, there was an anti-tank mine, bolstered with extra explosives. At another, Tommy hung grenades from trees which exploded as the Germans disturbed them. At a third he armed his guys with Sten guns so they could perform devastating hit-and-run attacks before disappearing quickly into the surrounding countryside.

Now it was Das Reich's turn to scream. At each blockade, the booby traps worked, maiming and killing the enemy forces who had previously committed such awful crimes.

For a handful of men to take on an entire division like this took true courage. And Tommy Macpherson was leading from the front.

Their mission was successful. It should have taken Das Reich three days to reach northern France. Thanks to Tommy and his men it took them three weeks.

By which time they were too late.

Tommy Macpherson continued to wreak havoc across France. He hijacked German supply vehicles. He blew up bridges and railway lines. His speciality was demolishing pairs of electricity pylons, so that they fell together and created a massive firework display.

And all the while, his habit was to drive round the French countryside, wearing his kilt and with his traditional Scottish dagger tucked in his socks. He even boldly pinned a Union Jack and a *croix de Lorraine* to his car. He was making the very clear point that Germans could not suffocate the pluck of the Allies, no matter how hard they tried.

He wound the Nazis up so much with his antics that they put a price on his head of 300,000 francs.

It didn't put him off.

Day after day after day he continued his relentless campaign of guerrilla tactics, and the Germans were simply unable to stop him. He became known as the 'lunatic Scotsman who keeps blowing up bridges'.

But Tommy Macpherson was no lunatic. He was a man with untold reserves of bravery and a total refusal to let the bad guys win.

But perhaps his greatest act of courage was yet to come.

By late July 1944 it was clear that the Nazis' plans for European domination were being scuppered by the Allies. The Germans were retreating.

But a retreating army can cause just as much bloodshed and mayhem as an advancing one. Not to mention the fact that they can always turn round and attack again. These retreating Germans needed to be stopped.

Trouble was, there were a lot of them.

When a German garrison of 100 heavily armed men came marching over the horizon Tommy knew he couldn't defeat them by force of arms. But he could, perhaps, defeat them by cunning.

He had discovered that if you held a Sten gun with a wet handkerchief, it made a sound not unlike a heavy machine gun. And plastic explosives, properly detonated, could be made to sound like mortar fire. Tommy and his guys let rip with their mock armaments.

And then, carrying a large white flag, Tommy walked straight up the hill to meet the Germans head on.

Adopting his best poker face he told the German commanding officer that he had a heavily armed force up ahead who could call up the RAF at any moment to blow the enemy to smithereens. The Germans' only option was surrender.

Which they did. *En masse.* Tommy waited for some French reinforcements to arrive and loaded the German soldiers into trucks to get them to a POW camp.

The bluff had worked. But it was only 100 men. What if he was faced with a considerably stronger enemy force?

Like, 23,000 strong.

That was the size of the army Tommy Macpherson and his band of French Resistance fighters soon found themselves facing. It consisted of more than 15,000 regular troops and more than

7,000 front-line troops, who were highly experienced in battle. If it came down to a fight, they'd make mincemeat of the French.

And a battle was looking very likely.

The army needed to cross a small bridge over the river Loire. It was manned by the French, but they had no chance of holding this bridge when push came to shove.

Their only chance was if the Germans could somehow, miraculously, be persuaded to surrender on the spot.

It was time for Tommy to bluff his way to victory yet again.

In order to approach the German command Tommy needed to make his way through five miles of road lined with trigger-happy German troops, not to mention their 1,000 vehicles. And so he commandeered a French Red Cross van. It was just about the only vehicle that could potentially make it through the massed ranks of the retreating German army without coming to harm. If he got lucky.

Tommy donned his full Scottish regalia, including his kilt and hat. He had good reason to do so. Dressed in his official Highland gear he could perhaps persuade the German commanders that the lie he was about to tell them was true: that, just over the bridge, he had a full Highland brigade, complete with tanks, heavy artillery and a full detachment of French troops.

Not only that, but he repeated the gambit he'd used before: one call and the massed ranks of the British RAF would be strafing overhead, reducing the 23,000 German troops to a pile of twitching corpses.

They swallowed it. Hook, line and sinker. Thanks to the gutsy effrontery of a single man, all 23,000 German troops laid down their arms and surrendered.

Now, that bluff took grit.

*

But even then Tommy's war wasn't over. Fresh from his experiences in France he was sent back to Italy, where his enemy were no longer the Nazis but communist partisans loyal to the Yugoslavian dictator Tito, who had his eye on vast swathes of Italian territory.

The enemy might have been different, but Tommy's methods of dealing with them were the same. In Italy, however, he came closer to death than he'd ever been when an Italian *Fascisti* took a pot-shot at him with his pistol.

An inch in any other direction and Tommy Macpherson's war would have ended right there, but luck was on his side: it bounced off his notebook and gave him a mere flesh wound. Leaving Tommy to deal – terminally – with the soldier who'd shot him.

He also dealt terminally with Tito's designs on the Veneto region of Italy. Tommy Macpherson wreaked such havoc with the dictator's plans that Tito went so far as to put a death sentence on the head of the man he contemptuously referred to as the 'Scottish major'.

You can tell a lot about a man by the nature of his enemies. To have Nazi war criminals and communist dictators baying for your blood, you must be doing something 'right'.

Without doubt, Tommy had pitted himself against some of the most ruthless and violent men of the modern era. That he came out on top is a testament to his remarkable persistence, his refusal to bow down in the face of superior numbers and firepower.

Above all, Tommy Macpherson showed an almost superhuman amount of sheer old-fashioned bottle, and, to me, he embodies everything that is best about the courageous men and women who fought for our liberty during the Second World War.

# BILL ASH: THE COOLER KING

'There is something very deeply ingrained
in me that can't resist a good escape.'

BILL ASH

March 1942. An American pilot, flying for the Canadians, fighting for the British against the Germans, is in trouble over occupied France.

Big trouble.

His name is Bill Ash. He's flying his Spitfire, with other members of his section, home to Hornchurch in Essex after a sortie that has taken him as far as Comines in Belgium. An urgent call comes over the radio:

'Break formation. Break formation!'

Ash pulls an immediate 180-degree turn, just in time to see a German Focke-Wulf 190 easing away below him. The Focke-Wulf is, at this time, the Germans' most effective combat aircraft. But that doesn't worry Bill Ash. He's about to give this pilot something to think about. He catches up with the plane, opens fire and watches with satisfaction as the 190 spirals down to earth, billowing smoke.

Then he sees another member of his section being tailed by a Messerschmitt.

He alters his trajectory and releases a flurry of rounds into the Messerschmitt's fuselage. But, as he fires, he hears an ominous, thumping sound from his guns.

He's been hit.

The Spitfire's engine starts to judder. His speed suddenly drops. He glances around the surrounding airspace. A group of Messerschmitts are flying towards him from several directions. They circle, like wild cats around a wounded beast, and prepare to finish him off.

Bill Ash doesn't intend to give them that satisfaction.

Here's the thing about bravery: you have to call on it when times are toughest. Ash knows that there is no point trying to outrun his enemy. In a situation like this, he has only one option.

Fly directly towards the Messerschmitts.

Head on, he will be a smaller target to hit. And, crucially, he will force his enemy to concentrate on not crashing into him.

Unfortunately, it also means he has to watch the incoming rounds pummel his Spitfire as he makes the most important decision of his young life to date.

Parachute out? Or crash land?

Parachuting would be safer, but it will give the Germans on the ground plenty of time to find him. So he goes for the riskier option. He picks out a flat field next to a small French village, and prepares to bring the juddering Spitfire back down to earth, the fast way.

The plane cartwheels as it hits the ground. One wing rips away from the fuselage. The fuselage itself tears in two just behind the pilot's seat.

Amazingly, the pilot himself is still alive.

One thing, however, is certain. Here, far behind enemy lines, German ground forces will be closing in on him any moment.

He needs to escape – and fast.

Bill Ash doesn't know it yet, but escape is something for which he has a definite flair.

*

A local French villager got to him before the Germans. She gave him some civilian clothes, but after that he was on his own.

And on the run.

Not knowing if the Germans had dogs, he waded deeper and deeper along what he thought was a canal, to hide his scent.

He soon realized that it wasn't a canal. It was a foul-smelling open sewer.

When he heard someone following him, he went under – head and all. He emerged a stinking mess, which wasn't helped when, the following day, he had to hide in a manure heap.

Smelling good, Bill. But not captured. Yet.

He wandered through northern France for three days, before falling in with members of the French Resistance. They smuggled him first to Lille, then to Paris where, for some weeks, he stayed with a French family and walked the streets of the capital, brushing shoulders with the Nazis. He hoped to remain 'hidden in plain sight'.

Plucky, but unsuccessful. In early June, Nazi soldiers broke into the apartment where he was staying. At gunpoint, they demanded his papers.

He had none, of course. His first escape was at an end.

The Nazis beat him viciously in the face with the butt of a rifle. Then they escorted him to one of the most terrifying buildings not just in Paris, but the world. The last place on earth a downed Allied pilot wanted to find himself.

Gestapo HQ was situated in a road that members of the Resistance dubbed the 'Street of Horrors'. If you ended up there, you were much more likely to be tortured then executed, rather than be set free. Bill was dragged into a small cell in the basement for a couple of hours, then taken up to be interrogated by a neat, grey-haired man in civilian clothes. Ash declared himself a prisoner of war, and requested to be treated as such under the terms of the Geneva Convention. His interrogator laughed.

'You are a spy,' he said. And everyone knew what the Gestapo did to spies. It was never pretty.

The Gestapo officer declared that he would only believe that he was a POW if he revealed the names and whereabouts of every French person who had helped him since he crash landed.

Of course, Ash knew exactly what would happen to anyone he shopped to the Nazis. With a twinkle in his eye, he apologized that he was simply terrible with names.

The Germans didn't see the funny side of Bill's disdain for the Nazis.

His guards went to work on him. One of them grabbed his arms and yanked them behind his back. The other smacked him viciously and repeatedly in the face, followed by even more brutal blows to the pit of his stomach and between his ribs. The guard paused for a moment, making Ash wonder if he'd had a sudden change of heart. He hadn't. He was just taking a moment to wrap a rag round his fist so he could continue raining blows down on every part of his body until his face and shirt were soaked in blood.

Then his interrogator returned. He was holding a piece of paper. It was an execution warrant. If Ash failed to cooperate, he would be shot the following day as a spy.

The terror of captivity is hard to describe – that feeling of being utterly powerless – knowing that either torture or death awaits you at dawn.

The feeling in the pit of your stomach as you hear those terrifying footsteps approach your cell door must be horrific to endure.

The following morning didn't bring death, however, but more interrogation.

Ash was shaking with fear by now. When his interrogator once more demanded some French names, the pilot gave him one. Monsieur Josef.

The Gestapo man's eyes lit up with triumph. Who was this Monsieur Josef? he demanded.

Bill Ash gave him a weak smile. 'My French teacher back in Texas,' he revealed.

Once again, the Germans' sense of humour was lacking. The beating that followed was even more brutal than the first one, culminating in repeated and agonizing blows to the kidneys that beat almost every drop of air and life out of his limp body. Unable to walk, he was dragged to his cell, where he lay bleeding – with the promise that tomorrow, he really would be executed.

Still the execution didn't come. Just a week-long orgy of violent beatings, blood and excruciating suffering as the Gestapo tried to coerce some names out of him. But despite the wretched pain and humiliation inflicted upon him, Bill Ash didn't give in.

The Gestapo rarely got bored of inflicting violence for no reward. If information wasn't forthcoming then they just intensified the torture. And they would have no doubts about having him shot in the end. But his salvation, such as it was, came from an unexpected source.

One morning he heard a voice outside his cell arguing with his Gestapo interrogator. When the door opened, a Luftwaffe officer stood there. He explained that Bill was now a Luftwaffe prisoner. He would be taken to a camp and treated as a POW.

Bill was taken to Dulag Luft near Frankfurt, and from there to the infamous Stalag Luft III. The camp commandant tried to explain that the war was now over for Bill Ash. But the commandant was wrong.

For Bill Ash, the war was only just beginning.

*

For a Spitfire pilot under attack by a Messerschmitt, the standard operating procedure was to fly straight at it so the enemy had something to think about other than firing his guns. For a POW of Bill Ash's make-up, the standard operating procedure was similar: to try to escape, because then you'd be diverting the enemy's attention from other matters of war.

But escaping was difficult, and dangerous. Get caught, and you risked a bullet in the head from the Gestapo. That didn't bother Bill. He set his mind to it the moment he became a prisoner of the Luftwaffe.

Food at Stalag Luft III was scarce. Ash knew that to be a successful escapologist, he needed a bit more meat on his bones. There were two foodstuffs that were so disgusting nobody would eat them: one was a foul, sloppy, green cheese; the other was klipfish – fish innards that had been dried out years before, which needed rehydrating into a revolting paste that smelled and tasted like wet dog hair. Ash guzzled it down, and once he had a bit more weight on, he started exercising hard to get himself fit.

What is most remarkable about Bill Ash's escape attempts from the many POW camps in which he found himself is not the volume of them. It's not even their audacity. It's his sheer, bloody-minded persistence. He felt honour-bound to disrupt the enemy in any way he could. And he was certainly successful in that, even if he was unsuccessful in remaining on the run for more than a few weeks.

His first attempt to escape from Stalag Luft III was concocted with the help of another downed Spitfire pilot called Paddy Barthropp. Together they presented their first escape plan to the camp's escape committee.

Beneath some of the prisoners' showers, where the water ran

off to the drains, was a small compartment for the mains taps. If they could hide there for long enough, the prison guards might assume that they had genuinely escaped and give up looking for them within the camp. This would make a real escape attempt easier.

Nice idea. Unfortunately they didn't count on the sniffer dogs.

When their absence was noted, the camp's Alsatians and their handlers burst into the showers and located the sodden hide-aways. Their reward: several days in solitary confinement – the 'cooler'. But that failed to dampen Ash's determination to escape.

Between his capture and the end of the war, Bill Ash made thirteen escape attempts from camps all across Europe. And he clocked up more weeks in the cooler than he could even count.

Ash was then moved to a new POW camp in Poland. He first tried to stroll out of the camp while the guards were looking the other way. Unfortunately they saw him and overtook him on their bicycles! The guards beat him horribly on that occasion, but were so preoccupied with violence that they failed to search him properly. He had a small file taped to his leg, which he used to cut the bars of his cell. He might have got away with it if the guards hadn't randomly moved him to another cell, by which time his file had grown blunt . . .

Ash made many escape attempts from that camp, including one that involved digging a tunnel 17 feet below the ground. The entrance to the tunnel was situated in the putrid-smelling latrines – the escapologists reasoned that their German guards wouldn't really fancy nosing around them much.

While one man sat on the toilet to keep guard, a dozen other men started digging a chamber right next to the stinking bowl of the latrine itself. In order to enter the tunnel and continue digging, Ash and his comrades had to battle a foul lake of human excrement. But the closeness of the latrine was also an advantage – it gave them somewhere to stash the earth they dug away as that treacherous, narrow tunnel moved slowly but surely toward the edge of the camp.

Picture it. No light. Cold clay and excrement pressing in on you. Barely enough room to move – the tunnel was only two feet wide by two feet high. The tunnellers kept the roof up by using slats from prison beds, but still showers of filth would fall on them, and there was the ever-present risk of collapse.

At the open end of the tunnel a prisoner would use a makeshift bellows to pump air down to the workers, but still: oxygen was scarce. And, of course, the latrines would overflow, and they'd find themselves crouched on a dribbling stream of rotting effluent.

But still they dug.

Thirty-three men escaped through that tunnel. But they were all captured. Ash himself managed six days on the run, before being found by a bunch of German farmers armed with pitchforks. Yet the escape attempt was by no means a failure. The German army had to divert massive resources to finding the escapees. These audacious attempts were a veritable part of their own private war effort.

And so Bill Ash kept them coming.

In the autumn of 1943 Ash found himself in a Lithuanian camp. This time, the tunnel he helped dig was more than 150 feet long. Ash escaped, along with fifty others, into the Lithuanian country-side. But for escape and evasion, you need to be fit. The months of physical labour involved in making the tunnels, not to mention the terrible lack of food and his long stretches in the cooler, meant Bill was anything but in shape by this stage.

Ash would later describe his journey through the unknown

Lithuanian countryside as like being in a daze. A nightmare, more like. In his weakened state he had to cross fast-flowing rivers, before sleeping in cold, damp clothes that froze his joints and sapped any remaining strength from him.

Night-time brought strange, terrifying hallucinations that startled him from his much-needed sleep. He suffered severe dizziness and lack of breath. As he stumbled through treacherous marshland, he had to follow the paths made by wandering goats in order to avoid being sucked down by quicksand.

When he could finally go no further, he collapsed in a farm outbuilding. But when he woke, he was being stabbed at with a pitchfork by a crowd of Lithuanian peasants, demanding to know if he was Russian or German.

If they thought he was either, they would no doubt have done to him what the Gestapo had refrained from doing. Despite his exhaustion, Ash persuaded them that he was neither German, nor Russian, nor British, nor American. He was a Texan! The peasants had never heard of Texas, but decided he was a friend and let him stay with them for several days. Then they set him on his way to the Baltic Sea, where he hoped that perhaps he could steal a small boat and continue his escape.

He made it to the coast. He even found a boat. But then he made the mistake of asking another bunch of Lithuanian peasants digging their garden to help him launch it. He was an escaped American pilot, he explained, being chased by the hated Germans.

The peasants looked at each other. Then they gave him the bad news. They weren't Lithuanians at all. They were German soldiers, and the escaped American pilot was standing on their vegetable patch.

Next stop for Bill Ash: the local Gestapo.

*

The Gestapo sent Ash, with a massive – and no doubt rather flattering – armed escort, to Berlin. Nazi heartland. He can't have expected to survive very long there.

The Gestapo certainly wanted to put him to death. Unusually, given the countless millions they had already exterminated, they wanted to do so 'legally'. So they put Bill Ash, serial escapologist, on trial. Happily for him, things were going badly for the Axis powers. In the winter of 1943, nearly 2,000 tons of ordnance were dropped on Berlin in a single day. The Nazis simply didn't have the resources to continue the trial. And so, with another impressive armed escort, the Cooler King returned to a hero's welcome at Stalag Luft III, before being slammed straight in the cooler once more.

And in a weird kind of way, his stretches in solitary confinement saved his life. Bill Ash was alone in the cooler when the sirens of Stalag Luft III blared to announce another breakout. This was the Great Escape, of which a fanciful Hollywood version would later hit the screens. (Bill Ash would later comment, wryly, that in all his escape attempts there never seemed to be a lone motorbike around when you needed one!)

Fifty men made it under the wire that day. Fifty men were captured. And fifty executed. But fortune was smiling on William Ash, alone in the cooler and not part of that escape attempt.

Despite his persistent attempts to escape, and his relentless beatings at the hands of his Luftwaffe and Gestapo enemies – any one of whom could have shot him with impunity – Ash made it through the war. He lived to tell his tale.

And it's a tale worth telling, because it teaches us something profound.

In our day-to-day lives, we all meet bullies and tyrants. Hitler and his Nazis were extreme versions of just that. And sometimes it is hard to stand up to the bullies. But the story of William Ash is a reminder of the value of persistence, ingenuity and good, old-fashioned pluck in the face of those who think they can get away with keeping you in the gutter.

He is a reminder that you can't keep a good man down for long and that good will eventually win through – if you get lucky.

# EDWARD WHYMPER: A DISASTROUS SUCCESS

*'Every night, do you understand, I see my comrades of the Matterhorn . . .'*

EDWARD WHYMPER

The date: 18 February 1880. The place: Cotopaxi in the South American Andes range. The world's highest active volcano. A man holds the ankles of his colleague as he hangs over the edge of the crater.

Twelve hundred feet below him rages a melting pot of lava and flames.

Most people would have wanted something a little more secure than just a friend holding their legs.

But Edward Whymper wasn't most people. He was a man whose thirst for exploration remained unquenched, despite the terrible tragedy he had once been part of.

Away from the mountains, he lived the quiet life of a book illustrator. But his quietness hid a character of steel. One that would embark on some epic quests of adventure, from the harsh mountains and volcanoes of South America to the frozen wastes of Greenland.

But his most celebrated expedition was, without doubt, the first ever ascent of the Matterhorn. It's a tale of persistence and courage, but also of disaster. A reminder that sometimes, glory goes hand in hand with sacrifice. And that it is not enough just to keep your wits about you on the way up. You must tread even more carefully on the way down.

*

The Matterhorn. It's up there with the Eiger as one of the most impressive peaks in the Alps. It rises to the sky like a great rocky pyramid on the border between Italy and Switzerland. It's like a siren. Beautiful, but very dangerous – and more than willing to kill all manner of climbers who, over the years, have found themselves drawn towards it.

The peak's flanks are so steep that snow and ice can only cling to them in patches. Avalanches – both of snow and rock – are commonplace. Its location and its height make it vulnerable to sudden and extreme changes in the weather. You can have perfect visibility one moment; the next you'll be climbing blind.

A winter storm in these mountains is not like your regular storm. Needles of ice blast and stab at your face. Chunks of ice a foot wide have been known to have blown vertically upwards from the glacier below.

Yet despite this, the mountain is a magnet, both for tourists and mountaineers. The tourists come because it's beautiful. The mountaineers come because it's deadly. Even today, people regularly die trying to climb it, their broken, blood-stained frozen bodies perfectly preserved in icy couloirs where nobody will ever see them.

But, for many a mountaineer, the danger only increases the allure. The Matterhorn is a formidable challenge, waiting to be tackled.

Nowadays, the ascents are well mapped. There are even fixed ropes on parts of the more awkward pitches. But, of course, this has not always been the case. By the middle of the nineteenth century, many people had taken up the challenge to climb the Matterhorn. None of them had achieved it.

This was a time known as the golden age of Alpinism. Intrepid mountaineers sought to conquer the most difficult peaks of the

Alps. But by 1865 the Matterhorn's summit still remained untouched by humans – not for want of trying.

The peak first came to the attention of the young Edward Whymper when he was dispatched to the Alps in 1860, to draw Alpine scenery for a series of book illustrations. It was his first visit to the region, and he soon became captivated by mountaineering.

One of his subjects was Mont Pelvoux, which a mountaineer by the name of Professor Bonney had attempted to scale, and failed. By 1861 Whymper had conquered the peak. He clearly had an aptitude for the sport. Armed with his simple gear and inexhaustible enthusiasm, Whymper went on to claim many of the greatest Alpine peaks.

One, though, still eluded him.

There was, at the time, a huge rivalry between the Italian and British Alpinists. They didn't just want to beat the mountains – they wanted to beat each other.

Whymper and his English contemporaries had bagged the first ascents of most of the main Alpine peaks. When only the Matterhorn remained, a group of leading Italian climbers decided that they should restore a little national honour and be the first to scale the peak.

Jean-Antoine Carrel was one of these mountaineers. Between 1861 and 1865, he and Whymper both attempted to conquer the Matterhorn via the south-west ridge. This was widely accepted to be the most accessible means of ascent. But neither had any success.

It's worth taking a moment to think about the gear those early Alpine explorers would have used. Nowadays, mountaineers have incredibly lightweight, reliable, well-tested equipment. Not

Edward Whymper. For him, the few bits of gear he had were some coils of thick (heavy!) manila rope; an 'alpenstock' – or a good, sturdy stick to you and me; wool gloves and hobnailed boots (he wasn't a fan of the crampon); a canvas tent or bivouac for protection (again, heavy!); and a compact spirit lamp – or 'Russian Furnace' – for light and heat.

With this, he was good to go.

On one occasion, Whymper attempted a solo ascent. It very nearly killed him. He slipped on a particularly treacherous ledge and tumbled down a 45-degree slope. His body smashed into some rocks before tumbling over a ledge and into a gully. As he fell, his skull cracked against rocks and hard ice. (No modern helmet for him!) He continued to crash down for more than 60 feet, until rocks broke his fall and brought him to a sudden, violent halt.

He was a mess. His body was covered in deep gashes – more than twenty of them. The worst were on his head. Blood gushed out of the wounds, blinding him, covering his skin and clothes. Turning the snow scarlet.

He would surely have bled to death if he hadn't hit on the idea of pressing a large chunk of hard snow against his face as an improvised dressing. It stemmed the bleeding enough for him to continue the descent.

Back in Zermatt, he tended his wounds with a mixture of raw salt and vinegary wine. Never fun on an open wound.

On another attempt, a storm blew up when Whymper and his companions were halfway to the summit. They pitched their tent as the storm raged around them. For twenty-six hours they stuck it out, nothing but a piece of canvas between them and the ferocious elements. In the end they had to turn back. Their survival depended on it. It seemed that whatever Whymper threw at the mountain, the mountain cast back in his face.

By 1865 Whymper had attempted the Matterhorn seven times. Each attempt had ended in failure.

But you know what they say. Fall down seven times, stand up eight. And Whymper wasn't going to be defeated.

By now, any Alpinist worth the name wanted to be the first to scale the Matterhorn. It led to huge rivalry and secrecy. Of all of them, Whymper was the most obsessed. One of his rivals described him as 'that fellow whose life seems to depend on the Matterhorn . . . suspiciously prying into everything'.

But what some people might call obsessive–compulsive, others would call thinking outside the box.

Was the south-west ridge, which had defeated everybody, really the only way up?

Nobody thought that climbing it via the so-called Hornli Ridge, which looked so forbidding from the ground, was even possible.

Whymper now considered it.

Sure, it looked deeply menacing from below, but mountains look different close up. And Whymper thought that he had maybe spotted a route. People thought he was mad. Whymper didn't care. He decided to give it a go.

Six other men joined Whymper's team. Three Englishmen: Lord Francis Douglas, Charles Hudson and Douglas Hadow. A French climber: Michel Croz. Two guides, father and son, both called Peter Taugwalder. They set off from Zermatt at dawn on 13 July 1865.

By midday, they had climbed to a height of 11,000 feet. So far, so good.

They pitched their tents and sat it out till the following morning. Just before dawn they packed up their camp. As soon as it was light enough to climb they started their final ascent. The conditions stayed good, their new route was working. By 1.40 p.m. the party had conquered the peak.

They stayed there for an hour, revelling in their success. Time passed quickly. They were euphoric. Ecstatic. Elated. Not quite literally on top of the world, but not far off.

Then the men started their descent. Which was when things went very horribly wrong.

The treacherous Matterhorn had reeled them in with a relatively easy ascent. Now she was preparing to spit them out.

She was about to show the mountaineers that she wouldn't be taken lightly.

★

Perhaps it was their euphoria that betrayed them. Perhaps it was fatigue. Or maybe it was just bad luck.

At Whymper's instruction the men roped themselves together. It was a good idea, in theory, and was typical of early Alpinists learning the fundamentals of modern-day mountaineering techniques through trial and error. The rope is there to stop a slip becoming a fall – as long as it is kept taut.

But the downside is that if the rope is allowed to fall too slack, and someone falls, then the force could rip those above them off the face. All of them. Like dominoes.

Croz led the way. Then Hadow, Hudson and Douglas, followed by the two Taugwalders – old Peter and young Peter. Whymper went last. But as they climbed down, Hadow – who was in second place and also the least experienced of them – lost his footing. Fatally, the rope above him had also been too slack.

As he slipped, he crashed into Croz, the leader. As the rope behind him pulled tight, it yanked Hudson and Douglas down the face.

It had only taken seconds. But on a dangerous peak like that, seconds is all it takes.

Further up the rope, Whymper and the two guides heard the desperate screaming of the men below. Immediately, they clutched at some rocks.

But their luck was not to hold. Nor was the rope.

The force of the falling men was too much for it.

It strained – drum-tight.

Held for a second or two.

And then it snapped.

Whymper stared, horrified. From his elevated position he saw Croz, Hadow, Hudson and Douglas tumble down the face.

They spread out their hands, trying to grab something that would halt their fall.

But there was nothing to grab.

And with the rope broken, there was nothing Whymper and his two companions could do.

Except watch.

One by one, Whymper's four companions slipped out of sight. Nothing could have saved them as they tumbled from one precipice to another.

They fell a total of 4,000 feet.

As they'd fallen, a single word had echoed up towards the remaining mountaineers. It came from the mouth of Croz.

'Impossible!'

'Impossible!'

Whymper had shown that climbing the Matterhorn was not impossible. But the costs can be impossibly high.

There is a special bond between men who set out on an expedition of that scale together. A kind of comradeship that is hard to find in everyday life. But then to lose any of those companions is a brutal blow that is hard to describe. It turns the victory sour, and any triumph hollow.

Whymper and his two guides shouted out the names of the fallen as they continued their dejected descent. But they knew it was in vain. Nobody could have survived a fall like that.

The broken mountaineers didn't reach Zermatt until the following day. There was no glory in their return home. In fact, there was nothing but controversy. They were accused of having cut the rope in order to save their own skins. People said that, rather than try to save their companions, they had betrayed them. It was a cruel twist for Whymper, the man who had risked his all.

Whymper's embittered success did not kill his enthusiasm for mountaineering or adventuring. But he never attempted another Alpine peak. And in the years that followed he could barely bring himself to talk about the climb that had made him famous – or maybe infamous.

His fallen colleagues haunted him nightly. In his dreams he saw them slipping away from him, to their deaths. And when he finally died, aged 71, in 1911, he was buried in Chamonix, not far from the scene of his greatest, and most dreadful, achievement.

Times change. So do people. But mountains don't. Not in the lifetimes of men. The Matterhorn still remains a great challenge today. And in the 150 years since Edward Whymper and his team first reached the summit, it has claimed the lives of more than five hundred climbers.

For me, the story of Edward Whymper serves as a reminder that, in extreme situations, you can't let your guard down for a moment. If you do, then mountains have a habit of coming up and biting you on your backside. Hard.

You may have reached your pinnacle, but a mountain doesn't care if it kills you on the way up or the way down. Never get com-

placent. Complacency kills. And remember that the time to concentrate hardest is when you are feeling weakest.

Edward Whymper's own words remain as true as ever: 'Climb
if you will, but remember that courage and strength are nought
without prudence . . . Do nothing in haste; look well to each step;
and from the beginning think what may be the end.'

Good advice for mountaineering. And good advice for life.

# GEORGE MALLORY: 'BECAUSE IT'S THERE'

*'I feel strong for the battle, but I know every ounce of strength will be wanted.'*

GEORGE MALLORY

The Nepalese call Mount Everest Sagarmāthā – the Goddess of the Sky. The Tibetans call her Chomolungma – Mother Goddess of the Universe. But whatever name she goes by, the reality is that her faces are a living graveyard.

It's no surprise. High above sea level, where the oxygen is thin, the air freezing and your muscles and mind are exhausted, death can feel strangely attractive. The final stretch of the climb is known as the 'Death Zone'. Here, your body enters a state of necrosis. It is, quite literally, starting to die.

The choice of whether to turn back or continue is down to the climber – and so half the battle of conquering the world's highest peak happens in your oxygen-starved brain. It is why the way to the top is littered with the bodies of those who didn't make it.

Near the very top is the body of David Sharp. In 2005 he nearly made it. Just short of the summit he stopped to rest. But the sub-zero temperatures were working their icy ways on him. His body started to freeze where he sat. Several other climbers passed him by – struggling to move themselves, let alone able to carry another.

Although Sharp's limbs were frozen stiff, he was gently moaning. The other climbers moved him out into the sun. There was little else they could do.

David Sharp still sits there today. An iced corpse, fully clothed in mountain gear. His hands on his knees. A gruesome landmark for anyone heading to the summit.

Most of the bodies are well preserved by the cold. Some aren't. There are corpses lower down on the slopes of Everest that have rotted away into skeletons. Their skulls protrude from their clothes with hideous rictus grins, snow settling on the rims of their empty eye sockets.

Some corpses have been mummified by the wind and the sun drying out their skin. Others lie face down, recognizable only by their clothes. One of them is nicknamed 'Green Boots'. He's an Indian climber who died in 1996, only identifiable now by the colour of his footwear.

More than two hundred people have died in their attempts to climb Everest. Nepalese law states that the bodies should be collected and properly buried, but that isn't always possible. Maybe it is somehow fitting that those who didn't make it remain on the mountain. Their own memorial to a dream they had.

In 1999, at 26,670 feet on the North Face of the mountain, one such corpse was discovered. Its well-preserved flesh was frozen as hard as rock. The skin was bleached almost white by the sun. It was lying on its front, pointing up towards the mountain. Its arms – still muscular – stretched out above its head. Its torso was frozen to the ground.

Two bones in the right leg were broken. The elbow dislocated. Several ribs were fractured. There was a hole in the skull, probably the result of a blow with an ice axe. Imagine how that one must have bled.

And inside the body's clothing was a name tag. It said: G. Leigh Mallory.

The frozen body of George Mallory was a revolutionary find. Not only was Mallory's attempt to reach the summit – nearly thirty years before Edmund Hillary set foot on the mountain – a truly inspiring moment in the history of human endeavour, it also led to one of the Goddess of the Sky's most tantalizing mysteries.

*

The young George Mallory came from a family of clergymen. As a child he displayed a flair for mathematics, and won a scholarship to Winchester College. There, a teacher introduced him to the sport of mountaineering, and took him on a trip to the Alps. The seeds of his future fate had been sown.

In 1905 he went to Magdalene College, Cambridge, to study history. He was clearly a talented, intelligent and fun young man. He fell in with the likes of Rupert Brooke, John Maynard Keynes and Lytton Strachey. And when he graduated he joined Charterhouse school as a teacher. One of his students was the young Robert Graves. Graves's recollection of his teacher tells us a lot about the kind of man Mallory was: 'He was wasted at Charterhouse. He tried to treat his class in a friendly way, which puzzled and offended.'

Graves was not the only man to speak of him with admiration. Lytton Strachey wrote that he had the 'mystery of Botticelli, the refinement and delicacy of a Chinese print, the youth and piquancy of an unimaginable English boy'.

The poet-mountaineer Geoffrey Winthrop Young gave him the nickname 'Galahad' after Sir Thomas Malory, author of *Le Morte d'Arthur*. He was becoming a romantic figure even before he stepped foot on the foothills of Everest.

But all that poetic stuff hid the fact that Mallory also had grit in abundance. His interest in climbing continued and he became an accomplished Alpinist. The Alpine peaks are not to be taken lightly. Mallory conquered many of them, including Mont Blanc. But then the Great War got in the way.

When the war started he wanted to join up. The headmaster – following an edict from the Minister of War Lord Kitchener, stating that school teachers should not be allowed to leave their posts – did not grant him permission. So Mallory was forced to sit in the comfort of Godalming while his friends (such as Rupert Brooke) and pupils (such as Robert Graves) went to war. He met, and married, Ruth Turner, who lived near Charterhouse. But the bliss of those first few months of married life was marred by what was happening in Europe.

Many of Mallory's friends and acquaintances died in the foul, brutal misery of the trenches. By 1916 he couldn't take it any more. He defied Kitchener's edict, joined up and was sent to the Western Front.

The horrors of trench warfare on the front line are another story for another day. But, given his ultimate fate, one letter home jumps out: 'I don't object to corpses so long as they are fresh. With the wounded it is different. It always distresses me to see them.'

Mallory survived the war and returned to continue his teaching. His love of the mountains, however, had not diminished. Nor had his sense of adventure. When, in 1921, the Mount Everest Committee financed the British Reconnaissance expedition's attempt on the summit of the world's highest peak, Mallory was an eager participant.

The expedition failed to reach the summit. So, the following year, he tried again, this time as part of a group led by Brigadier-General Charles Bruce. And although this attempt also failed, Mallory reached a record-breaking altitude of 26,980 feet without oxygen.

A third attempt in the same year also failed but, by now, Mallory was a celebrity. When a reporter from the *New York Times* asked him why he wanted to climb Everest, he replied with the three most famous words in mountaineering. Three words that are the beating heart behind why many explorers or adventurers do what they do.

'Because it's there.'

And it was still there, of course, in 1924, when George Mallory made his fourth and final attempt. He knew that, at the age of 37, this might well be his last opportunity. And he promised his wife Ruth that, if he made it to the summit, he would leave a photograph of her there.

Then he set out for glory.

The omens were good. On 7 June, Mallory wrote in a letter from Base Camp that it was 'perfect weather for the job'.

It needed to be.

The mountaineers of the day were not clad in lightweight modern clothing or equipment to protect them from the elements. Rather, a mixture of tweed and cotton. No modern mountaineer would consider the boots *c.* 1924 up to the job. This time, though, Mallory at least agreed to trial some early oxygen apparatus. It was heavy, but experience told him he couldn't manage without it.

Charles Bruce led the 1924 expedition, as he had in 1922. Mallory's partner was Andrew Irvine. One of their colleagues, a geologist by the name of Noel Odell, followed at some distance behind them in a support role.

Little is known about what happened next. Mallory and Irvine had no means of communicating with other members of the expedition. All we know for certain is that they never made it back. But I can tell you, from my own time on Everest, something of what they would have experienced.

The upper faces of Everest are treacherous. Crevasses – giant cracks in the ice – can open up beneath your feet with no warning.

It happened to me. If I hadn't been attached to a rope, I'd be another statistic of the mountain. It took two companions to help drag me out. One wouldn't have been enough.

If your oxygen runs out in the Death Zone, you can expect immediate delirium, lethargy and, finally, death. The weight of the oxygen canisters, which are keeping you alive, feel like a constant and cumbersome burden. Yet the benefits of the oxygen narrowly outweigh the weight of the bottles. In 1924 the weight was far, far greater still.

Frostnip is run of the mill up there – even today I still feel its effects in cold weather from my time on Everest. Numbness followed by intense pain as blood floods into the weakened capillaries.

And at that height your body also loses the ability to process food. It starts to deteriorate. Entering the Death Zone is like setting off a time bomb. Stay up there too long, and you will die, no matter who you are.

The weather can be wildly unpredictable – even with modern forecasting. In 1924 there were no forecasts. And the winds on Everest can be easily strong enough to blow a man off his feet – and then the only way is down.

Being up that high, in those conditions, hurts.

Man, it hurts.

Your muscles cry for relief.

Your lungs burn.

Your extremities ache with the extreme cold.

Your head throbs, and your mouth and throat grow raw with the thin air.

It's a kind of torture. You feel like you'd do anything to make it stop. It's like the mountain itself is willing you to quit. And, as the air grows thinner and the temperature colder, she makes you feel like you just don't care any more.

Everest makes death seem like an attractive option.

And you have to fight that. You have to fight it with all your might.

When I climbed the mountain, I had advantages that Mallory and Irvine never had. Proper footwear and mountain gear. Communication with other climbers on the mountain. A deeper understanding of how the body reacts in extreme environments. Proper weather reports. The ability to receive messages from my family at home. For me, all that makes the attempts of those early pioneers all the more awesome.

I can see Mallory and Irvine, their teeth gritted, their minds locked in battle with the mountain as she sucks the life, the energy and the will to win, out of them. And doing all this alone.

History and science tell us that Mallory and Irvine, although they may have made it very close, probably never reached the top. The world would have to wait another twenty-nine years before Edmund Hillary and Tenzing Norgay finally conquered the world's highest peak.

There's no doubt that Mallory and Irvine died on the vicious slopes of Everest. Nor is there any doubt that back in England their brave attempt turned them into national heroes. They even had a memorial service at St Paul's Cathedral attended by the Prime Minister Ramsay MacDonald and King George V.

But are history and science telling us everything? Or is there more to the story of George Mallory than meets the eye?

Noel Odell, their support climber who was following behind them, reached a height of 26,000 feet on 8 June. As he was gazing up towards the summit, the cloud cover cleared for a moment. He later recorded what he saw: 'One tiny black spot silhouetted on a small snow-crest beneath a rock-step in the ridge; the black spot moved. Another black spot became apparent and moved up the snow to join the other on the crest . . .'

On the high faces of Everest, there are three distinct rock and ice outcrops: the First, Second and Third Steps. Many people think Odell was describing an area between the Second and Third Steps, which means Mallory and Irvine were very close to the summit.

Close enough to reach it, before perishing on the descent?

We know from the story of Edward Whymper that a mountain will as happily kill you on the way down as the way up.

And we know that Mallory had the guts to go for it. He was all in. Glory or bust.

With the discovery of Mallory's body, we know some other things too.

It was just before one o'clock in the afternoon that Odell saw Mallory and Irvine striking out towards the summit. There's little doubt that, at this time of day, they would have been wearing their goggles to protect them from snow blindness. But Mallory's goggles were not fixed to his corpse. Nor were they found nearby.

They were in his pocket.

Does that suggest that he was making an evening descent, at a time of day when the goggles weren't necessary? Many people think so.

And what of Mallory's promise to his wife, that if he made the summit he would leave a photograph of her up there. That would surely mean that he'd have had the photograph on him when he left camp. And it should have still been on him when his body was discovered.

Only it wasn't.

Is it too romantic to imagine that Mallory did indeed make it to the summit of Everest?

That there, for a short while, the image of his wife lay in that lonely, desolate, beautiful place before the winds blew it away or the snow covered it.

Before her husband died on the descent.

No one knows. But perhaps one day Irvine's body will be found, with the camera they took with them. It will either show pictures of them on the summit, or it won't.

For now, only Everest holds the key to the mystery. And the Goddess of the Sky does not willingly give up her secrets.

One thing's for sure: Hillary and Tenzing were the first to climb Everest and return safely. The glory of that achievement is theirs for ever. But whether Mallory reached the top or not, his assault on the mountain – just like that of all those who try – is no less awesome or epic. It was a goal he had set himself. Maybe he succeeded, maybe he didn't. But what's important is that he got out there and gave it his best shot.

We all have our own Everests to climb. And just like there's no shame in being defeated by the real one, there's no shame in being defeated by our own personal mountains.

It is all about never giving up, and acting with courage and dignity in the big moments.

The only real shame lies in refusing to try.

And no one can accuse Mallory of that.

# TONI KURZ: THE MURDER FACE

'We must have the wall,
or it must have us.'

TONI KURZ

The Eiger.

Translated from the German it means 'the Ogre'. For a climber, the very name evokes terror and respect. If it doesn't, you're in the wrong game.

This 13,000-foot mountain in the Swiss Alps has attracted the most determined mountaineers for as long as the sport has existed. Not because of its height, but because of its unrelenting difficulty. And it is one of the few mountains whose fame extends beyond the fraternity of mountaineers.

Like Everest, the Matterhorn and K2, young children learn its name. And they learn that it hosts one of the most fearsome, epic climbs in the world: the North Face.

In German, it's called the Nordwand. In the 1930s, it was nicknamed the Mordwand. Which means 'Murder Face'.

This is not the story of how the North Face of the Eiger was finally scaled in 1938 by a brave German–Austrian team. It's the story of a failed attempt just a year before that. A cautionary tale – that sometimes extremes of courage are not enough when you're battling against the natural world for your own survival.

And a reminder of the many, horrible ways in which a mountain can kill you.

*

Toni Kurz was a handsome 23-year-old in July 1936 when he decided, along with his three companions Willy Angerer, Edi Rainer and Andreas Hinterstoisser, to make an attempt on the North Face.

These were the sports stars of their day. Their exploits were recorded on the front pages of newspapers.

When the day of the climb arrived, crowds of people stood at the foot of the mountains with telescopes and eye-glasses to watch the death-defying entertainment.

The four men knew that if they conquered the Murder Face they would be heroes. As they set out, they were overheard telling the local climbers, 'We will have to climb your wall for you, if you will not climb it yourself.'

But mountains require respect. Fail to give it, and Mother Nature has a habit of reminding us – often the hard way.

The climbers started off roped together as two pairs, but before long they chose to rope themselves together as a foursome. It was more than just a mountaineering decision. It was almost as if they were making a statement: they were in this endeavour together. Any triumph would be theirs to share.

So, too, would any tragedy.

They started off well. They climbed the early stages of the North Face, across areas whose names – the First Ice Field, the Second Ice Field – were well known to Eiger-watchers. But then the mountain sent a warning shot clean across the climbers' bows.

It was a warm day. And on the Eiger that's not a good thing. As the sun's rays hit the face, the ice melts and the meltwater starts to pour down the cliffs, bringing with it rocks and ice-debris. It is a big part of what makes the North Face of the Eiger so treacherous.

One small rock, falling like a bullet, smacked into the side of Angerer's head. A shower of blood spurted out. He was alive but bleeding badly. Rainer was forced to hold back from the group and tend to Angerer's injuries.

Soon he had staunched the wound, and the team decided that Angerer's bleeding head wasn't serious enough to abort the mission.

Despite this incident, they made good progress on the first day. They had scaled half of the North Face before they bivouacked for the night.

The following morning, the crowds at the base of the Eiger were even bigger. They knew that Angerer had been injured, so perhaps they'd come out to witness a retreat. But there was to be no retreat, and the team continued to climb.

It was apparent that Angerer was flagging, but still, by the end of the day, the climbers had reached the Third Ice Field. They bivouacked there for the night.

The following day, the spectators watched as Kurz and Hinterstoisser pushed on towards an area of the North Face called the 'Death Bivouac'. But their companions, Angerer and Rainer, didn't move. The wounds that Angerer had sustained on the first day were now taking their toll.

And so, despite being so close to success, the two leaders retreated back down to their companions.

The team might have started the North Face with an air of cockiness about them but, as climbers and as friends, they knew that Angerer's life was worth more than the glory of scaling the North Face. The mountain was teaching them humility – and fast. If Angerer was unable to climb, he would need the help of all his companions to get back down to safety.

And they were there to give him that help. All for one.

*

If you've read the stories of Edward Whymper (see page 173) or Joe Simpson (see page 223), you'll know by now that descents can often be as dangerous, if not more dangerous, than ascents. To help an injured and weakened companion down the sheer North Face of the Eiger would be a mammoth task.

At first, it seemed they were up to it. The Second Ice Field – a large, sweeping slope of compacted snow – seemed to the watchers below to present no great difficulty. They crossed it fairly quickly. But when they reached the area known as the 'Rock Step', which led to the First Ice Field, they started to slow down. Dramatically. At the top of that ice field, they had to bivouac for another night.

That day, they had only descended 1,000 feet. There were still 4,000 to go.

That third night, stranded on the North Face of the Eiger with an injured man, must have been a frightening one. Not only were they wet, cold and sapped of energy, but they also knew that the following day they would have to 'carry' their companion across some of mountaineering's most fearsome climbs like the 'Traverse' and the 'Difficult Crack'. Each man knew that it would be the hardest climbing of their lives – much harder than their original goal of the summit.

It would either make them or, quite literally, break them.

Dawn came. The spectators down below watched through their telescopes as the four men emerged from their bivouac. They descended the First Ice Field with reasonable speed. Things were looking promising, after all. But as they approached the Traverse, the weather took a turn for the worse. The mountain hadn't finished with them yet.

Tendrils of mist started wrapping themselves around the North Face. Avalanches of powder snow, ice and rock started cascading down the mountainside.

Cloud continued to cover the mountain. The temperature at the rock face dropped dramatically. The streams of running water turned to bullet-hard ice. The observers down below could only catch occasional glimpses of the foursome.

The situation was getting brutal for the climbers. As they battled against the cold, the wind and the exposure, clinging to the sheer face for life itself, the reality of their predicament must have been beginning to dawn on them: they were going to struggle to get themselves off this mountain, let alone with their injured partner.

When the clouds parted, the crowds could see that only three of the climbers were attempting the Traverse. The fourth – Angerer – was at the rear.

Then the clouds covered them again.

As the mist unfurled once more, it revealed that the three able-bodied climbers had been forced to give up on the Traverse. Covered with treacherous ice, it had proved impossible to cross. The three men had spent the whole morning trying, but had succeeded only in exhausting themselves further. The stricken climbers were going to have to find another route of descent.

The trouble was, from their position, there was only one.

Vertically, straight down.

Straight down was the lesser of two evils, but it was still evil.

It meant that three able-bodied and one injured man would have to rappel 700 feet down a rock face that they couldn't see the end of. And that is one hell of a long way to rappel.

In places, where outcrops of rock bulged out from the vertical, the climbers would be forced to rappel over overhangs with no idea whether their rope would lead them back to the face. And even if it did, they had no idea whether there would be anywhere for them then to anchor their next section of rope to, in order to continue down.

With no communications or guidance on whether the route was viable, they would effectively be rappelling blind. And, all the while, the falling stones and avalanches would be raining down on them like skittles in a bowling alley.

To attempt this rappel, and in a blizzard, would be suicide – but they had no other option.

They went for it.

At first, it looked like the team might pull off the impossible. Down on the ground, onlookers heard the group yodelling that everything was fine. As they got lower, they even sounded excited, as if they were starting to believe they could actually now make it.

What happened next occurred behind a veil of thick cloud, and we can only try to piece together the unfolding tragedy. But we do know that it was an avalanche that killed the first of them.

As the brutal weight of the tumbling snow smashed mercilessly into Andreas Hinterstoisser it ripped him free from his rope. He plummeted to his death, falling like a rag doll through thin air. His body slammed on to the rocks, thousands of feet below.

Hinterstoisser's death was no doubt a devastating blow to the three remaining survivors when they were so close, but they couldn't allow it to break them. They could mourn him later. For now, they had to survive. But survival was much more difficult with only two of them left to help their injured companion.

It wouldn't stay like that for long.

The wounded Angerer was the next to die. Quite how it happened is not clear, but it seems that he slipped and fell, and the rope that was meant to save him ended up strangling him. Now he was suspended in mid-air, a hanged man, his corpse limp and gruesome.

The mountain was teaching some harsh lessons to those bold enough to have attempted the Face.

And the mountain hadn't finished yet.

Rainer had been on the top end of the rope securing both Kurz and Angerer. But the combined weight of the men on the rope below him – one living, one dead – was crushing his chest. The pressure must have been immense and there was no way he could fight it. The force and the weight of the rope around him squeezed him in a vice-like death grip. He died of asphyxiation where he lay.

Only one man was left. Toni Kurz. Surrounded by cloud and death. But alive.

He was suspended in his harness, hanging from a rope thousands of feet above the ground on the Eiger's brutal North Face. One dead body was attached to the rope above him, one dead body attached to the rope below him. He couldn't move up. He couldn't move down. And he couldn't swing in to the rock face.

He could do nothing but hang there, and hope that somebody had the guts to come to his rescue.

There were mountain guides in the area, but their chief refused to force anybody to join the rescue mission. Kurz and his companions had known the risks of their undertaking, after all.

But the mountaineering community has always been close-knit, and it's testament to the bravery of those guides that they agreed to mount a rescue mission, despite the very real dangers involved.

The guides struggled through snow-blasted winds to reach a point 300 feet below where Kurz was hanging. They called up to him through the screaming wind, and Kurz yelled back down. He explained what had happened to his three companions. Then he told the guides that their only hope of rescuing him was by coming down from above. He explained that he had left some climbing pitons (spikes) embedded in the rock above, from which the guides could lower themselves.

But the day was drawing to a close, and such an ambitious rescue would take time. To attempt it in the dark would be suicide. The guides yelled a question up to Kurz: 'Can you manage one more night?'

The response was definitive, and delivered with a clear, strong voice. 'NO!'

But the guides knew they didn't have a choice. A rescue attempt in the dark was impossible. If Kurz was to live then he had to figure out how to survive one final night.

The guides yelled up at him that they'd be back at first light the following day, but as they descended, they heard Kurz's voice echoing against the rocks and through the gale.

'NO!'

That surely must have been one of the longest nights ever. Hanging in agony in his harness. Surrounded by death and darkness. Frostbitten and frozen on to the rope. Your friends, all corpses, hanging above and below you. Buffeted by the gale, swinging backwards and forwards. Backwards and forwards.

It was so cold that icicles, eight inches long, formed from the soles of his boots, as his wet clothes seeped and then froze. At some point during that interminable night, one of his gloves slipped from his hand. A cruel blow. Kurz must have known he was now in real trouble.

The cold then ripped into his flesh. First it froze his fingers, then his hand, then crept up his arm.

All the while, wave after wave of powder snow poured over him from the mountain above.

Hypothermia is a silent killer. It steals your ability to move.

Then your ability to think clearly. Then it sucks away your will to stay alive. But Toni Kurz refused to give in to it. When the guides returned at first light, he was still there, frozen but alive – still able to shout back to them, albeit in a much weaker voice than before.

The rocks of the wall were now frosted in an icy glaze. Kurz still insisted that the only way they could rescue him was from above, but the guys knew it would take an expert mountaineer to descend that way, even in the best of conditions. And so, four of them ascended from below Kurz's position.

They got to within 130 feet of him. So close.

They couldn't see Kurz because of an overhang, but they knew his only chance was if he could somehow get more rope to rappel down on. If he could descend just a little further, they would be able to reach him.

They tried to fire some rope out at him, but the ropes just shot into empty air before falling limply back down.

Kurz had only one other option. One final chance at life.

He would somehow have to lower himself down to where Angerer was hanging and cut the rope. Then he would have to climb back, as high up the rope as he could, and cut the rope that had joined him to Rainer. Then he would have to tie the two ropes together and rappel the final section down to the rescuers.

It was an almost impossible task for an exhausted, frostbitten, hypothermic man with one arm frozen solid.

Almost impossible, but not quite.

The astonished rescuers soon heard the hacking of an axe against rope. The rope split, but Angerer's body did not fall. It had been partially resting against the face, and had frozen solid to the rock. It took an avalanche – which only just missed the guides – to break the frozen corpse free.

It hurtled with snow down into the abyss.

Then, slowly and painfully, Kurz hauled himself up the rope and hacked away at it, separating himself from Rainer's body.

Using just his teeth and his one good hand, he unravelled the rope he had freed. So far, the whole operation had taken him five hours. Five hours of unimaginable courage and determination.

Agonizingly, slowly and painstakingly, he tied the ropes together. It would normally have taken a man like Kurz seconds. But his body was shutting down. It took over an hour.

Amazingly, with his reserves of strength almost depleted, he managed to lower the rope down to the rescue team. And then, little by little, he started to lower himself down towards them.

It was slow, excruciating work. Kurz's body was almost frozen solid. Just moving his limbs a few inches took Herculean willpower. But he fought against the pain, the fatigue and the menacing embrace of death and, little by little, he edged his way down.

And he so nearly made it.

He was in view of the guides, and in easy earshot. But there was a problem. Where the two ropes had joined, there was a large knot. In order to get past it, Kurz had to squeeze the knot through the snap-link on his harness.

Perhaps it would have been possible if one of his arms hadn't been near frozen solid, or if his utterly spent body was not so totally drained of all his last reserves of willpower. The guides screamed words of encouragement at him over the wind.

'Keep trying! Keep trying!'

He did keep trying, so far as his body would let him. He was mumbling incoherent words as he did so. The guides couldn't make out what he was saying. His face had turned purple with frostbite and his lips could barely move.

His body could barely move.

And the knot wouldn't move.

The guides watched, willing him on, but powerless to help. Kurz's movements grew slower still. More laboured, still.

His frozen left arm jutted out from his body, stiff, immobile – and useless.

In a final attempt to push the knot through his snap-link, Kurz summoned up his last reserves of strength and leaned forward to grab the knot with his teeth.

But the attempt failed. Toni Kurz knew he was about to die. He raised his head towards the guides and spoke once more. This time it was not a feeble muttering. The guides heard his words quite clearly.

'*Ich kann nicht mehr*,' he said.

I can't go on any more.

Then Toni Kurz, having given it everything, slumped immobile and waited for death to sweep over him.

Toni Kurz is not the only person to have lost his life trying to defeat the North Face of the Eiger. But he makes it into this book not because of the ambitious courage of his original endeavour, but because of his stubborn refusal to surrender, even as the mountain and the elements threw their worst at him, beating the very life out of him.

Toni Kurz died trying, and his courage and raw determination have always been a humbling and inspiring example to me of a man who gave real meaning to the words: true grit.

# PETE SCHOENING:
# THE BELAY

*'The team might have failed, but they failed
in the most beautiful way imaginable.'*

REINHOLD MESSNER

In 2006 twenty-eight people had a party. They were celebrating something very special: their own existence.

These were the descendants of an eight-man mountaineering team who, fifty-three years previously, had made an attempt on the second-highest mountain in the world, K2. These twenty-eight people knew that they would never have been born if it hadn't been for one man's miraculous feat of strength on the slopes of that fearsome peak.

For a mountaineer, the term 'belaying' refers to the use of ropes between climbers to ensure their safety as they ascend and descend. And on the unsuccessful 1953 attempt on K2, 'the Belay' – as it became known in mountaineering folklore – was critical.

Make no mistake: K2, on the border between Pakistan and China, might be only the world's second-highest mountain, but it's widely regarded as the most difficult Himalayan giant for any mountaineer.

Climbers regularly die on its faces, even today. And for every four people who reach the summit, one dies trying. It's never been climbed in winter and, back in 1953, it hadn't been climbed at all.

An eight-man American team led by Charles Houston was aiming to be the first.

You've heard it said that there's no 'I' in 'team'. Well, this was Houston's guiding principle as he put together his companions. They weren't selected solely for their climbing brilliance – many technically better climbers were overlooked for the expedition – but more for their ability to get on with others in adverse conditions.

Houston made the call that when the chips were down, he wanted men of character by his side.

He could not have foretold how important this decision would turn out to be.

Among the team he assembled were a nuclear scientist from Los Alamos and a ski instructor from Seattle. There was also a geologist from Iowa called Art Gilkey, and the youngest of their company, a 27-year-old chemical engineer called Pete Schoening.

It was Schoening's name which would go down in mountaineering history.

The attempt on the summit occurred just after Pakistan's partition from India. This was significant. It meant that the Indian Sherpas – who, up until partition, had acted as porters on Himalayan expeditions – were not welcome in Pakistan. Conversely, the Pakistani Hunza porters were not considered to be such skilled mountaineers.

The company decided, rather than use unskilled porters to help them haul their gear, that they would travel light. This meant no unnecessary equipment and no oxygen canisters.

But abandoning local guides had its advantages. The route they were going to take was an ascent called the Abruzzi Spur. There would not be space to pitch many tents on the way up, so the fewer people in their group, the better. Or so they thought.

There's an old Army saying: fail to prepare and you prepare to fail. For Houston's team, preparation was key. It had all the hallmarks of an immaculately planned expedition.

The team arrived at base camp on 20 June. They would need to establish eight camps in order to crack the summit of K2. These guys spent the next six weeks climbing methodically up and down the mountain, selecting and maintaining the route, pitching the camps and making sure that the vital supplies were in place. Only on 2 August did the team finally make it to Camp 8, less than 1,000 metres from the summit, ready for the final push to the top.

Everything was looking good.

But there are some things no amount of preparation can fully predict. The weather is one. It had been deteriorating for a few days, but now, almost from nowhere, a massive storm circled round the climbers. They were forced to sit it out in the 'Death Zone' – the altitude above 8,000 metres where your body can no longer metabolize effectively and literally starts wasting away. All the team could do was hope that conditions would improve – and fast.

They didn't.

The freezing, oxygen-starved air was taking its toll on the climbers' weakened reserves. At that height the human body is dying, and everything becomes a battle. A fight just to stay alive. On the fourth day, one of their tents collapsed in the wind. On the sixth, with heavy hearts, they had no choice but to prepare to retreat – or die.

On the seventh day, the storm abated. Should they continue their ascent?

It was almost as if the mountain was toying with them.

Then fate played a deciding card.

The human body isn't designed to spend extended periods at altitude. Nor does it react well to extremes of temperature. On high peaks most people think of frostbite, hypothermia or altitude sickness. In truth, there are countless ways your body can fail up a mountain. Thrombophlebitis is one of the worst.

There are no good illnesses to have in the Death Zone, but even if there were, this wouldn't make the list.

It's a severe inflammation of the veins caused by a blood clot. It's sometimes called 'White Leg' and it requires immediate medical treatment. If the blood clot moves through your system and into your heart or lungs, it's game over. In the mountains, where the air is thin and the blood thick, this illness is exponentially more serious than at sea level. Fatally serious. When one of the group's number, Art Gilkey, collapsed in front of their tents that day, Houston was quickly able to diagnose the disorder.

The team had a choice to make. Gilkey's chances of survival if he remained in the Death Zone were nil. Carrying him back down to base camp was almost impossible. In addition, the brief break in the weather had gone and the storm had now returned with renewed and worsening fury.

Mountaineers could argue that the logical thing to do would be to leave Gilkey to the mountain, in order to save the rest of the team: why let eight people die when only one death is certain?

But let's not forget Houston's criteria in putting these men together. This was a real team. Eight men who had agreed to stick together. No matter what.

The guys didn't need to discuss it. There was no way they would leave Gilkey there to die. They would attempt the impossible and bring him back down to safety.

Or they would die trying.

The team couldn't leave Camp 8 immediately. The storm had kicked off again, and there was an ever increasing risk of an avalanche. They were forced to remain in their cramped, freezing camp for another three days. But time was running out for them all.

The Death Zone doesn't cut you any slack. The longer you remain inside it, the less likely you are to survive.

Gilkey's condition was getting worse. Much worse. He was showing signs of pulmonary embolism. This meant the blood clot was in the region of his lungs. He was now coughing up blood. Death was closing in.

The storm had still not abated. But the team had no choice. They had to start their descent or perish.

They say that necessity is the mother of invention. And that's never more true than in a survival situation. The team needed a stretcher, so they were forced to improvise one. They used some ropes, canvas from their tents and a sleeping bag to fashion a kind of cradle in which Gilkey could lie as they lowered him down the slopes. As his life was hanging by a thread, his body was hanging by a rope.

Both were completely at the mercy of his friends' courage and resolve.

The distance between Camps 8 and 7 was only about 300 vertical metres. It doesn't sound like a lot, but just try covering that distance under those conditions, at that altitude – and with a casualty. In order to get to Camp 7 they needed to traverse a treacherous ice face, which ended in a sheer rock cliff some 2,000 metres high. Not a place to fall.

It was tough, unforgiving climbing at the best of times, and these were the worst. Blinding gusts of wind and snow whipped up into their faces. The climbers could barely see where they were kicking their crampons in. They relied solely on the crunch and feel of the metal spikes on their boots biting securely into the ice to confirm their next step. One step at a time. Steadily. Methodically.

Four members of the team roped off in two pairs. Pete Schoening was attached to Gilkey and one other. The final man, Robert Craig, was climbing alone. Together they were trying to pendulum Gilkey across the ice face and back down to Camp 7.

Schoening was taking the weight of two men: one able-bodied, one far from it. He needed to anchor himself securely as the others tried to get Gilkey across the traverse. He drove his ice axe deep behind a frozen rock, fixed his rope to the axe, then to him, and started to pay out the rope to his colleagues from his improvised belay.

Then disaster struck.

One of the four guys slipped on a patch of highly compacted ice. Along with his partner, he went hurtling down the ice field towards the rocky precipice below. The falling climbers flew past the other paired team and somehow became entangled with the rope joining them together.

Entwined, the four climbers were now careering and screaming down the slope to their fate.

As they fell, they crossed the rope leading from Gilkey to his partner and then to Schoening far above.

Within the blink of an eye, six men were suddenly plunging towards the abyss. Six men were about to die. The only thing that might potentially save them, at the top of this tangled mess of rope, was Pete Schoening.

Schoening threw his weight on top of the axe and held on to it with all the strength in his weakened body. Any second now the combined force of six men – not to mention all the gear they were carrying – accelerating down a frictionless slope would come on to his axe with the force of a runaway train. If the ice axe remained embedded in the rock under that sort of pressure, it would be a miracle.

His teammates continued to slide.

Fifty metres.

A hundred.

Schoening gritted his teeth and waited for the rope to tighten.

It came suddenly, jarring his entire body, feeling like it would rip his limbs apart, as the rope snapped drum-tight like a metal cable. Amazingly, Schoening withstood the force and kept hold of the combined weight of that massive load. We're talking more than 500 kilogrammes, which must have felt much greater considering the speed that the men had been accelerating downwards.

The conditions were appalling. Schoening's hands were frozen. He was acting on pure adrenalin and through a fog of utter exhaustion.

This was 'the Belay'. One of the most astonishing examples of strength a mountain has ever seen from mortal man. Little by little, Schoening's teammates managed to regain their positions while he battled to hold their weight. If he hadn't managed that Herculean feat of human endurance, all seven of them would undoubtedly have plunged to their death.

In later years Pete Schoening would say that he'd simply been lucky that day on the slopes of K2. His companions knew otherwise.

Heroes wear their laurels lightly.

The story wasn't over. The guys continued to make their way down towards Camp 7 slowly. Once down, they fixed Gilkey to the ice face so that they could set up camp.

But, as they were erecting their tents, the men heard him shout weakly.

Two of the team returned to Gilkey's position. But the ailing mountaineer was no longer there. The ice axes that were fixed into the slope were gone. It appeared that Gilkey had become the victim of an avalanche.

Or had he?

This was a group of men who had been specifically selected for their ability to act as a team. To pull together. To think of each other. It's worth considering what might have been going through Art Gilkey's head as he hung, slumped in a sleeping bag, high up on the icy faces of K2.

He would have known, of course, that his life was in the balance. But he would also have known that his companions were risking their own lives to save him. Already they had come very close to falling to their graves on that belay. If it had not been for Pete Schoening's superhuman act of strength, they would all be dead.

They were still a long way up the mountain. Was Gilkey's condition likely to threaten his buddies' lives again?

Almost without doubt.

Would they listen to him if he told them to leave him on the mountain and continue without him to save themselves?

Definitely not.

Gilkey was drowsy with morphine. Even so, I can imagine him forcing himself to a sitting position in his makeshift stretcher.

Extending his arms to grab the ice axes that were fixing him to the mountain.

Using his final reserves of energy to work those axes loose.

The weakened shouts that his companions heard: Gilkey's ultimate adieu.

Maybe Pete Schoening's was not the only act of outstanding courage on the high faces of K2 that day. Perhaps Art Gilkey had decided that his friends had risked enough, and that there was only one course of action open to him.

A course of action that would lead to his own grisly death, smashed to bits on the frozen rocks below.

Nobody knows what really happened. All we know for sure is

that the climbers continued their descent. They owed him that much at least – to survive.

The only evidence the team saw of Art Gilkey's fate was a broken ice axe and some blood-stained rocks. His remains were not discovered for another forty years.

Years later, members of the team, including their leader Charles Houston, stated their belief that Gilkey had sacrificed himself in order to save his friends.

Heroes are born on mountains – and they often die on them as well.

It took another five days for the team to reach base camp. They were weighed down and beaten, from frostbite, hypothermia, grief and exhaustion. But, finally, they made it.

Before they left base camp, the survivors erected a small cairn to the memory of Art Gilkey, and held a simple service of thanksgiving for his courage and life. Today, it is the burial site for many climbers who have died on K2.

And to me it's a memorial to more than just one man. It's a memorial to an ideal of loyalty and companionship. Pete Schoening's belay turned him into a mountaineering icon, but he always downplayed his achievement, as great team players and heroes tend to do.

Charles Houston would later say of the members of that expedition that 'we entered the mountain as strangers, but we left it as brothers'.

And Reinhold Messner, one of the greatest mountaineers ever, got it in a nutshell. The team might have failed, he said, but 'they failed in the most beautiful way imaginable'.

And those sorts of qualities always outweigh the successes.

# JOE SIMPSON: CUT THE ROPE OR DIE

'Life can deal you an amazing hand. Do you play it steady, bluff like crazy or go all in?'

JOE SIMPSON

In 1956 the mountaineer and author Sir Arnold Lunn said of Toni Kurz's struggles on the Eiger, 'In the annals of mountaineering, there is no record of a more heroic endurance.'

And, in 1956, that was probably true.

But those words were written before Joe Simpson and Simon Yates travelled to the Peruvian Andes. Their exploits would become a bona fide modern mountaineering legend.

Joe Simpson was no stranger to dangerous mountains.

In 1983 Simpson and a companion called Ian Whittaker had been climbing the Bonatti Pillar in the French Alps. It's a 2,000-foot granite spire that you can see from the Chamonix valley, and a magnet for thrill-seekers. Their first day's climbing had gone well. They decided to overnight on a ledge, where they could enjoy a view of the stars before finishing the climb the following day.

It didn't happen quite like that.

The ledge itself formed the top of a rocky outcrop bulging from a sheer cliff face. It was only four-feet wide, but long enough for them to lie down next to each other in their bivi bags. They took the usual safety precautions – I mean, four foot doesn't exactly give you much room to roll over, and on one side was a very long, sheer drop – so they tied themselves to their anchor point, which they had fixed into a crack in the solid rock behind them.

They were just settling down to sleep when the whole ledge that they were lying on suddenly broke clean away from the cliff face. For a few seconds of blind terror Simpson and Whittaker found themselves plunging into the void below. Then, suddenly, the ropes bit and stopped their fall.

They were alive, but hanging helplessly, unable to do anything to save themselves. If they tried to wriggle free and ascend the rope, their anchor point could easily break free from its crevice. They were trapped. Hanging free by a precarious thread of rope.

Beneath them was 2,000 feet of darkness. They could only hope and pray that someone might have seen what had happened or heard their screams, and call for rescue.

They were hanging for twelve dark, sickening hours before finally a rescue chopper came for them. The two petrified climbers were brought down alive. Ian Whittaker lost his desire for mountaineering after that narrow scrape with death. And who can blame him?

Joe Simpson, however, still had it. That strange, inexplicable, burning drive that forces adventurers on to bigger and greater endeavours.

Bigger and greater ascents.

What follows is a story of fear and bravery. Fear of the unknown. Fear of suffering. And fear of death. But it's also the story of how one man refused to bow to that fear. And how Joe went on to pull off one of the biggest escapes in mountaineering history.

Siula Grande. The clue's in the name. It is indeed Grande.

More than 20,000 feet high, it's an imposing peak in the Waywash mountain range, deep in the Andes of Peru. And, like all

magnificent peaks, its summit beckons out to the boldest mountaineers out there.

Joe Simpson was one of those. So was Simon Yates. Together
they had set themselves a formidable challenge: to be the first men
to climb Siula Grande by the as-yet-unclimbed West Face. Several
mountaineering teams had attempted this. They'd all failed. But,
in June 1985, Simpson and Yates were out for the summit's blood.
And they got it.

Blood, that is.

Joe Simpson and Simon Yates became the first men to climb
Siula Grande by that formidable West Face route.

But this is not the story of that ascent.

It's the story of one of the most gruelling descents of all time, as
the pair battled to make it down off the peak and back to their
base camp.

Bear in mind that at this point the team of two were exhilarated
but exhausted, having just pulled off one of the fiercest and most
demanding climbs the mountaineering world had ever seen.

As they left the summit, events were already beginning to stack
up against them. After three and a half hours of treacherously
difficult and slow down-climbing they had made very little
progress. It was just after 5 p.m., as they were struggling along
a particularly technical and awkward ridge, when Joe felt the
snow suddenly break away beneath him. He tumbled out of
control down towards Simon's position, and then came to a
violent stop.

The pair were completely exhausted by now. And they knew
that the fall could have been much worse. It was a lucky break.

They needed to rest up, so the two climbers started to make an
improvised shelter for the night by digging out an ice cave and
hunkering down.

But there were problems. Simon had frostbite on both his

hands. By morning, the tips of his fingers had turned black. They ate the remainder of their food and used the last of the gas in their stove to melt snow for drinking water. They both knew that, in terms of mountain survival for two men at the limit of their fatigue, it was crucial that they made it down to base camp that day.

They set out at 7.30 a.m. but, once again, the terrain was dictating their descent, and their progress was excruciatingly slow. Joe, who was now in the lead, was attached to Simon by one length of rope, and was using his ice axe to ease his way over the edge of, and down, a sheer section of the ice face.

It was from this position that Joe slipped. And found himself in freefall.

When he smashed into the base of the cliff, he felt the bones in his right knee shatter. He didn't know it at the time, but his tibia had speared itself right into the heart of the knee joint.

He screamed in agony, but already he was falling backwards again, head-first down the icy face. As he fell, his thoughts turned to Simon. He knew they were tied together. At the end of the rope, the force of the fall would surely rip Simon off the mountain after him . . .

But then Joe came to a sudden and violent halt.

His whole right leg was burning with pain. He looked down. He could make out that the lower half of the limb was jutting out at an angle. When he tried to move it, he felt bone crushing against bone. Unimaginable pain. Like fire burning through his veins. It was clear that the bones and sinew were a total, mangled mess.

But above the pain, there was another overwhelming thought. They were 19,000 feet up in the mountains. If his leg was broken – and it surely was – he would have zero chance of getting down. Simon, if he wanted at least one of them to live, would have no choice but to leave Joe there to die. It was a hard but untenable situation. Joe knew that if Simon tried to help him off the mountain then, without doubt, they both would perish.

Is it any wonder Joe started to cry?

*

Joe had come to a halt because Simon had managed to drive his ice axes deep into the snow just in time. Steadily, he eased himself down to where his injured partner lay howling.

He immediately saw that Joe didn't stand a chance. Not with that kind of injury. Not here.

Few people in the climbing fraternity would have blamed Simon for leaving his partner there. They had no radio or sat phone to call for help, and no one they could signal to for assistance. The only choice would be for Simon to get down and attempt to get help back up the mountain to Joe. Either way he would have to leave his injured buddy. It was certainly what Joe expected him to do.

Simon didn't see it that way. Instead he started lowering his partner down the mountain.

They knew they needed to move quickly, but that was just not possible. Darkness was coming and the weather was now getting worse. The plan was this: Simon would repeatedly dig himself a snow seat where he could anchor himself, take the strain on the rope and lower his injured partner, length after length, down the slopes.

To make things quicker, they tied together two 150-foot lengths of rope. When the 300-foot rope ran out, Joe would hunker down and wait for Simon to down-climb to him.

It was a wildly ambitious plan and, in all truth, it was doomed to fail in those freezing mountain conditions. But Simon refused to leave Joe. And the plan seemed to be working.

At least for a while.

The weather continued to deteriorate – as weather in the mountains has a habit of doing when you most need calm. The clouds were bubbling up ominously in the east, and it was now snowing hard. The loose powder was being driven by the biting wind into every crack in their down jackets and glasses. The conditions were blinding them.

Joe's fingers then began to freeze, adding frostbite to the list of problems.

They finally reached a col – a ridge between two peaks – but here their descent became more difficult. With each movement, stabs of searing pain shot up Joe's mangled leg, leaving in its wake an incessant, unbearable throbbing. He found himself howling impotently into the wind as the freezing snow bit into his skin. But no one could hear him – not even Simon.

Several times Joe's boot caught on a rock, twisting the broken leg awkwardly, forcing more yells from the injured man's throat.

The pain pushed every other thought from his mind. It consumed him.

The broken leg started to shake. Joe couldn't stop it. His frostbitten hands were getting worse by the minute. Nausea and dizziness surged through him.

But still the pair continued their 300-foot descents.

Soon the conditions were a white-out. They could see nothing above them nor, crucially, below them. Should they continue their descent without knowing what kind of terrain Simon was lowering Joe into? Or should they wait, and surely both freeze to death?

They continued. It grew fully dark. The pair estimated that they had descended nearly 3,000 feet. Another lowering of the rope, maybe two, and they'd reach the top of a glacier. Here they'd be able to find a snow cave to last out the night, before aiming to finish their descent the following morning.

But, again, it never happened that way.

As Simon lowered Joe down the next section of mountain, Joe noticed that the slope was particularly steep. Suddenly he found himself sliding particularly fast. He tried to slow himself down with his arms, without success. He screamed up at Simon to slow him down, but his voice went unheard.

Suddenly, he was in empty air. Falling.

Showers of snow fell over him as he plummeted into darkness.

Then, with an abrupt yank of the rope, he came to a halt. He was spinning uncontrollably on the end of the rope, round and round in the void. By the light of his torch he could see an ice wall six feet away, coming in and out of focus as he continued to twist.

When the spinning stopped, he looked up. He was about 15 feet below the lip of the cliff that he had tumbled over.

Then he looked down. It was hard to tell in the darkness, but he reckoned there was 100 feet of empty air beneath him. Below that, the silhouette of a deadly crevasse – a massive tear in the ice leading down into the heart of the glacier.

Joe's torch beam flickered and then died as the batteries wore out. An ominous jolt, as the rope bit into the snowpack at the lip of the cliff, reminded him his leg was broken and causing him agony.

The rope could break at any moment. Simon could break at any moment – and then they'd both go tumbling into the unknown.

But despite his pain, the frostbite, and the wretchedness of the situation, Joe didn't give up. He knew that if he did, he was dead. And fear can be a powerful motivator.

His only option was to try to climb the rope from which he was suspended. He tried to do this using an improvised climbing knot called a prusik, but his hands simply wouldn't work. They were frozen in place. Immobile. He knew he had no chance of climbing up.

The freezing wind spun him round. Loose snow blasted his

face. The taut rope from which he was hanging dug mercilessly into his freezing body.

He felt dread, exhaustion and cold seep through his veins. Any moment now, he told himself, he'd be dead.

Above the edge of the cliff, Simon Yates was locked, unable to move. Joe was a dead weight at the end of his rope, unable to go up, unable to go down. A frozen and terrifying hour passed before Simon realized he had the Devil's choice.

He could wait here to die, at which point they would both go tumbling into the void. Or he could cut the rope, and give at least one of them a chance of survival.

The pair had no way to communicate. They were out of visual and vocal contact.

What do you do?

There was a penknife in his rucksack.

The rope was taut. The knife sharp. If any semblance of life was to be salvaged from this disaster, there was only one choice.

The blade cut through the rope with no pressure or difficulty. The dead weight at the end of it was suddenly no more.

Simon felt no guilt. He had done what had to be done. He dug himself a snow cave and prepared to weather the harsh mountain night.

Joe knew the fall was coming. One way or another, it was the only thing that could happen.

The silence seemed to last for ever. He wondered if this was what death felt like, and for a moment he wasn't scared.

Then he hit the ground with a solid thump.

The fear returned. He realized he was skidding down into the deep crevasse. He screamed again, as his body slid faster and faster into the deathly heart of the glacier.

Any moment now, he would surely be dead . . .

But, suddenly, he came to a halt.

His chest went into a spasm of retching and gagging. He tried to get air into his lungs as pain from his mashed-up leg surged through him once more. Somewhere, far above the ledge on which he'd landed, he could see stars twinkling.

In the pitch darkness, he touched the icy wall of the crevasse on one side. But he also sensed a dangerous drop right beside him. And then, when it hit him that he was still alive, he actually started to laugh. The sound echoed up around the chamber of the crevasse. Then he found his spare torch battery, and shone it down the black opening to his side. He stopped laughing.

The torch lit up 100 feet of empty space below him. One hundred feet of nothing. He could only guess the true depth of the crevasse.

He saw the cut end of the rope that had fallen with him, and understood what had happened. Then he turned off his torch to preserve the battery, and started to cry in the darkness.

There was no way Joe could climb out of the crevasse with his broken leg. Which left him two options: lie there and die, or abseil further down into the crevasse until he could find . . . something. He had no idea what was down there, and the prospect of finding out was terrifying.

He would later say that he wasn't brave enough to look down. But, to me, his next act was one of sheer courage.

At dawn, having endured the darkest of nights, lying twisted and broken on that freezing ledge, he twisted an ice screw into the wall of the crevasse to fix his rope to, and then started to lower his broken body further down into the darkness of the abyss.

He tied no knot into the end of his rope. If he didn't reach anything solid by the end of his rope then he would simply abseil off it to his death . . .

Dread pumped through him. Claustrophobic and frozen, he abseiled further and further into the unknown.

And the ultimate risk paid off.

His rope lowered him on to a snow-covered floor. Just then, a shard of sunlight cut down from the top of the crevasse.

It's amazing how simple things can give you hope.

Joe promised himself there and then that he was going to get out of there. He didn't know when, or how, but he was going to survive.

His broken leg had grown stiff. It hung shorter than the good one. Walking was out of the question, but somehow he managed a kind of excruciating hop, aided by the use of his ice axes.

His progress was horribly slow. He saw a slope ahead of him of about 100 feet. With two good legs it would have taken him ten minutes to climb. As it was, it took him five hours. But it led him to a hole in the crevasse. He pulled himself through it. He was back in the sunshine on the mountainside.

He felt a sense of jubilation, but his escape from the jaws of death was far from over. He had no water, save the handfuls of snow and ice he could suck on. But he knew that, at this altitude, he required at least a litre and a half per day to stave off dehydration. He knew nobody was coming to rescue him, so his only choice now was to crawl and slide down the mountain.

At one point he tried to walk, having wrapped his sleeping mat round his bad leg as a makeshift cast. Bad move. As soon as he put pressure on it he almost vomited through the pain.

Joe hopped and crawled through the snow and ice. His jubilation faded as he realized how lost he was. He seemed to be in a sea of crevasse openings. Surely he would never survive a fall into these scars of the mountain.

But he didn't fall. He just kept going. Past one crevasse and then past the next. Precariously dragging his limp and frozen body inch by inch through the minefield.

When he tried to sleep he was haunted by nightmares. And all the while, the physical pain was unspeakable. For three days, he crawled and hopped. Stubbornly. Tenaciously. He was at the very edge of endurance, not just physically, but also mentally. But somehow, through sheer doggedness, courage and unbending determination, he crawled his backside off that mountain.

Simon had since made it to safety too. He was at their original little base camp with a companion who had been looking after their tents. He knew he'd made the only decision he could, but it couldn't have been an easy time for him. Certainly he had never expected to see Joe again in a million years. He'd even ceremoniously burned all his clothes.

When he saw his companion crawling towards them, sobbing with agony, barely able to see through snow blindness and exhaustion, it must have been like seeing a ghost, back from the dead.

And in many ways, that's exactly what it was. In the course of that one descent, Joe Simpson had beaten death countless times. More than that, he'd done so having sustained injuries that would surely have killed off someone who didn't have his resilience and fortitude.

Experienced mountaineers consider Joe's escape from the crevasse on Siula Grande one of the greatest feats of mountaineering. I think it's actually one of the greatest feats of survival ever.

*

A word must remain for Simon Yates, the man who cut the rope.

When he and Joe returned to the UK, there were words of criticism for the way he had consigned his companion to an almost certain death. Joe quickly quashed those criticisms by saying he had done exactly the right thing – just what Joe himself would have done in the same situation. It's true. Simon Yates's decision was not an act of cowardice. It was an act of courage. You could even say that the decision saved both their lives. If he hadn't cut the rope, it's unlikely either would have survived.

To keep a cool enough head to make the right call under extreme pressure is a mark of true grit. And, for me, the story of Joe Simpson and Simon Yates is a reminder that sometimes, at the edge of endurance, when the natural world is bombarding you with everything it's got, and death seems the only option, humans have shown themselves capable of summoning up truly extraordinary reserves of courage.

One day that might be a powerful thing to remember.

# CHRIS MOON: KIDNAPPED, BLOWN UP . . . AND STILL GOING

*'I asked myself the question, "What is life all about?" I decided it was about doing the best we can, reaching our full potential and making use of our talents.'*

CHRIS MOON

Chris Moon was brought up on a farm. And growing up, he always thought that farming would be his life. It wouldn't.

In 1986, at the age of 23, he decided to join the Army. He enrolled at the Sandhurst Military Academy. Once his training was complete, he joined the Royal Military Police, and also served with a number of infantry units. He was stationed in Northern Ireland and, trust me, to be a member of the British Army in the Province at that time took more grit than most people ever get to display.

But this isn't a story about Northern Ireland. Because Chris Moon's life would take him far further afield than that. And he would pit himself against dangers that even Army life could never have prepared him for.

Chris left the Army a few years later and took a job in the City. Sitting behind a desk was no way of life for a man like him, so he made a typically brave decision: to volunteer for a charity called the HALO Trust.

HALO: Hazardous Area Life Support Organization.

Mine clearance to you and me.

Land-mines are a scourge of the modern world.

Nowadays they are banned by international law. And with good reason. Buried in the earth, you don't know they're there until you step on one. And then you *really* know about it. If you're still alive.

A land-mine doesn't care if you're an enemy combatant or a small child on their way to school. And once they're planted, they're there for years. Decades. Long after a war zone has ceased to be a war zone, land-mines continue to kill innocent citizens.

Locating and getting rid of them takes untold reserves of courage.

The HALO Trust employed former servicemen and women, trained them up in the difficult techniques of land-mine clearance, then sent them out to perform this high-risk work.

The de-miners worked in metre-wide strips. They crawled along the earth feeling for trip-wires, cutting through vegetation as they went. When they found a trip-wire, out came the metal detectors. And when the mine was found, it would be detonated – a controlled explosion where it lay.

But that wasn't the end of it.

It's the nature of land-mine clearance that those involved find themselves working remotely in the world's hot spots. Some spots, however, are hotter than others. Chris Moon's first deployment as a member of the HALO Trust saw him in Cambodia.

And Cambodia, at the time, was still recovering from a regime so brutal that the stories of its crimes against humanity are beyond sickening.

The Khmer Rouge came to power in the 1970s. They effectively turned Cambodia into one big concentration camp. Their leader, Pol Pot, outlawed foreigners, anyone with an education (including anyone who wore glasses), anyone with a religious faith and anyone who disagreed with his edict that all Cambodians should work the land rather than live in the cities. Anybody who contradicted these rules was sent for 're-education' in horrific prison camps, where they were tortured and then executed.

The entire country was put to work in the rice fields. They were overworked and underfed. Untold numbers starved to death.

All teachers were murdered. All money was burnt. Schools and hospitals were shut down.

If more than two people gathered together and talked, they were executed on the spot. If members of a family showed any affection towards each other, they met the same fate.

When they killed their prisoners the Khmer Rouge preferred to save bullets. Instead they used pick-axes, sharpened bamboo sticks, poison, spades . . .

Or if these tools were lacking, the victims were simply bludgeoned to death by having their faces slammed repeatedly against trees.

If a parent was killed, then his or her children would be executed too. That way, they couldn't grow up to take revenge on the regime.

You've probably heard of the Killing Fields. These are the horrific mass graves where the tortured corpses who fell victim to the Khmer Rouge were disposed of. In the four years that the Khmer Rouge ruled Cambodia they killed about three million people.

Even when Pol Pot was toppled, the Khmer Rouge didn't disappear. They continued to wage a guerrilla war against the people of Cambodia, especially in the more remote parts of the country. Foreigners were most at risk from these guerrillas. If they were kidnapped by the Khmer Rouge – and they frequently were – they knew what to expect.

Torture. Then death.

So Chris Moon's decision to volunteer to clear land-mines in Cambodia in 1993, I think you'll agree, took some guts.

But he'd need even more courage to survive what happened next.

*

Chris was driving a Land Rover. Beside him was an interpreter, Mr Houn. In the back were six other de-miners. Behind him, another vehicle, driven by a man named Sok, containing twenty women and children.

And ahead of him, 250 metres away, approximately twenty Khmer Rouge militants. They were carrying Kalashnikovs and rocket-propelled grenades.

If Chris tried to retreat now, there would be a bloodbath.

His only option was to stop.

The guerrillas gathered their prisoners and forced them to remove their clothes. Chris obeyed. He had no choice.

The Khmer Rouge soldiers had faces filled with hate. They stole Chris's belongings before telling him that he, Mr Houn and Sok were to be taken into the forest to 'meet' a Khmer Rouge commander.

They had been kidnapped. And to be kidnapped by the Khmer Rouge was, to all intents and purposes, to be killed.

As they journeyed through the forest, they overheard some of the soldiers discussing whether or not they should just kill them there and then. But they clearly feared their commander, and the journey continued. Chris kept calm, telling himself that, when he finally came face to face with this commander, he'd be able to talk him round. To explain that he was no threat to the Khmer Rouge. He was just here to help people.

That the guerrillas should just let them go free.

No chance. The commander told them they were to be taken to Khmer Rouge headquarters. Why? Because he didn't have the authority to kill them. 'Yet,' he said.

They spent the night in the forest. When dawn came, Chris went to the stream to drink. He realized he wasn't being watched. He had a chance of escaping. But if he did that, he would give the Khmer Rouge a reason to start shooting. He would be putting the lives of Mr Houn and Sok at risk.

To escape takes a lot of guts. But sometimes *not* to escape takes more. Chris stuck by his fellow prisoners.

They drove deeper into the forest. Word reached them that the bosses at Khmer Rouge HQ believed Chris to be an enemy Russian soldier. They were being taken for interrogation.

Their interrogators called themselves Mr Red, Mr Keun and Mr Clever (because he was the only one who had attended primary school). They told Chris and his companions that they were prisoners of war. And Chris knew that the Khmer Rouge were not exactly likely to abide by the Geneva Convention.

His gut told him that he was about to become another statistic of the Khmer Rouge's brutality.

In the face of that kind of fear some men crumble. Others, however, stand up to it. Chris refused to be bowed. He refused to be a victim. Rather than shrink back into a cocoon of terror, he engaged with his captors – he tried to befriend them.

He stopped hatred from entering his soul, and replaced it with understanding.

That must have taken some doing. And it was a massive gamble.

But the gamble paid off.

Chris Moon and his companions were kept prisoner by the Khmer Rouge for three days and three nights. Thanks to his determination to engage and negotiate with men who would kill him and his fellow prisoners without a second thought, he achieved what most people would have thought impossible.

He persuaded the militants that he was in their country for peaceful reasons. He refused to become a victim, because he knew that would give them the upper hand. He stood up to the mark, and successfully negotiated their release.

Not many people were captured by the Khmer Rouge and lived to tell the tale. Chris Moon did. And because of his bravery, mixed with some hefty good fortune, Moon, Sok and Mr Houn were set free.

But being captured by those gun-toting guerrillas was not Chris Moon's closest brush with death.

That was still to come.

Nobody would have blamed Chris Moon for getting straight out of Cambodia after such an ordeal. But he had come to do a job, and he fully intended to finish it. He bravely completed his tour of Cambodia, even when he heard that the Khmer Rouge had decided to put a price on his head.

Many people like to think they might risk their own lives to save others, including those whom we might never even meet. But how many of us actually would do it when push really comes to shove?

Fast forward to Mozambique.

In March 1995 the south-east African country was emerging from twenty years of civil war. Famine had also battered the population, not to mention the mindless and horrific violence that had been waged against women and children.

Both the government and the rebels had laid endless land-mines in order to destroy and maim each other. There were more than

100,000 mines scattered across the country, lying in wait, primed to destroy innocent and unsuspecting victims.

Chris Moon was neither innocent nor unsuspecting. He knew *exactly* what he was letting himself in for when he volunteered to travel to Mozambique to help rid the country of this curse.

This was how he found himself in a part of the country where the fighting had been particularly bad during the civil war. Government forces had laid an untold number of mines to 'protect' themselves from the rebels.

These were Russian mines, each one containing 240 grams of TNT.

Easily enough to blow your leg clean off. And, in a remote part of the world like this, the chances of one of the locals getting medical aid were almost zero. People were losing their lives on a daily basis.

Enter Chris Moon.

On 7 March 1995 Chris and his team had cleared the best part of a minefield. They had established a safety lane, and Chris – never one to ask his men to do anything he wouldn't do himself – was walking carefully along this lane through the dusty African scrub.

He stopped. At his feet was a thick patch of dried blood. Flies were swarming hungrily around it. He knew that a local man had stepped on a mine here just a few hours ago. The man was now dead.

Yet Chris felt a strange chill. Here in the middle of the safety lane, he knew that something else was wrong.

He instinctively turned to go back. Took one step.

Two steps.

Three.

And then he heard it.

An ear-shattering bang.

He was thrown to the ground.

The smell of burning TNT reached his nostrils. So did the smell of burning flesh.

His own.

At first there was no pain, but he knew he had stepped on a mine. He looked at his hand. It was a bloodied, lacerated mess.

Then he looked down at his right leg. His foot was nowhere to be seen. The lower leg was mangled and shredded. He could see his bone sticking out from below his knee. It was surrounded by ragged, bleeding, pulpy flesh.

Then the pain hit.

His body started going into shock.

Life was draining from him as fast as the blood was from his body. But he managed to find the strength to get on the radio and call for help.

Soon the medics were there, risking their own lives as they made their way up the supposedly clear safety lane. And then a casualty-evacuation helicopter was on its way. Even so, Chris knew his life was slipping away from him. And fast.

He could do nothing but pray. 'God help me,' he whispered.

Then the pain got serious. Pain like he'd never known. At a local hospital, and without any kind of anaesthetic, an orderly snipped off the flesh around his stump to prepare him for surgery. Like a butcher trimming a piece of meat with a sharp knife.

As he lay on the hospital bed, he saw the amputation kit to one side. It looked as brutal as you might imagine. A huge hacksaw. Chisels. Files for smoothing the rough bone where it has been cut.

As the doctors prepared to give him an anaesthetic, a nurse soothed his brow. She told him that the pain was about to go away. That everything was going to be all right.

But Chris had grown up on a farm. He had whispered the same words to sick animals as they were being put down.

He slid into unconsciousness, not knowing if he would ever wake up again.

*

The medics saved his life. But it was never going to be the same again.

The doctors amputated his right arm four inches above the wrist, his right leg just below the knee. He had prosthetic limbs fitted, and had to learn how to walk again. He had to deal with the pain – phantom and real – as well as the realization that his life had taken, by anyone's standards, a severe turn for the worse.

Nobody could blame Chris for feeling despondent.

But that kind of emotion didn't seem to be part of his make-up. The land-mine might have taken away his limbs, but it hadn't taken away his spirit.

Every amputee has a mountain to climb. Their own Everest. I never fail to be humbled by the quiet courage of those many soldiers who have lost limbs in Afghanistan. We hear so little about them. Their stories are many but their daily struggles remain largely untold. For them every day is a mental and physical battle.

The determination and endurance they display is mind-blowing. And Chris Moon is a great example of the iron will that these people epitomize.

Chris gave serious thought to returning to Mozambique and continuing his work in mine clearance. It was only the fact that the metal in his prosthetic limbs would interfere with the metal detectors used on the minefields which persuaded him his calling now lay elsewhere.

Chris insisted on looking at his injuries and amputations not as a hindrance, but as an opportunity. The chance to challenge the preconceptions of both disabled and able-bodied people alike.

Have you ever run a marathon? Tough work, even with two good legs. Try running it with a prosthesis. That's what Chris Moon did less than a year after leaving hospital.

Now try running a series of six marathons, back to back, in the burning heat of the Sahara Desert. It's called the Marathon des Sables (Marathon of the Sands), and it's one of the toughest foot races on earth. Temperatures can top 50°C, and sandstorms regularly reduce progress to a crawl.

Anyone who completes it has proved themselves to have strength and endurance beyond most ordinary men and women.

To complete it as a double amputee must be almost indescribably hard.

And yet that's what Chris Moon did.

Interestingly, more people completed the Marathon des Sables that year than any other. Chris's explanation: 'They couldn't stand being beaten by a one-legged git!'

It takes a lot of heart to keep your sense of humour, when you've lost so much else.

In total, Chris Moon has now run more than thirty marathons, and raised hundreds of thousands of pounds for charities such as BLESMA – the British Limbless Ex-Service Men's Association – and the Red Cross.

But, in achieving these remarkable feats of endurance, he's raising something else, too. Awareness. A special kind of awareness: not of how terrible things can be, but of how *great* they can be, despite the adversity.

He is a living example that storms can make us stronger.

*

Twelve years after being captured by the Khmer Rouge, Chris returned to Cambodia. The mine-clearance programme had, by and large, been effective. The Cambodian countryside was mostly free of land-mines. During his visit, Chris came face to face with one of the Khmer Rouge guards who, if things had gone just a little differently, would have killed him without a second thought. He was able to look him in the eye and shake the man's hand.

In doing so Chris Moon showed that not only did he have guts, but he also had grace.

It's amazing how often the two go hand in hand.

# MARCUS LUTTRELL:
# HELL WEEK

*'I will never quit.'*

FROM THE NAVY SEAL CREED

When Marcus Luttrell was 15 years old he already knew that he wanted to be a US Navy SEAL.

There's nothing like aiming high.

The SEALs are one of the toughest, most skilled fighting forces in the world. And that means they take only the toughest, most skilled American recruits.

Marcus and his twin brother Morgan knew this, even as teenagers, so they enlisted the help of a former US Army soldier who lived nearby. He instructed them in the principles of fitness and endurance. They would be essential qualities when it came to the gruelling task of SEAL qualification training . . . and beyond.

Different special forces around the world have different training regimes. The SEALs start out with a twenty-four-week Basic Underwater Demolition/SEAL course, or BUD/S for short. This includes a physical 'conditioning' phase, part of which comprises a week of intense and sleep-deprived training known as 'Hell Week'.

During Hell Week, you're only allowed to sleep for a total of four hours – not per night but per week! The rest of the time is spent undergoing extreme physical training, including more than 200 miles of running (that's nearly eight marathons) over a period of five days. You're exercising over twenty hours a day. You're always hungry, wet and exhausted. You eat 7,000 calories a day and still lose weight. Your skin is blasted with sand and mud. There are medical staff on hand day and night, because some bodies just aren't made to endure that kind of intensity.

Hell Week tests your physical fitness, of course, but it's also designed to test something just as important: your mental strength. I call it 'spirit'. Lots of candidates drop out of BUD/S during Hell Week. The stress beats their bodies and their minds.

Marcus Luttrell didn't make it through BUD/S the first time, but it was nothing to do with lack of fitness or endurance. He broke his leg halfway through. It didn't put him off. As soon as the bone was healed, he returned for second helpings. He was that kind of guy.

Sure enough, Luttrell made it through BUD/S the next time, and eventually became a SEAL. But, as any special-forces soldier will tell you, qualification is just the beginning. If you think Hell Week is as bad as it's going to get, think again. You put yourself up for selection every time you step into your boots, and it's when you start the job proper that the hard work really begins.

As Luttrell was soon to find out, the rigours of Hell Week at Coronado, the SEAL training facility in San Diego, are nothing compared to advancing to contact in the badlands of Afghanistan.

When it comes to inhospitable parts of the world, Afghanistan takes some beating. The terrain in this war-torn country is one of the most hostile on earth. Arid, sweltering deserts. Freezing, almost unpassable mountains. But that's what the SEALs train for.

There were three other men in Marcus Luttrell's unit that day in the summer of 2005: Mike Murphy, Matthew 'Axe' Axelson and Danny Dietz. When they fast-roped into the Hindu Kush – the unforgiving mountain range stretching from central Afghanistan to northern Pakistan – from an MH-47 helicopter on the night of 27 June, they did so as part of Operation Red Wings. Their mission: to carry out surveillance on a group of buildings known to be used by a local Taliban commander called Ahmad Shah.

Shah was a highly trained militant and a known associate of Osama bin Laden. He needed taking out.

The unit was to find him, check out how big his militia force was, then call in an airstrike to finish the job. And, if it looked like Shah was getting away, then they were to take him out themselves.

A typical special-forces mission, deep in enemy heartland.

Their insertion point was 10,000 feet above sea level, where the air was oxygen-deficient. But Luttrell's unit was well trained to cope with such environments. After they had inserted, they moved off on foot towards their objective. But almost at once, events started to slip from their control.

A small group of Afghan goat herders stumbled upon them. It would have been immediately obvious to the locals that these were American soldiers, so the SEAL unit took the herders captive while they discussed what to do with them. There were really only two options:

1) Let them go, and hope that they kept quiet about what they had just seen.
2) Kill them.

They took a vote. It's a testament to the humanity as well as the courage of those four men that they made the decision to spare the goat herders' lives. Sure, they were acting in accordance with the rules of engagement. Sure, they had no evidence that these were Taliban sympathizers. But Taliban sympathizers don't walk round with T-shirts declaring their loyalty. Arguably, the correct military decision would have been a swift, silent execution.

The soldiers knew letting the herders go was a risk. But that was the call they made. It was a decision that would come back to haunt them.

Did the goat herders shop them to the Taliban? Almost certainly. Because within the hour, the SEAL unit entered a particularly treacherous area with high ground on three sides. And there, waiting for them, and with the advantage of height, were Ahmad Shah's forces.

Some reports say that there were fifty Taliban in that ambush. Others say that there were two hundred. The numbers are academic. What matters is that the four soldiers were facing a hardened militia force armed with machine guns, assault rifles, 82 mm mortars and rocket-propelled grenades. These militants knew how to use their weapons. You don't need many guys packing that kind of hardware, and firing down on you from an elevated position, for the outcome to be a fast annihilation.

An ordinary military unit would have been wiped out in seconds. But this was not an ordinary military unit. This was SEAL Team 10.

Luttrell and his colleagues engaged the Taliban, cutting down their numbers with a barrage of accurate fire. But their only real option was to retreat. Trouble was, the way back was an almost sheer drop down the mountain. As Luttrell and Murphy retreated rapidly and under intense fire, they tumbled out of control for 200 yards before literally falling over the lip of a cliff. Luttrell somersaulted twice in the air before slamming down on to the rock-hard ground.

Amazingly, both men survived the fall. Luttrell had lost all his gear except his rifle. The skin had been ripped clean away from one side of his face. He was covered in blood and bruises and he hurt like hell. Murphy was worse. He'd been shot during the fall, and blood was pumping from his stomach. When Danny and Axe joined them, it turned out Danny's right thumb had also been blown off.

There was no time to tend their wounds. Taliban rocket-propelled grenades were incoming. The guys were directly in the kill zone and were forced to hurl themselves over another precipice. During this manoeuvre, Danny was shot for a second time. A Kalashnikov round, in through his back, out through his stomach. Blood was everywhere, spurting from the wound and dribbling from Danny's mouth.

Still they carried on fighting.

Danny took a third bullet. Straight in the throat.

They tumbled down another precipice.

The rounds kept coming. Hundreds of them. Thousands. It was a miracle that only two of them had been shot. But then Danny took another round in the neck.

And then in the face.

Blood spilled out of his head. Life out of his body.

Four had become three.

They couldn't stop for even a beat to mourn him. Bullets were raining down everywhere. They continued their tactical retreat, trying to find defensible ground.

Mike Murphy took a round to the chest. Axe one to the head.

Things were now looking really bad.

Their only real chance was to get backup. But that meant getting into open ground to find a signal. Mike Murphy knew that. He knew that he was sacrificing himself. With blood spurting from his chest he staggered out into that fatal but essential open ground. He made the distress call back to base. Then he took a final, fatal shot to the back. Blood exploded from his chest. He tried to continue the withdrawal, but the life was pouring from him as fast as the bullets continued to come. He died screaming in agony.

Three had become two.

And Axe was clearly dying too. He had managed to fit a bandage to his head, but his eyes had turned black as blood from the wounds seeped into the sockets. His last words? 'Stay alive, Marcus. And tell Cindy I love her.'

Stay alive. After a brutal two-hour firefight that had killed his three buddies, that was exactly what Luttrell was determined to do.

But the Taliban had other ideas. They knew his location. He heard the ominous fizz of an RPG heading in his direction. Then the sudden thunderclap as it exploded right next to him.

The blast blew him over the edge of the ravine. He lost consciousness before he hit the ground.

Luttrell woke up upside down in a hollow. He was in a bad, bad way. His trousers had been blasted off, but that was the least of his problems. He couldn't feel his left leg. Its flesh was riddled with shrapnel from the RPG and blood was gushing relentlessly from his wounds.

He had a broken nose, a broken shoulder and a broken back. That hurts. Trust me. Every time he moved, he left a trail of blood. He packed his wounds with mud to stop the blood leaking out. But he was a gruesome, mashed-up mess.

The gunfire had stopped. It was scant comfort. The mountains were crawling with Taliban and they would hunt him down.

There was just one glimmer of hope. Murphy's heroic distress call had made it back to base. A QRF (quick reaction force) was being dispatched. Right now, they looked like Luttrell's only chance.

The QRF comprised a Chinook containing eight SEALs and eight special-forces air crew. The Chinook was chaperoned by Apache attack helicopters. A serious team flying in to serious work. The Chinook is an amazing piece of equipment, but it's not invulnerable. It took real guts for those guys to fly straight into the kill zone. They knew they were a highly visible and anticipated target for the insurgents who had just killed three of their comrades.

It only took a single rocket-propelled grenade to bring the Chinook down. It was fired straight into the open tailgate as the guys were preparing to fast-rope to the ground. Then it hit the fuel tank. In seconds, the Chinook was an inferno. Burning men fell screaming from the aircraft to the ground. The helicopter itself veered out of control before slamming into the mountain.

All sixteen men died.

So far, Operation Red Wings had seen the SEALs' biggest loss of life in a single day. An unbelievable tragedy for all involved. But one man was still going. Just.

Marcus Luttrell.

Marcus was alive, but he was torn to bits: light-headed through his blood loss; parched with thirst having lost his water bottle; barely able to walk with three shattered vertebrae, numerous fractured bones and shrapnel sticking out of his flesh. To move an inch was unbearable torture, but staying still wasn't an option. The Taliban were hunting him. If they found him, they'd kill him, and brutally. If they didn't, he'd still die, either of his wounds or of thirst.

He needed to get to the top of the mountain: a defensible

position where a helicopter could land. And he needed to find water.

Luttrell started to hike, or hobble. Never mind that the terrain was rocky and unforgiving. Never mind that the high-altitude air was thin. Never mind that his back was broken.

If he found grass, he licked the mountain dew from it. If he found a tree, he broke off the thinnest twigs and tried to suck out the sap. He even tried wringing out his socks to get some liquid. Still, the thirst was all-consuming.

He navigated using the stars, and hobbled up the mountain all night, well aware that the Taliban were tracking him. He fought to ignore the indescribable pain his body was in.

By first light he was so thirsty that his tongue had stuck to the roof of his mouth. He was afraid that if he moved it, he would tear the skin. The sun grew hotter. And hotter. His thirst grew worse. He somehow ignored it, as well as the agony of his shattered bones. Instead he focused on his escape and evasion.

And on finding water.

All the while, the Taliban were combing the mountains for him. Ahmad Shah and his men knew the surrounding peaks like the backs of their hands. They'd grown up there. The heat of the Afghan summer was nothing to them. And, of course, their bodies were whole and unbroken.

Afternoon came. Somewhere in the distance Marcus heard the unmistakable tinkle of a mountain stream, and desperately started making his way towards it.

Suddenly, a shot rang out.

A brutal thud in his leg.

Pain, screaming through his body.

He had been shot by a Taliban sniper.

The force of the bullet knocked him back down the mountain, opening up his wounds as AK-47 rounds flew everywhere.

He could only crawl now, so that's what he did. Over hills,

down gullies, blood pouring from his wound and leaving a trail behind him, AK-47 bullets pinging over his head. When a Taliban scout caught up with him, Luttrell managed to shoot him in the chest. When he realized two more were nearby, he lobbed a grenade in their direction and took them out. Somehow, despite everything, he was still able to fight smart.

Now he was starting to black out. Still he crawled, somehow managing to evade his hunters. Towards late afternoon he found a waterfall, but before he could reach it he slipped an excruciating 1,000 feet down the mountain – and then had to climb up it again. He did so on all fours.

Finally he reached the precious water, where he drank deeply. The sweetest water, he would later say, that he ever tasted.

As he looked up he saw three Afghan men watching him.

Like a wounded animal, he prepared for his final stand.

He tried to shoot them, but blood trickled down his forehead and into his eyes, blinding him. More blood from his brutalized body was turning the ground around him red. The world started to spin.

He might have gone down fighting, but now, he knew he was finally defeated.

Only he wasn't. These people were not Taliban. They were mountain tribal people and were well-disposed towards Americans. They would help him.

Here, in the most hostile region on earth, at the end of a truly incredible escape and evasion, surrounded by killers who wanted him dead, could it possibly be that Luttrell had found friends?

**✶**

I don't know about you, but if I'd just been double-crossed by four Afghan goat herders, I'd be wary of mixing with any more locals. Luttrell had put his trust in human nature once, and it had failed him. Should he now put his trust in the kindness of strangers? Did he have a choice?

He had no option but to pray, and to trust them.

Good move.

When a Pashtun tribesman offers you help, he means it. That offer of help brings with it an unbreakable promise to defend you to the death.

Those men and women gave Marcus shelter in their village. Even when it was surrounded by Taliban, they refused to give him up. They smuggled him out of the village into some nearby caves to keep him from the enemy's clutches. Those simple Afghan villagers repaid his trust in them a hundredfold.

They tended his wounds as best they could, but the truth was that Luttrell needed specialist medical treatment, and soon. He needed to let the Americans know where he was. The nearest American base was in Asadabad, 40 miles over the mountain. There was no way Luttrell could make that journey. And so the village elder, a tough old man who had no time for the Taliban's violence, volunteered to make the journey himself.

That is hospitality. That is grace.

The man eventually managed to alert American forces to Luttrell's presence, and they came to his rescue. It had been six days since the contact that had killed the rest of his patrol.

Six days of pain, danger, sand, fatigue and fear. You could call it Hell Week.

Marcus Luttrell returned home a hero. But a man does not easily lose nineteen of his colleagues on the field of battle. The guilt for the survivor can be the toughest battle to face. People deal with it in different ways. Luttrell's way was inspiring.

After a second tour of duty in Afghanistan (yes, he went back for more!) Marcus Luttrell started the Lone Survivor Foundation. It's an organization that aims to help wounded soldiers and their families as they try to make the difficult readjustment to life back home. That's a cause worth fighting for. These men and women go into battle to defend our liberty. Some pay a very high price. Arguably the ultimate price.

To take a stand, get back in the fight and to determine to help those most in need, takes courage, heart and determination. Men like Marcus Luttrell have those qualities in spades.

# ARON RALSTON: SELF-SURGERY SURVIVAL

*'It was a hundred times worse than any pain I'd felt before. It recalibrated what I'd understood pain to be.'*

Aron Ralston

Canyonlands National Park, Utah, 26 April 2003.

The dusty, sand-filled canyons are parched. The wind, which has had 100 miles of open land to whip up speed, is fierce. A lone, 28-year-old man struggles against it on his mountain bike, pounding the pedals as hard as he can.

He's wearing cycling gear and carries a heavy backpack. Inside, he has all the gear he needs to rappel down into the deep, treacherous canyons in this remote part of North America. Rope, carabiners, belaying devices, a pocket-tool with two blades and a pair of pliers.

He's hardly ever had to use that final item, but it's good to be prepared.

He has three litres of water in his CamelBak pouch, an extra litre in a water bottle, and enough food to last him for the day. Because that's how long his little expedition into the hard-baked desert of Utah is going to last. A day.

Aron abandons his bike – he'll collect it later – and hikes for a few hours towards the main object of his day's trek: the 'Big Drop', a 65-foot rappel down to the floor of a weather-beaten canyon.

First, though, he has to lower himself down a narrow slot. There'll be some down-climbing, and at one point he'll have to squeeze himself through a section where the two walls of the canyon are no more than a claustrophobic 18 inches apart.

But that's OK. Aron is an experienced canyon man. He's doing it solo, no problem.

So now, Aron is on his own. He is far from the beaten track. A lonesome part of the world. He hasn't told any of his friends where he is. To all intents and purposes, he's off the grid.

Many people like it like that. And it's true that out there, surrounded by the bleak but magnificent desert landscape of red dust and deep canyons, there is a unique peace to be found.

But what happens when things go wrong and you need your buddies around?

Aron Ralston was about to find out. Big time.

You've heard me say it before: survival is rarely pretty. So, if you're of a squeamish disposition, stop reading now!

At the edge of the slot, Aron gets his gear together. Rope, belay device, harness, multi-tool and water bottle. He fits a lamp to his head – important, because it will allow him to check any cracks in the rock for hidden snakes or scorpions before he puts his hand into them. You don't want a bite at any time, but especially not during a solo rappel.

But, as Aron lowers himself deeper and deeper into the canyon, there are no snakes. And, to start with, no problems. In places he finds himself chimneying – where you climb down the narrow gap between two rock faces by pressing your body against one face and your feet against the other, then slowly edge your way down, as if free-climbing down a chimney.

He reaches a ledge. Just below it, a large boulder is wedged fast between the two vertical rock faces. Nine feet below the boulder is the canyon floor. If Aron can step out on to the boulder, he reckons he'll be able to hang from it, then simply fall that short distance to the ground.

He chimneys down to the boulder. Before he steps on to it, he kicks it to check it's not loose.

The boulder doesn't budge.

He lowers himself on to it.

A slight wobble, but it feels pretty secure.

Moving carefully he grabs hold of the boulder and lowers himself over the edge.

Then the boulder shifts with his weight. This is bad news. Aron immediately lets go, and allows himself to fall.

He thrusts out his right arm – almost a reflex action to stop the boulder crashing on to his head.

But then the boulder bounces off one wall and slams with a sickening thud into his right arm, crushing it against the opposite wall. And holding it fast.

Silence. Just the sound of his frenzied heart beating and his breath coming in short, terrified gasps.

Then the pain hits – deep and burning, like lightning bolts of pure agony flashing up his arm – and he screams.

But even as the pain is consuming his mind, he knows what he must do while his blood is rich with adrenalin: try to move the boulder.

He grabs it with his left hand and yanks it with every ounce of strength in his body. It shifts just a tiny fraction of an inch. Then it judders back down heavily on to his right arm.

Another searing blast of pain.

Then everything is silent – and still.

Aron is sweating profusely. Anyone would be. He needs water, but his CamelBak is empty. He has a litre water bottle in his backpack but it's strapped over his right shoulder. He has to wriggle his head through the straps to gain access, then instinctively gulps down several mouthfuls.

Bad move. He's just consumed a third of his remaining water and he doesn't know how long he's going to be here. Without water, in the desert heat, he can expect to be dead in three days. If he's lucky.

He turns his attention instantly to the arm. It's already going numb. He can see his right thumb. It has turned grey. He doesn't think any bones are broken, but the soft tissue is mangled and mashed. More importantly, it's completely trapped between the boulder and the rock face.

He looks on the positive side. At least he's not bleeding. Sure, he can see some patches of blood on the rocks above where he scraped his skin during the fall. But there's no blood loss from his crushed right hand.

With his free hand he pulls out his multi-tool and extends the larger of the two knives. Maybe he can hack away at the rock and loosen the limb. He gives it his best shot, but the rock is just too hard.

The afternoon wears on. He tries to use the file on his multi-tool to crack into a fissure on the rock. He creates a little powder, but more than anything he's just blunting the file.

He tries not to dwell on the hard truth that he's trapped.

And he tries not to think about the stark reality that, the way things are looking, he has only one option if nobody comes to rescue him: to hack off his own arm.

But surely it won't come to that.

Night falls. Aron keeps hacking at the boulder. A small piece comes away. But it's just that: a small, insignificant piece. The arm itself is still stuck fast.

The temperature drops. He empties his rucksack and wriggles it back over his head again. Desert nights can be cold. The pack will help insulate him a little.

At 1.30 a.m. he allows himself a mouthful of precious water. It refreshes him, but he's getting exhausted. He's been standing for more than twelve hours. His knees are threatening to collapse beneath him.

In survival mode, sometimes you have to improvise. He wriggles into his harness and creates a makeshift grappling hook from his mountaineering gear, which he slings upwards. It bites into the rocks above and creates a swing that takes the weight off his feet.

But the relief doesn't last long. The harness starts to cut off the blood flow to his legs. He has to stand again.

The night-time drains all the warmth from him. Exhausted, he makes it through till morning.

With the sun warming his cold skin, he continues chipping away at the boulder. He doesn't really think he'll have enough time to break through it before he dies.

But the alternative is too awful to think about.

Day two.

The daytime heat rises. Aron is no longer chilled. He's burning hot.

He tries to improvise some sort of lever system with his climbing gear to move the rock. No luck.

He thinks he can hear climbers and screams at them to help him. But it's just a wild animal scurrying through the canyon.

It would be easy to despair. He doesn't. Instead he turns his mind to the gruesome possibility of amputating his own arm.

Not a fun prospect by anyone's standards.

Aron instantly sees that there are problems. Obviously he'd need some sort of tourniquet to staunch the flow of blood if he ever got free. He improvises with a piece of webbing and a carabiner, which he twists tight around the region just below his elbow. But the resulting tourniquet doesn't feel tight enough to stop the blood flow completely.

And, in any case, he's jumping the gun. His little knives might be up to cutting through the flesh, but he'd need some kind of saw to get through the bone of his forearm. He has nothing of the sort.

And even if he managed this monstrous surgery, he would still have to rappel down the Big Drop, and then hike eight miles to where he had left his truck.

It would be impossible.

Once he realizes this, his morale saps.

He's going to die here.

He has a camcorder in his pack. Reaching for it, he switches it on and records a farewell message for his mum and dad, explaining what has happened, and that he loves them.

Then he settles down and concentrates on staying alive.

On the third day, he prays, begging God for guidance as crowds of mosquitoes swarm around him and suck at his flesh. But, for now, it doesn't seem as if the prayer is going to be answered. The day plods excruciatingly into night. The temperature drops again. He shudders violently, and his teeth chatter.

When he allows himself a sip of water, he has to fight the urge not to gulp down what remains. And now, when he chips away at the rock, he does so because the movement warms him up – not because he thinks he has any hope of shifting the rock.

By 7 a.m. he calculates that he's been trapped for forty hours. His mind turns once more to amputation.

His CamelBak is insulated with neoprene tubing. He removes it and uses his left arm to tighten the neoprene just below the elbow. His forearm turns white. This could be an effective tourniquet.

He picks up his multi-tool and extends one of the knives. Then, slightly gingerly, he slices the blade across his forearm.

Nothing happens. It's too blunt even to break the skin. He gives up that line of attack, for now.

He feels the need to urinate, and does so on the canyon floor. Later that afternoon, the urge to pee comes again. He realizes that he shouldn't waste this precious resource. He urinates into his CamelBak. It's fouler smelling and more concentrated than this morning's urine, but that can't be helped. Over the next few hours, it separates into layers: golden liquid at the top, thick sludge at the bottom.

At midnight he has his first taste. It is cold and bitter, but he thinks he can stomach it when the water runs out. Which it will, soon – he only has a few mouthfuls of fluid left.

The night passes, slowly, painfully. The next morning, Aron picks up his multi-tool. If he can't use the blade to slice through his skin, maybe he can use the point to gouge into the flesh.

Almost before he knows what's happening he has slammed the knife point deep into his forearm.

The blade is jutting out perpendicular from the arm now. It doesn't hurt as much as he thought it would. He can feel it against the bone in the middle of his arm.

Slowly, he pulls the knife out. There isn't much blood – the flow has been cut off – but he can see the yellow layer of fat beneath the skin. He reinserts the knife and taps it against the bone. It vibrates up and down his arm. Pain. And the feel of it confirms what he knows to be true. He can't cut into the bone, nerves and tendons. It just won't work.

He awards himself another gulp of water. Now it's all gone.

\*

At midday on the fourth day he prays again. Not for guidance this time, but for patience as he waits for death.

\*

As night-time approaches yet again, his mind is filled with hallucinations, a result of sleeplessness, pain, dehydration and severe cold. In his moments of clarity he sips at his stash of urine just to moisten his mouth. Then he falls back into a horrific trance.

He starts to hallucinate. He imagines he's with his friends, that he's being given refreshing drinks. It's almost as if he's at a dinner party, surrounded by people he loves.

Except, of course, he isn't. He's deep in hell.

The long, horrific night turns into another long, horrific day. At 2 p.m. he picks up his camcorder to record his last requests. And as another freezing night falls, he carves his name and date of birth into the rock face. Then he carves the date: 30 April. It's his own memorial, because he fully expects not to live to see morning.

But he does.

And it's on the sixth day trapped by the rock that the solution comes to him. Like a revelation. An epiphany.

There's no way he can cut through the bones in his forearm with his knife. But if he can put enough pressure on his upper arm, perhaps he could snap the bones in two.

He barely gives his new plan a second thought.

Aron crouches down. He presses his left hand against the boulder. Then, with his crushed hand fixed in place, he slowly, but with great force, yanks the right arm down and to the left.

Then, crack!

The sound of the first bone breaking in his forearm is like a gunshot. It echoes around the canyon.

He uses his good fingers to feel the break. There it is. The snapped bone is sharp and jagged. His fingers confirm what the terrible pain is telling him: it's definitely broken.

There are two bones in the forearm: the radius and the ulna. He's broken one. Now he has to do the other.

Crack!

Another gunshot.

Aron screams with the pain. Sweat mingles with his agony. Then he touches the break point and feels a strange kind of elation. He can twist his upper arm while the forearm stays solid.

The bones are broken. But the forearm is still attached with veins, sinew and skin. To complete the amputation he has to cut through this with the blunt knife of his pocket tool.

He saws at the skin around the break point, trying to slice cleanly. Once this is done, he inserts his good fingers into the gory hole he's created. He explores the warm wetness inside his arm, feeling for the break and the exact sinews he needs to cut in order to butcher himself as cleanly as possible. He slices, trying to avoid the bigger arteries. He'll leave these till the end. For now, it's a matter of patiently slicing through the pink, bloody strands of sinew to cut himself free of his useless, dying hand.

Twenty minutes pass like this. He cuts through one artery. Then a second. His blood is starting to ooze out more aggressively now. He comes to a particularly tough tendon, so he takes a break from his bloody work to reapply his improvised tourniquet.

Then back to the tendon. It's too tough for the knife, so he folds that back in to the multi-tool and removes the pliers. Little by little, he clips and twists tiny clumps of tendon.

Back to the knife. He concentrates hard on the bloody mess his arm has become. He has one more artery and a little bit of muscle left to cut through.

And a nerve.

He knows this is going to be the most painful bit.

Just touching it makes him scream with pain.

But he cuts through. More pain than he's ever known floods through him. Intense. Blinding. Burning. For a moment he can do nothing but give in to it.

But now he only has a few scraps of skin and gristle to go. He continues his appalling work.

And suddenly, after nearly an hour, the amputation is complete.

Aron Ralston is free.

\*

But he's still alone, and a long way from anywhere.

Leaving his amputated forearm crushed in the rock, he wraps his stump in a white shopping bag he has with him. Then he improvises a sling with his CamelBak then gets moving. Time is everything. He needs help before he bleeds to death.

With only one good arm and a whole world of pain, he somehow manages to rappel down the Big Drop to the canyon floor. Here, he finds a pool of stagnant water to rehydrate himself. Never a good move to drink water you don't trust. But these are desperate moments for a man on the brink.

Almost immediately, his bowels expel the filthy water. Then he starts to stagger across the desert.

Mile after mile.

The intense heat burns down. Blood drips from his wounded

stump, and the constant pain takes everything out of him. But he keeps walking, past the limits of endurance, for a full six miles. Then he sees figures up ahead – a family of three. He calls out to them, yelling for help. They are aghast when they see what has happened. But they run ahead and fetch help.

A helicopter finally arrives and airlifts Aron out of there. The air crew stare at him in disbelief and horror. And when he touches down at the nearest hospital, the doctors stare at him in wonder.

It is 127 hours since the rock first fell on him.

By rights, he should be dead.

There are so many lessons to be learned from Aron Ralston's 127-hour feat of endurance. Some are simple – like, always let someone know where you're going to be if you're heading out into the wilderness.

Some are more complex.

Aron Ralston would later say that he believed if he'd amputated his arm earlier, he would have bled to death because the helicopter that lifted him to hospital wouldn't have been in the area. At his nadir, he prayed for inspiration and patience. At the time, it didn't seem like either prayer had been answered. But sometimes hindsight can show you something beautiful among the suffering. Aron Ralston needed patience first, and then inspiration. He was given both.

He had something else, too: an instinct for survival. When the chips were down, he would do whatever it took – literally, whatever it took – to stay alive.

That instinct for survival is buried deep in all of us. Sometimes it takes an extreme situation for it to come to the surface. And, invariably, we are all stronger and more resilient than we might imagine.

Aron Ralston discovered, through incredible pain and hardship, that as humans we are made of much more than just flesh and bone.

# SIR JOHN FRANKLIN: DEATH IN THE ARCTIC

'The fate of Franklin no man may know
The fate of Franklin no man can tell
Lord Franklin alone with his sailors do dwell.'

FROM 'LADY FRANKLIN'S LAMENT'

This story starts with the opening of a coffin.

But not just any coffin.

This was a coffin perfectly preserved in ice. It was buried in the permafrost of an island in the Canadian Arctic called Beechey Island. Inside was a corpse. It belonged to Petty Officer John Shaw Torrington, who died on 1 January 1846.

You'd expect, after more than 150 years, that his body would have rotted away to leave just a skeleton. But this body had been deep frozen. Mummified by the ice. The skin on its face was blotched with black and yellow, but was otherwise perfectly preserved. Its lips were slightly curled back to reveal tombstone teeth, fully intact. A mass of curly hair surrounded the frozen head. In most respects, John Torrington's body was almost exactly as it had been the day he died.

And he had died badly.

The body was frozen so hard that the team who dug it up had to thaw it with water before they could examine it properly. Torrington was desperately thin. His ribs stuck out against his meagre, waxy skin. He had been close to starving at the time of his death. He'd also been very ill. Cutting open the body, they found that his lungs were horribly scarred, the ravages of tuberculosis.

His brain had turned into a thick, yellow ooze. He was riddled with lead poisoning, which can drive a man insane.

Petty Officer John Torrington was one of 129 members of an audacious seafaring expedition that took place in the middle of the nineteenth century, led by the Royal Navy officer and explorer Sir John Franklin.

And what is most remarkable about Torrington's corpse is not how perfectly preserved it was – rather, that it is one of only a handful of bodies of those 129 ever found.

What happened to the rest of his companions is a mystery. A mystery that endures to this day.

(Although, as a side note, on an expedition I led to the Northwest Passage a few years back, we discovered what we believe might potentially have been the remaining corpses, but that's all another story! See: www.fcpnorthwestpassage.com.)

But here's the thing: even though Petty Officer John Shaw Torrington clearly met his end in a miserable way – thousands of miles from home, frozen, poisoned and diseased – the chances are that he was one of the lucky ones.

In 1845 the Holy Grail of exploration was the Northwest Passage.

The Northwest Passage is a route through the Arctic Sea, along the northern coast of Canada. A century and a half ago the frozen seas stretching up to the North Pole were solid with ice, but it had long been thought that a navigable route existed.

Whoever found it would have untold glory and wealth heaped on them, because such a passage would supply a new (and much faster) link between the Atlantic and the Pacific. A short cut from Europe to Asia would be a very profitable trade route, especially for Britain.

Nowadays, huge exploration ice breakers have been able to plough their way through these ice-bound seas. Back then, you needed to be both brave and mad even to contemplate exploring this part of the world.

Temperatures could easily reach –50°C, and, combined with freezing sea spray and huge storms, the hazards of cold-weather endurance were amplified: frostbite, hypothermia, dehydration, snow blindness and muscle wastage.

Plus, of course, there was the sheer scale of the Arctic: thousands and thousands of square miles of desolate, ice-bound, blizzard-swept wasteland, with any open water being a swirling cauldron of floating icebergs.

In short: the Arctic, uncharted, unexplored, in wooden ships, with no communications, no maps or GPS, and with limited, substandard rations, was not a fun place to endure.

And if an iceberg could rip a hole in the hull of an ocean liner like the *Titanic* several decades later, imagine what it could do to the timber frames of HMS *Terror* and HMS *Erebus*.

These were the two ships Sir John Franklin commissioned to take him on what everyone in England fully expected to be a gloriously successful mission to locate that elusive Northwest Passage.

*Terror* and *Erebus*. One named for fear, the other for a Greek god of the Underworld. The names were strangely prophetic, though nobody knew it yet.

Because surely nothing, not even nature, could withstand the might of the Royal Navy when all its wealth of resources and most determined officers were thrown at such an endeavour.

The discovery of this elusive Northwest Passage was a prized jewel, destined to be uncovered by the British Empire.

*

Sir John Franklin was a seafaring hero. Not only had he fought at the Battle of Trafalgar at the age of 18, he was also the grizzled veteran of some unbelievably brutal expeditions to the Arctic.

Some were massively successful – on his third trip there he succeeded in mapping 1,200 miles of coastline, recording valuable geological information and taking notes on more than 600 new species of plants.

Others weren't.

Take the Coppermine expedition of 1819, which gave Franklin a fair idea of just how abominable the Arctic region could be.

Franklin and his men had set out to explore the northern coast of Canada, where they expected to receive help from friendly indigenous people, and then sustain themselves by living off the land and the sea. But the indigenous people were far from friendly, and the weather conditions so harsh that hunting for food became impossible.

Close to starvation they were forced to retreat, with only lichen to eat. And then, in desperation, they also resorted to eating the leather off their shoes. This earned Franklin the nickname 'the Man who Ate his Boots'.

If the story is true, then his boots saved his life. Of the twenty men that set out on the Coppermine expedition, eleven died. Franklin was one of the nine survivors.

But he had the soul of an adventurer, which meant his longing for exploration would not be dampened by minor inconveniences such as starvation, hardship and the death of his comrades.

Franklin's enthusiasm was undimmed.

When he was offered the opportunity of one last crack at the Northwest Passage, he jumped at the chance.

At the age of 59 he was desperate to make sure his name would go down in those history books.

Many others signed up to sail with him. Franklin was a hero.

To join him on his greatest, most ambitious expedition, would be a chance to walk straight into the same history books with him.

And it was. Just not as any of them intended.

Franklin certainly had everything going for him – not least, two of the most advanced ships of the day. HMS *Terror* and HMS *Erebus* had steel-coated prows to help them grind through the ice.

Although they were sailing ships, they were also fitted with steam-powered motors and supplied with enough coal to break through the ice for twelve days. And they carried sufficient supplies to last for three years, including 8,000 tins of food.

Remember those tins of food. They'll be important later on.

They set sail from Kent in May 1845. At the end of July the ships were spotted by the captain of a whaling ship near Baffin Island, off the Canadian coast and at the edge of the Northwest Passage.

And then, just like that, the two ships lost all contact with the outside world.

It's easy to forget, in these days of satellite phones and navigation, how an expedition like this meant entirely cutting yourself off from civilization. Nowadays you can tweet from the space station. Back then, a voyage of exploration meant being out of touch for years. Literally.

So, back in England, nobody was surprised that they hadn't heard from Franklin and his men for six months.

Or a year.

Or even two.

But by 1847 people started to worry. The first of many rescue parties was sent out to the Arctic to try to locate HMS *Terror* and *Erebus*.

It found no trace of them.

More and more rescue parties followed.

Same result.

It was as if they had vanished from the face of the earth.

*

For the next century and a half, hundreds of people would try to piece together what happened to Franklin and his crew.

Gradually, a picture has emerged of gruesome, lingering deaths in that most inhospitable of regions. And it seems likely that their problems started with those 8,000 tins of food they had so carefully stashed in their stores.

The tins, it transpired, had been cheaply made by an unscrupulous supplier. They contained an unusually high amount of lead. This meant that, from the moment the first one was cracked open, the sailors were being slowly but surely poisoned.

Lead poisoning is a nasty thing. It leads to blinding headaches, vomiting and diarrhoea. It makes you hallucinate and suffer from delirium and insomnia. It makes you depressed, and robs you of your ability to make clear-headed decisions.

All in all, it's not what you want on a lonely, demanding expedition across the frozen Arctic, or to sustain you through the long, cold, dark Arctic winters.

Despite these symptoms, the explorers did not turn back. As they pushed further and further into the ice-strewn passage they still believed that it was worth enduring the suffering for the ultimate prize.

We now know that they overwintered on Beechey Island, a bleak, unfriendly chunk of rock and ice in the Canadian Arctic Archipelago. It was on Beechey Island that the body of John Torrington was exhumed more than 150 years later. He and two others perished that first winter, and, as described above, lead poisoning and tuberculosis played a significant part in his death.

The remaining men were also in very poor shape as they sat out the winter.

But they didn't turn back. They determined to carry on.

Franklin and his men set sail from Beechey Island at the end of that harsh winter. For several months they vainly probed and sailed the frozen labyrinth of the archipelago, desperately trying to find a way through. But they couldn't.

By the September of 1846 their ships had become frozen solid in the Arctic ice.

HMS *Terror* and *Erebus*, with their crews of 129 men, had become icebound. They would never sail again.

What did the sailors do? How did they spend their days? It seems they had nothing to eat except poisoned food that was sending them gradually mad. The isolation would have made things a hundred times worse. They were lost, trapped, in an unending sea of ice, hundreds of miles from civilization.

And they knew that nobody would be coming to rescue them any time soon.

Days turned into weeks. Weeks into months.

Picture it. Nothing but ice and blizzard, as far as the eye could see; the encroaching certainty that if something didn't change, the frozen ships that were their refuge would soon become their tombs.

All the time, watching their shipmates deteriorate and die before their eyes.

In May 1847 we know that at least some of the men ventured out from the ships to build a small cairn marker. Here Franklin himself left a small but characteristically plucky note.

It said: 'All well.'

But all was not well. Because within a month John Franklin, England's hero of the day, was dead.

And the men he left behind were also gradually dying. One by one, exposure and starvation would have picked them off, gradually but inexorably.

More horrific, solitary months passed. Still no release from the ice or cold. Still no hope of escape or rescue.

Nearly a year later, in April 1848, two of Franklin's officers left a second note in that cairn. It was reserved and unemotional. It told nothing of the horrors of the solitude and death on those frozen ships. It simply stated that another fifteen men had died. They had made a decision to abandon their ship and trek across the ice in an attempt to reach the coast of Canada.

Even in their lead-poisoned, delusional state, none of them could have ever really believed that they would survive such a bid for freedom.

*

We can only imagine the state of them as they tried to fight their way across the ice to safety.

Poisoned and starving.

Frozen.

Staggering.

Continually battered by the Arctic weather, day and night.

They would have been riddled with scurvy: their gums bleeding, and oozing wounds erupting all over their bodies. Tuberculosis would have infiltrated their lungs and the infection would have spread around their bodies.

They were dead men walking.

Franklin's wife, Lady Jane, was determined to find out what had happened to her husband. She refused to believe that 129 men could simply vanish. She spent her entire fortune paying for search parties, including one led by Captain Leopold McClintock.

McClintock managed to gather tantalizing scraps of information from the local Inuit people who lived among the frozen wastes of the north. They told stories of two ships that had been crushed by the moving ice; of white men staggering across the ice, falling down dead as they walked. The Inuit handed over a small collection of buttons, knives and jewellery that had been worn by members of Franklin's crew.

Even today, the few indigenous Inuit people who populate that region tell tales handed down to them by their ancestors. They speak of a bedraggled column of men trying to head south. The legends say that their eyes were wild with madness, and I don't doubt that is true. The lead would have steadily driven them mad, but so too would the desperate solitude and utter hopelessness.

McClintock also found a small whaling boat frozen into the ice. It was full of books and chocolate that had been taken from either the *Terror* or the *Erebus*.

It also contained the skeletons of two sailors.

The boat itself was pointing towards, not away from, the location where the ships were thought to have frozen. Were these men trying to sail to safety? Or had they simply resolved to head back to the ships to die with their comrades?

Sir John Franklin's expedition to find the Northwest Passage was the start of the longest search and rescue mission ever launched. The last days of Sir John Franklin and his crew have captivated those with a passion for exploration ever since his ships disappeared.

And they have disappeared. Most likely, the ships were systematically crushed by the shifting, groaning ice. Having lured and then trapped the unfortunate sailors, the Arctic then swallowed their ships down to the icy depths.

The few bodies that *have* been found have, however, revealed some startling secrets.

Such as the knife scars in their bones, which suggest that in their final, desperate days, some of Franklin's crew probably resorted to acts of cannibalism. Eating their friends in order to buy themselves a few precious extra days or weeks of hopeless existence.

In terms of survival in the face of overwhelming hardship, hunger, misery and madness, there are few stories that rival the desperate fate of Franklin's men. But then not all stories of true grit end in triumph. Some – in fact, many – are endured to the grim end with heroism, stoicism and quiet courage.

And to those brave souls: we salute you.

# CAPTAIN SCOTT: 'GREAT GOD, THIS IS AN AWFUL PLACE'

*'Had we lived, I should have had a tale to tell of the hardihood, endurance and courage of my companions which would have stirred the heart of every Englishman. These rough notes and our dead bodies must tell the tale.'*

FROM THE JOURNAL OF CAPTAIN SCOTT

November 12, 1912.

An Antarctic search party has just discovered a tent pitched on the frozen ice, many hundreds of miles from civilization. Inside the tent are three bodies. They are wrapped in their sleeping bags, and look for all the world as if they've just fallen asleep.

In fact, they've been dead for eight months.

On closer examination, their skin looks yellow. It's covered with frostbite.

Two of the men look peaceful. The third, lying between the others, appears to be stretching out in agony, as if he had died wrestling against death itself.

In life, their names were Lieutenant Henry Bowers, Dr Edward Wilson and, lying between them, Captain Robert Falcon Scott.

Scott of the Antarctic.

The epic story of his doomed expedition to the South Pole is a humbling reminder of the sheer grit of a team of men who pitted themselves against the worst nature could throw at them, and lost.

A team that, even when they knew they were defeated – both by nature and by their rival explorers – remained dignified, and resolute to the last.

*

Before we hear the story of Captain Robert Falcon Scott, let's hear about the Antarctic. Because it is arguably the toughest, most hostile place on our entire planet.

The continent is massive. Take Britain. Then multiply it by fifty. Or take Australia, and double it.

Next, consider that it's 99 per cent covered in ice. In some places the ice is three miles thick.

Temperatures in the Antarctic can reach 89°C below freezing. On average, nowhere on earth is colder than that. And yet, technically, it's a desert. No camels, but not much rain either, which is why it is classified as desert terrain.

And in many ways the climate is more dangerous than any normal desert. Not only does the daytime last for twenty-four hours for part of the year but, just like in the desert, the Antarctic will dehydrate you fast. The sun, reflecting brutally up off the permanent sheets of ice, will also scorch your skin and burn your eyes. And then there's the altitude, much of the continent being above a body-draining 10,000 feet.

And you get blizzards too. Like you never saw. Shocking, violent white-outs of snow and ice, kicked up by biting, gale-force winds. Winds that would spin humans up into the air like dust.

Even today, Antarctica is almost totally unexplored. The vast majority of the continent has never seen human footfall upon it. If ever a place is to be called wild and unforgiving, it is Antarctica. And nothing prepares you for when you first land on its surface. I know. The beauty. The scale. The cold. It takes your breath away – literally.

The Antarctic is surrounded, almost guarded, by the Southern Ocean, where the winds are stronger than anywhere else on earth. The waves rise like mountains and crash with Newtonian forces that are hard to imagine.

It is the only place on earth that has no permanent human

inhabitants, and no indigenous people. For a good reason. Nobody could live here for long. For a human to live off the land in the vicinity of the South Pole is almost impossible. There's simply nothing there to hunt or forage.

Some of the bravest explorers have tried, and failed, to make headway into the Antarctic. Even Captain Cook attempted it during his Pacific voyage of 1772–4. He braved the rigours of the Southern Ocean, but only managed to circle the Antarctic, without ever landing on the continent itself.

Whenever he tried to get close to the ice shelves his ship became enshrouded in a menacing and potentially deadly cloak of ice and fog. If the winds and seas picked up, as they often did, his would be a grizzly fate, smashed against the 500-foot shelves of vertical sea ice that surround and protect the land mass itself.

He didn't get within 1,000 miles of the South Pole, and declared that it was most likely impossible to get any closer.

'Impossible', of course, is not a word that sits comfortably in the minds of the great explorers. But impossible or not, one thing's for sure: any man or woman who pits themselves against the Antarctic is going into battle with nature at its most vicious and violent.

In 1912, Captain Scott and his four companions – Captain Lawrence Oates, Bowers, Wilson and Petty Officer Edgar Evans – did just that. History tells us that the wild won that battle.

But sometimes, great and gutsy deeds are performed on the road to defeat. The deeds of Captain Scott and his men were among the greatest and the gutsiest ever told.

*

Robert Falcon Scott was a born adventurer. He came from a fairly well-to-do family, and both sides of his family had a history of seafaring. Even so, he must have been unusually eager to see the world, as he first went to sea at the age of 13. This was on HMS *Boadicea*, where he served for two years as a midshipman. As his teenage years progressed he worked his way up the ranks of the Royal Navy, and when the opportunity came to join HMS *Discovery* on the National Antarctic Mission of 1901–04, he grabbed it.

The seeds of his future fame were sown, and within only a matter of years he would be known all around the world as Scott of the Antarctic. It was a name that would come at the cost of his life.

The *Discovery*'s voyage was celebrated as a great success, though it was not without its troubles. The ship itself became ice-bound in the frozen waters of the Southern Ocean. But that didn't stop the men setting foot on the Antarctic continent – a landmark moment for the Navy.

The men had taken dogs along, hoping the beasts would pull them as close to the South Pole as possible. But they didn't know how to manage these dogs effectively, and soon they became weak. The crew were forced to slaughter the weakest of the animals and feed its warm flesh to the others just to keep them alive and working.

Add frostbite, scurvy and snow blindness into the mix, and you'll get some idea of what that early Antarctic voyage was like. The explorers spent a total of ninety-three days on the unforgiving ice. On the way back, all the dogs died and one of the men collapsed with scurvy.

Despite all this, however, they did go further south than any man had ever gone, and Scott's appetite for exploration had not been quashed by the hardships he'd undergone.

For a second time, he and his companions then stepped out on to the Antarctic ice, this time on an expedition that would last for fifty-nine days. On their return journey to *Discovery* Scott and two companions almost died when the ice collapsed beneath them and they fell down a deep crevasse. But miraculously they clawed their way back out and survived.

Even this could not dampen Scott's ardour to endure the worst, in order to achieve the best. He would conquer the South Pole somehow – or he would die in the process.

Both eventualities would come to him soon enough.

Captain Scott had been bitten by the Antarctic bug. Crucially, though, on this second journey, the explorers found that they had covered more ground per day on foot than when they'd been pulled by dogs. This was a fact that Scott would remember on his next journey to the Antarctic, nearly ten years later.

The members of the *Terra Nova* expedition, named after the ship that would return Scott and his new companions to the Antarctic, had just one objective: to be the first men to reach the South Pole. They knew, however, that they were not the only people with the same idea. A Norwegian explorer, Roald Amundsen, had the same plan. This was a race to the Pole, pure and simple.

The two teams employed different tactics. Amundsen would rely on dogs to pull his men and their supplies over the bleak Antarctic ice. He ordered a hundred of the animals, knowing that, as he approached the Pole, some of them could be shot and the meat fed to dogs and humans alike.

Scott had strong feelings about that. Perhaps the gruesome image he had of feeding a weak hound to its pack-mates had stuck with him, as had the memory of the remaining dogs dying on the ice. But more than that, he felt that relying solely on dogs was somehow less noble. As if it were 'cheating' their way round the challenge.

Scott and his men did, however, decide to use some horses. But Scott planned only to employ this mix of horse and dog in order to help establish the team's supply camps. For the final push, the dogs would be sent back and the horses shot. For the last march, the men would carry their equipment themselves.

It was a fatally heroic and brave decision. And whatever the reasoning, Scott emphatically believed it gave him the best chance of success.

The *Terra Nova* was beset with problems as it headed south towards the Antarctic. It got trapped in sea ice for twenty days. As they waited for the ship to break free, the weather started to get worse.

Already the horses were showing signs of strain. Once the men had unloaded their supplies on to the Antarctic ice and started towards their first supply depot, six of the beasts died – either through cold or because they were slowing the men down and had to be shot.

It was looking as if Scott's decision to rely more on ponies than dogs had been a bad one.

On 1 November 1911 Scott's five-man team set out on the final push towards the Pole. The conditions were dreadful. If they weren't blinded by blizzards, the men were blinded by the sun. The terrain was practically impassable, especially as, unlike Amundsen, they were hauling their own heavy supply-sledges rather than using dogs.

Heroic, perhaps, and a massive feat of physical endurance of its own. But it meant they were slow. And getting weaker with every step.

Still they struggled through the bitter cold, and through their own all-consuming exhaustion.

The air was not only cold but strangely damp. It felt like it was freezing their bones. The bleak monotony of their surroundings pummelled their morale: to see nothing but a frozen wasteland in every direction, knowing that there was no warmth or shelter or extra supplies anywhere, must have surely played deadly tricks with their minds.

But they dealt with it. And on 17 January, incredibly, they reached the South Pole. A phenomenal achievement of courage, endurance and sheer bloody-mindedness.

But there was a problem.

'The Pole. Yes,' Scott wrote in his journal, 'but under very different circumstances from those expected.'

To their anguish they saw a small tent mounted with a black flag. They had lost the race. Amundsen had reached the South Pole a full four weeks before them.

It was devastating news to the exhausted men.

Captain Scott's journal for 17 January tells us just what a body blow this discovery was.

> We have had a horrible day. Add to our disappointment a head wind 4 to 5 with a temperature –22 degrees Fahrenheit [–30°C], and companions labouring on with cold feet and hands . . . Great God, this is an awful place!

To have reached the Pole was, of course, a remarkable achievement, but they had no reason to celebrate. They consumed 'a fat Polar hoosh' – a revolting mixture of lard, oatmeal, beef and vegetable protein, salt and sugar – and then they could do no more but apply their exhausted minds and bodies to the business of the epic return journey that awaited them.

If reaching the Pole in second place had been a bitter blow for Scott, he was about to encounter conditions that would make any thought of glory, or of the race, melt away into nothingness.

Scott of the Antarctic was about to encounter hell itself.

*

The story of Scott's retreat from the South Pole has gone down in legend. But the true horror of his final weeks and days is sometimes forgotten. Scott was a proud man, and even in his own journals – which were found perfectly preserved in the snow, months after his death – we can hear his stiff upper lip as he describes the team's deteriorating circumstances.

But you can also sense that stiff upper lip begin to quiver, ever so slightly.

Having borne the crushing disappointment of knowing Amundsen's team had beaten them to the Pole, they faced the morale-sapping knowledge that they now had to drag their gear eight hundred miles back across the ice. Eight hundred miles.

They were now facing months of exhausting, demoralizing hell-hauling through the most unforgiving and harsh expanse of wilderness in the world. Fighting the cold and the wind, across broken, crevasse-ridden glaciers, with not even the promise of glory when they reached the *Terra Nova*. And all on ever-dwindling bare rations.

It's a wonder they survived so long.

As they retreated, they grew tired. And as they grew tired, they started to stumble. Scott damaged his shoulder. Wilson ripped the tendons in his leg. Evans lost his fingernails. They sound like manageable things, but when you haul with your shoulders, march with your legs and handle everything with your fingers, you can see how such extreme conditions magnify small problems a hundredfold.

This was turning into a perilous death march.

On 17 February, a month after they left the Pole, they suffered what Scott referred to as 'a very terrible day'. The conditions were especially bad.

There had been a fresh fall of snow, and the powder clogged up their sledge, making it twice as hard to pull. The sky was overcast. Visibility was poor. One of their number, Edgar Evans, looked to be in a bad way. He was dragging behind. When the team stopped to erect their tent, they saw that Evans was a long way back, so they returned to help him.

They found a man on the brink of madness.

He was on his knees. It looked like he'd tried to tear his clothes off, and his hands were open to the frozen air and completely frostbitten. There was a wild look in his eyes, and his speech was slow and slurred. One of the men thought he must have injured his brain in a fall.

They helped Evans to his feet, but he only managed a couple of steps before collapsing again on to the ice.

There was clearly no way he could walk. The men went to fetch their sledge, then dragged their comatose companion back to the tent. They tried to make him comfortable, but he was past their help.

Edgar Evans died just past midnight. It says something of the state of mind of the others that Scott noted: 'There could not have been a better ending to the terrible anxieties of the past week.'

The remaining four men struggled on. The weather deteriorated still further. So did their snow blindness, their frostbite, their hunger and exhaustion. All these elements got worse every day. Relentlessly. More pain, more hunger, more cold and more exhaustion. Scott knew his men were losing hope.

He forced Wilson, who was carrying lethal doses of morphine and opium, to hand over his supply. He could sense that everyone's thoughts were turning to suicide, but Scott would not allow them that luxury.

No matter how bad things looked, they would carry on.

And they did. Day after day. Through grim pain and with true grit.

Then, one month after Evans's death, disaster struck again.

Captain Oates was failing. He was unable to hide the agonizing pain that every feeble, frostbitten step caused him. He asked the others to leave him to die in his sleeping bag. They could not bring themselves to do it, and they helped him struggle on for another day.

As they made camp that evening, however, it was obvious that for Oates the end was very near.

Oates knew it too. Without him holding the group up, his comrades stood a slim chance of survival. But at the crawl of a pace that Oates could barely maintain, he knew they would all starve and perish.

Oates made it through the night, but awoke to another howling blizzard outside. It was a bridge too far. He turned to his companions and uttered perhaps the most famous last words in history: 'I am just going outside and may be some time.'

He staggered out of the tent, into the white-out, and disappeared.

Now only three men were left: Scott, Wilson and Bowers.

In his journal, Scott said of Oates, 'He has borne intense suffering for weeks without complaint . . . He did not – would not – give up hope till the very end.'

The same could be said of the rest of them. They knew their chances of survival were minuscule. The easiest way out would be to lie down in their sleeping bags and let death take them.

But they refused to do this. They would continue to battle against the worst the wild could throw at them, and they would perish in the attempt.

'We all hope to meet the end with a similar spirit,' Scott wrote, 'and assuredly the end is not far . . .'

The day after Oates's death, Scott's right foot became consumed by frostbite. Still, they struggled on. The rations were now almost negligible. The men were like skeletal ghosts, shuffling, agonizingly slowly, through the blizzard. Running on empty.

They were now close to one of their pre-supplied depots – the infamous one-ton depot. Only 11 miles.

But 11 miles might well have been a thousand in those conditions. The blizzard grew worse.

On 22 March the three men were literally unable to leave their tent because the conditions were so harsh. Scott refused to be bowed. He knew death was near, but was still determined to choose the manner of it: 'It shall be natural – we shall march for the depot with or without our effects and die in our tracks.'

But they didn't march that day. They couldn't. The fierce blizzard and the continuing, howling gale kept them pinned into their tent. And the gale just would not relent.

Another whole week passed. We can only imagine the bitter desolation of those final starving, freezing days as they lay there, stubbornly resisting death, but knowing it was closing in.

We know nothing of Scott's final moments, other than what is written in his last journal entry:

> We shall stick it out to the end, but we are getting weaker, of course, and the end cannot be far. It seems a pity, but I do not think I can write more. For God's sake, look after our people.

It is a mark of the man that his final words were for those loved ones he'd left behind in England.

His body was shutting down. The cruel Antarctic had won. But he'd faced it with total courage and humanity.

\*

As he lay dying in that freezing tent, Scott did not just write in his journal. He also wrote letters to those closest to him, and one stands out in particular, which he dubbed a 'Message to the Public'. This is what he said:

> We took risks, we knew we took them; things have come out against us, and therefore we have no cause for complaint . . . Had we lived, I should have had a tale to tell of the hardihood, endurance and courage of my companions which would have stirred the heart of every Englishman. These rough notes and our dead bodies must tell the tale . . .

But even though he didn't survive, the story of Scott's endurance caught the imagination and won the respect of a nation. He would forever be known as Scott of the Antarctic.

As Robert Baden-Powell, founder of the Scouting movement, said, 'Are Britons going downhill? No! There is plenty of pluck and spirit left in the British, after all. Captain Scott and Captain Oates have shown us that.'

We all need examples and inspirations in our lives, to make us better and stronger. And for me, it is not Scott's successes, failures or flaws that move me. Rather, it's the courage of his final weeks which, as an example of grit, valour and dignity, is hard to surpass.

# ROALD AMUNDSEN: THE GREATEST ANTARCTIC EXPLORER EVER

*'Victory awaits him who has everything in order – people call it luck. Defeat is certain for him who has neglected to take the necessary precautions in time; this is called bad luck.'*

ROALD AMUNDSEN

The Amundsen Sea. The Amundsen Glacier. Amundsen Bay. The Amundsen Basin. The Amundsen Plain. Mount Amundsen.

Any explorer with so many parts of the world named after him has to have been doing something right. This guy even has a crater named after him on the moon!

So what's the big deal? Why is it that the name Amundsen is plastered all over the most hostile parts of our planet, and beyond?

Well, you've read the story of Sir John Franklin and his attempt to find the Northwest Passage. You've read the story of Scott of the Antarctic, and his famous attempt to be the first to reach the South Pole.

The final expeditions of both Franklin and Scott were failures. Glorious failures. Courageous failures. Failures that would mark them down in history as some of the toughest, most resilient explorers ever. But failures all the same.

So it only seems right that a word must remain for the one man who achieved what neither of these men was able to do: to navigate the Northwest Passage *and* be the first to reach the South Pole – and then, of course, to make it back safely.

He is the success to the failures. The yin to the yangs.

Let me introduce you to Amundsen. Roald Amundsen. And he

was, by any measure, one of the greatest, most efficient explorers of all time.

\*

Roald Amundsen was Norwegian. Elsewhere in the book you'll have read about Jan Baalsrud and Thor Heyerdahl, and you'll have found out that Norway has been home to some of the toughest, most extraordinary characters out there. Amundsen was no exception. People called him 'the last of the Vikings', and it was a nickname he cherished.

He was born into a seafaring family, and he always knew that polar exploration was the life for him – so much so that as a young man he used to sleep with the windows open during the bitterly harsh Norwegian winters, in order to acclimatize himself to the life he had chosen.

As a kid, he set himself a goal: to be the first person ever to set foot at the North Pole. 

I like a kid that aims high.

In 1899, he made his first trip to Antarctica as part of the *Belgica* expedition. This was not a trip that went down in history, but it could have done. Even before the explorers reached the Antarctic, they had to plough through storms so terrifying and seas so massive that the freezing cauldron of waves literally swamped the vessel. One of the crew was washed overboard by a crashing wave, and swept to his death.

And then they reached Antarctica.

The *Belgica* expedition was the first to spend an entire winter on the Antarctic ice. They didn't have any option: their ship became trapped in the sea ice and was forced to drift wherever the pack took it. In the total darkness of an Antarctic winter.

The crew certainly weren't prepared for the lonely months of solitude, with scant supplies and the constant fear that the ice might eventually crush the ship. Its hull was stuck fast and the masts and rigging covered in thick frost. Returning alive was looking unlikely, as the ship began to get squeezed.

It was a formidable test of character and resolve for the young Amundsen.

Many of the men went insane through solitude and terror. One of them jumped off the ship and on to the ice, announcing that he was going to walk home to Belgium. Another man died of heart failure. Many became so ill that they started writing their wills.

Scurvy – the bane of an explorer's life – hit the crew. The captain was laid low, so Amundsen and Frederick Cook, the ship's doctor, took command. Crucially, Cook had insisted that they hunt for seals, and had stored their frozen flesh on board. Nobody knew what caused scurvy, but Cook was convinced this seal flesh would do the job, so he fed mouthfuls of the blubber to all the men. Gradually, the scurvy subsided.

But their difficulties weren't over yet.

Winter turned to spring. Daylight returned. But the ice – some of it more than two metres thick – still held the ship fast. If they couldn't loosen their vessel and get out into open water, they would have to spend another winter trapped there. Which would, surely, have killed them all.

Have you ever tried to dig a car out of the snow? Well, try digging a ship out of the Antarctic ice. That's what Amundsen and the others did. They used metal tools and even dynamite to blast their way out, before starting their arduous, nine-month journey home.

The Antarctic had shown that it wasn't a place that welcomed humans – unless you had a strong streak of steel running through you.

But in showing that humans *could* survive over the winter in such a bitter and hostile environment, the expedition set the scene for the great Antarctic exploits of Scott, Mawson and, of course, Amundsen himself.

It also established Amundsen as a great leader, and a master of the ice.

He had taken the first step on his path to greatness.

*

Every explorer worth the name wanted to find the Northwest Passage – that long-sought-after seafaring route across the Arctic Circle between the Atlantic and Pacific. Hundreds of men had died trying to do so, and many people thought such a route was simply not possible.

But in the soul of any great pioneer is a refusal to believe that *anything* is impossible. A refusal to be beaten, no matter how many people have been beaten before you.

Amundsen set out for the Northwest Passage in 1903 with just six other men. They sailed in a small fishing vessel called the *Gjøa*. The *Gjøa* must have looked impossibly tiny stuck in the endless ice of the frozen north, but it turned out to be a smart call. In order to navigate the Northwest Passage, the crew had to pass through very shallow waters. A bigger ship would have run aground.

The *Gjøa* was fitted with a small outboard motor but, even so, the journey took them three long years. During each winter the sea around them froze, and they had to wait for it to thaw sufficiently for the ship to move on. But Amundsen had a plan, and he kept to it. He hugged the coastline and he trusted that patience, in the end, would bring him victory.

He was right. But Amundsen's heroics on that voyage did not end with the successful navigation of the Passage. When the ship hauled anchor on the Pacific Coast of Alaska, Amundsen was eager to send a message back to Norway to let people know that he had completed this amazing endeavour. Trouble was, the nearest telegraph station was 500 miles away.

Amundsen wasn't fazed. He simply donned his skis and travelled the full distance across the ice, then back again to the *Gjøa* once his telegram was sent.

Like I said: he was tough.

He was clever, too. During his travels in the Arctic, he took the time to learn what he could from the indigenous people who lived in the area. He saw how they used dogs to pull their sledges, and how they used animals to keep warm. If you want to know how to survive an extreme environment, you'd better look carefully at the people who have been doing it for hundreds of years.

Amundsen did that. He was a man who liked to prepare, and it would stand him in good stead in the expeditions to come.

Amundsen had ticked the Northwest Passage off his list. But the two great challenges of polar exploration still remained: the North and South Poles. And it was the first of these that Amundsen had always wanted to reach, ever since he was a boy. He turned his sights to the north.

An assault on the North Pole would take careful preparation and substantial financing. It would also take guts – especially to do it in the manner Amundsen planned. His intention was to drift towards the Pole in a ship that had become frozen in the pack ice. But ice can eat a ship up so completely that nothing remains. Amundsen's solution was to use a round-bottomed ship that would be pushed upwards as the ice closed in around it, not crushed by the immense forces.

Would it work? Nobody knew for sure. But Amundsen was willing to give it a shot.

He never got the chance, however. His careful preparations took time, and while Amundsen was hesitating, devastating news reached him: two other explorers – rivals by the name of Frederick Cook (whom Amundsen knew from the *Belgica* expedition) and Robert Peary – had claimed the North Pole.

These claims were disputed, but that didn't seem to matter much to Amundsen. He wasn't the type to play second fiddle to anyone. So, although it must have been a body blow to learn that the achievement he'd set his heart on ever since childhood was not to be his, he immediately turned his sights to the South Pole.

Amundsen was crafty. He knew other men – Scott of the Antarctic, in particular – had their sights on the South Pole. He kept his plans a secret even from those closest to him. Even from the men who were joining him – he only told them the true objective of their expedition a month after they left Norway. And, having set out for the Antarctic eight weeks *after* Scott, he only cabled him at the very last minute to let his rival know that he had competition.

Amundsen and his men reached the Bay of Whales in Antarctica on 14 January 1911. Here, again, we can see the importance of careful planning, and more than a little cunning. Amundsen's Antarctic base was 60 miles closer to the Pole than Scott's. In a race like that, 60 miles could make a critical difference. The Bay of Whales also played host to colonies of penguins and seals. In other words: food. It was one of the few places on the continent where they could live off the land.

Amundsen had done his homework.

Once *in situ* he continued putting into action everything he had learned up until now.

He had enough provisions for two years. He also had almost

one hundred dogs, having noted how the people of the Arctic used those animals to pull their sledges and get around. (The dogs had another advantage – when the going got tough, they could be fed to each other, and also to the men.)

First, though, Amundsen and his men had to overwinter on the Antarctic ice. He knew from his first expedition what a dark, lonely experience that could be. As always, he was well prepared. He kept his men occupied with preparations for the assault on the Pole throughout that long winter, ensuring that they were too busy to let the cold, the dark and the loneliness get to them.

Their days were filled with a strict working routine, starting at 7.30 in the morning and ending at 5 p.m., six days a week. Amundsen had brought with him everything he needed to build a large winter hut for them all to live in. He made sure that their rations were wholesome and tasty – because nothing is likely to hack away at a group's morale more than poor and insufficient food.

He brought thousands of books for them to read. Musical instruments. A gramophone. There is something inspiring about the idea of these rugged men, holed away thousands of miles from civilization, listening to scratchy old records in the freezing darkness.

Amundsen even brought a portable sauna, just big enough for a single man – and once they'd had their sauna, the men had to run naked back across the ice to their hut. Bracing, but exhilarating, in an Antarctic winter!

When August came, the men were in good shape and ready to take on the South Pole. But the Antarctic is wild and unpredictable. Even when they were ready to make a dash for their first depot, and then on to the Pole, the weather took a turn for the worse and pinned them back in their winter hut. It wasn't until September that Amundsen judged it safe enough to set out.

At first, the going was good. They covered 31 miles in three days. However, the following morning they woke to find the temperature had dropped to a breathtaking (literally) 70°F below freezing.

It was so cold that the liquid in their compasses froze solid. Two of the men suffered frostbitten heels.

And two of the dogs froze to death.

It was too dangerous to head any further south. The men returned to the Bay of Whales. But Amundsen was not the type to accept defeat for long.

And his second attempt met with success.

It's often said that Amundsen was blessed with good conditions during his final onslaught to the Pole. That's the kind of thing people who've never been to Antarctica might say. Trust me: *any* conditions in that part of the world are incredibly punishing.

But what Amundsen did was also very smart. He showed careful, considered judgement and incredible leadership. He bided his time. He waited for a break in the weather. He held his nerve, kept his ego in check and, when the moment came, he went for it.

All in.

Heart, soul, grit and determination.

Amundsen, his four companions and more than fifty of their dogs had then to deal with the harsh reality of their endeavour. With the constant threat of hidden crevasses in the ice, and ever steeper, more unforgiving terrain.

On 11 November, a mountain range rose into view across the horizon. Amundsen named these peaks after the Queen of Norway. But, royal or not, these mountains would have to be crossed.

With gritted teeth, the men went for it, urging their dogs onward and managing to carry their ton of provisions to an altitude of 10,000 feet.

Here they shot twenty-four of the dogs. The men skinned them and prepared the meat. It was depressing and unpleasant work. They called this area 'the Butcher's Shop', but this was more than just butchery. They'd grown fond of these dogs, and had no desire to reward them with such a grisly end.

But the dogs were there for a reason: to aid and sustain the men. Amundsen and his team feasted on their meat. They needed all the strength they could get.

They had intended to rest for only two days. In the end they were forced to stay at the Butcher's Shop for four. A terrible blizzard was blowing all around them, but they knew that each day they put off their final push to the Pole was a day lost.

A day's less rations. A day closer to death.

They couldn't hesitate any longer. It was now or never. The time had come to go for it – total commitment. Amundsen and his men stepped out into the ferocious white-out of the blizzard and relentlessly pushed south.

For ten days they forced themselves through the blinding snow. On, into the blind white. Every step was a risk. The icy plateau on which they found themselves was riddled with deadly crevasses, and the swirling fog reduced their visibility down to inches.

They named this the Devil's Glacier.

But the Devil still had yet more dangerous terrain in store for them.

They found themselves on a vast sheet of thin ice. The ice itself resounded with a hollow echo when it was struck: there was a substantial gap beneath the sheet, and under that, a network of deadly deep crevasses.

Amundsen named this the Devil's Ballroom. They skated across it nervously, then continued their dogged march south.

On 14 December 1911 they finally made it. An incredible feat of guts, obsessive planning and meticulous calculations, coupled with bold but smart decisions in the big moments.

They erected the Norwegian flag and pitched their tent – the same tent that, only a few weeks later, would give Scott of the Antarctic visual confirmation of his heroic failure.

And yet, when Amundsen later looked back on that moment, it was with a certain melancholy. 'Never has a man achieved a goal so diametrically opposed to his wishes. The area around the North Pole – devil take it – had fascinated me since childhood, and now here I was at the South Pole. Could anything be more crazy?'

But maybe it's not so crazy, after all. Our lives seldom follow the exact path we might expect, yet sometimes some things seem almost meant to be. And one fact had been abundantly clear for a long time: Roald Amundsen was always going to be the sort of man to achieve the extraordinary.

It just didn't quite turn out how he had always expected.

Amundsen's hunger for adventure was not totally satiated by his conquest of the South Pole. As it always had, his heart led him back to the north. He continued his exploration of the Northwest Passage, and he became increasingly fascinated by air travel. So it was a natural development that he became part of a team that flew across the Arctic – and crucially the North Pole – for the first time.

And here's the thing: all the previous claims to have reached the North Pole by land remain disputed to this day. We still don't know whether Cook and Peary actually reached the Pole. But if – as many people think – they didn't, then it would appear that Amundsen did indeed achieve the goal he'd dreamed of ever since childhood.

He was certainly part of the first *undisputed* team to cross that landmark.

And that just shows us the power of dreams and the often inevitable consequences of hard graft and true grit.

Amundsen was not born a hero. Heroes never are. But he sure died as one. On 18 June 1928, an airship went down in the Arctic, returning from the North Pole. Amundsen was part of the rescue mission.

But the rescue mission never made it.

His plane crashed in the thick Arctic fog. Only bits of it were ever discovered, floating off the Norwegian coast.

Amundsen's body was never found.

A nation mourned him. But it seems to me that maybe it was a fitting death for a man whose life had been devoted to adventure and the exploration of the forbidding extremes.

The frozen wastes of the polar regions had eventually claimed Amundsen's body.

But not before the man had proved himself worthy of the title: the greatest Antarctic explorer of all time.

# DOUGLAS MAWSON: WHITE HELL

'We had discovered an accursed country.
We had found the Home of the Blizzard.'

DOUGLAS MAWSON

S cott. Shackleton. Amundsen.

These are names that history will remember as long as tales of Antarctic exploration are told. But the name of one man has been largely forgotten. That man is Douglas Mawson.

It's a shame, because Mawson was as tough as any of the great Antarctic explorers.

Maybe even tougher.

On the 1908 *Nimrod* expedition Ernest Shackleton sent a party of some of his toughest guys to climb the summit of Mount Erebus. Douglas Mawson was one of those men.

Mount Erebus was the only active volcano in the Antarctic. To an accomplished mountaineer its steep, ice-covered slopes, leading up to a height of 12,448 feet, would have been a significant challenge. But Mawson and his companions were not accomplished mountaineers.

Nor did they have much in the way of equipment – just ice axes and a little mountaineering rope. In place of crampons they poked nails through the strips of leather that they attached to their boots. In place of backpacks they tied their sleeping bags to their backs. They pulled their food on a sledge, ignoring the cold that was so bitter it stuck their socks to their shoes.

Plus, they were in the Antarctic, and if you've read this far you'll know what a punishing place that is.

So you get the picture – hardy, tough men, unwilling to be bowed by a lack of experience, and ready to improvise with what they have. Douglas Mawson was that kind of guy.

While Shackleton made his failed attempt to become the first person to reach the South Pole, Mawson had another objective in mind: to be the first to reach the magnetic South Pole. Along with his companion, Alistair Mackay, he succeeded.

That, in itself, was an incredible achievement on an incredibly dangerous route. The area through which they had to travel was an endless maze of deep and often hidden crevasses. Their team regularly fell into them, but somehow always managed to save themselves – often by throwing out their arms across the narrow spans of those scars in the ice.

They lived off seal meat and penguin, and their lips bled from the cold – Mawson noted that every biscuit he ate became smeared in his own blood.

Frostbite, snow blindness, nausea and fatigue were their constant companions.

But throughout it all Mawson kept his head and, despite the conditions, he made careful notes about his progress. It tells us a lot about him. He was more scientifically minded than his contemporaries Scott and Shackleton. The magnetic South Pole was of more scientific interest than the geographical Pole. It was this that captivated him – not the promise of fame and fortune. He was willing to put his body through month after month of unimaginable hardship – all in the name of science.

And perhaps this is why he turned down the invitation to join Captain Scott's ill-fated *Terra Nova* expedition, preferring instead to lead a more scientific expedition of his own, known as the Australasian Antarctic expedition.

It would lead to one of the most brutal stories of survival you'll ever hear.

*

The Australasian Antarctic expedition lasted from 1911 to 1914. It comprised various teams of explorers, spread out over three different permanent bases across the Antarctic. The idea was that the teams would sit out the unbearably harsh, dark Antarctic winters in these bases. Then, when the warmer weather arrived, they could set out to explore and gather the scientific data that was their aim.

On 12 November 1912 Mawson set out from the camp based at Commonwealth Bay to recce an area of the Antarctic called King George V Land. He took with him two companions: Xavier Mertz and Lieutenant Ninnis. They also had a pack of twelve dogs and two sledges, which carried all the supplies they would need for their journey.

At first, things went well. They had covered more than 300 miles over the polar plateau in the five weeks since they had set out. But then, on 14 December, disaster struck.

Lieutenant Ninnis was driving one of the sledges. It carried the lion's share of the team's supplies, and was being pulled by their six best dogs. Suddenly, and without any warning, Ninnis, the sledge and the dogs fell into an unseen crevasse.

Mawson and Mertz ran to where their teammate had disappeared. For hours they screamed into the dreadful crack in the ice, trying to locate Ninnis. No scream came back.

Just an ominous silence.

They tried to fix a rope to lower themselves into the crevasse and catch sight of their friend. Without success.

As they peered into the void, all they could see were the

smashed-up bodies of two dogs 150 feet below them. And a smattering of their gear, lost for ever.

If Ninnis was still alive – and that seemed unlikely – there was no way they could get to him.

They had no choice but to leave his body there, and try to make it back to base in safety. Minus all of their lost equipment and food.

They took stock of their supplies. Ten days' rations. No dog food. No tent. No ice axe. Vitally important articles of waterproof clothing had also disappeared into the crevasse with Ninnis.

This loss of gear was bad. Very bad.

The guys improvised a very basic tent out of Mertz's skis and a sheet of cotton. There was room inside for two one-man sleeping bags. Just.

But it was minimal protection against the elements, especially the Antarctic elements.

Only six dogs now remained. Mawson and Mertz knew that, for the return journey, they would have to slaughter the animals one by one, to provide food for themselves and for the other dogs.

The dog they'd called 'George' was the first to go. They shot him with their rifle, cooked his tough, stringy meat and devoured it to give them strength. It was, the men decided, 'permeated with a unique and unusually disagreeable flavour'.

The other dogs ate it ravenously.

And so they started their retreat. The 300 miles they had to travel back to base must have seemed impossible. It's thought that they had cyanide tablets in their packs to give them an easy way out if the worst came to the worst.

If they'd known what was to come, they might well have been tempted to take them . . .

*

Mawson was the first to suffer physical symptoms. Two days after Ninnis's death he complained of dreadful pain in the eyes. He diagnosed himself with conjunctivitis, but decided to deal with it the same way they dealt with snow blindness: take some tablets of zinc and cocaine and get your buddy to insert them into the tender jelly under your eyelids. Painful, but necessary.

Suddenly starved, the dogs grew instantly weak. Now the men had to pull their own sledges. When a couple of dogs became too feeble to walk, they killed and skinned them. 'A wretched game,' Mawson wrote in his journal. It can never be fun eating animals that you love and have depended upon so much.

The dogs that remained grew so thin they slipped out of their harnesses. When the men threw them the carcass of one of their pack-mates they devoured the bones and skin till there was nothing left.

Nine days after Ninnis's death Mawson and Mertz decided to reduce the weight of the supplies that remained. This meant discarding, among other things, their rifle. From now on, when they killed a dog, it would have to be with a knife, spilling the howling animal's blood all over the ice. 'A revolting and depressing operation,' Mawson further observed.

It then started snowing. Hard. Zero visibility.

Even worse, the wind started howling. Gales of 50 mph meant the men had to cook in their tiny, cramped, improvised tent. This was a big problem. The heat from the stove melted the snow settling on the cotton sheet, which dripped through on to them.

Their clothes became soaked through, and there was no way to dry them. Being cold and constantly wet is a brutal and morale-sapping situation to deal with. You just get drained of all your strength, and sleep is impossible. There was no respite. Worse still, the small amount of heat the stove gave off also melted the ice underneath their sleeping bags, which duly absorbed the water and became heavy and sodden. Then, when they extinguished the stove, all the soaked-up water immediately froze. Sleeping bags of ice.

They carried on by day, painfully slowly. Mawson watched his partner's physical state get worse.

Mertz couldn't stomach the dog meat. While Mawson nibbled at nutritious lumps of dog liver, Mertz ate nothing but fragments of dry biscuit. It started to show. Mawson could see the skin peeling off his companion's legs – a symptom of malnutrition. It left glistening raw flesh below.

Mertz's fingers became frostbitten. In shock, he bit a chunk off one end of his finger. He felt nothing. His body was dying.

After three weeks, Mertz could barely get out of his icy sleeping bag. He could only manage to eat small amounts of the powdered baby food they had among their scant rations.

Mawson persuaded his friend to sit on one of the sledges while he pulled. It was that or leave him. Mertz reluctantly agreed, and Mawson hauled. But then Mertz's condition grew worse. He contracted dysentery and would soil his own pants. Mawson was forced to scoop out by hand the foul, watery faeces from his companion's sodden clothes.

Mawson himself was also deteriorating. The damp conditions in their tent, combined with the relentless marching and malnutrition, meant that his skin also started to peel away, especially between the legs where there was much chafing. Agony. And because he was so undernourished, the skin that grew in its place was, as he put it, 'a very poor, undernourished substitute'.

His hair and skin would readily peel away and collect at the bottom of his trousers and in his socks. He had to scrape it out in great, stinking clumps.

By 7 January Mertz was continually soiling his pants with his own malodorous, malnourished watery waste.

He was suffering from fits, and shrieking with delirium.

The end was clearly near.

He died at two in the morning on 8 January.

Mawson buried his body in the snow, read out loud from his *Book of Common Prayer*, and left his friend's body to the harsh Antarctic elements.

Then he turned his attention to himself.

Ten days' rations had lasted twenty-six days. He was now desperately weak. His body was giving out on him. And he still had 100 miles to go.

He knew he was probably going to die. But he wrote this note in his journal: 'I shall do my upmost to the last.'

For two days Mawson couldn't move. The wind was too bad, the snow drifting.

Whenever his skin now broke, it didn't heal. He had sores and cuts all over his nose and lips. The skin on his scrotum had totally peeled away because of the chafing from trudging in wet clothes.

When he finally got moving, he was forced to stop after only a mile because his feet were in agony. He removed his socks to find that the entire soles of his feet had completely peeled away. The socks themselves had become soaked with blood and a watery discharge.

Mawson didn't know what to do. Surely he couldn't walk on suppurating raw flesh. He had to treat his feet somehow. He smeared the raw, bleeding tissue with fatty lanoline – a waxy substance you strip from sheep's wool – then lay the peeled-off skin back against the soles to protect them. He bound them with bandages, and put his socks back on. And then, gritting his teeth against the dreadful pain on the gruesome sandwiches of skin, blood and fat that his feet had become, he continued to walk.

The next night, Mawson found he had forgotten to wind his watch. He needed to know the exact time to calculate his longitude. Now he couldn't even do that.

Not only was his body breaking down but now, to heap fire on burning coals, he was also lost.

Still he carried on.

After one gruelling day's march he boiled up some dog sinews to make an 'extra supper of jelly soup'. That he found this such a great treat tells us something about his condition. Each day he had to dress his fetid, weeping feet. It was true agony – like torturing yourself, for hours at a time.

Then a few hours later he would have to start moving again.

The Antarctic was throwing everything it had at him – but it hadn't yet delivered its final sucker punch.

It happened just before noon on 17 January. Mawson was dragging the sledge behind him, using a rope harnessed to his body, when he felt the ice collapse beneath his feet. He had stepped on a thin ice bridge over a crevasse.

The opening was six feet wide – which meant there was nothing to hang on to.

He plunged downwards.

Sometimes, in a survival situation, the only thing that will save you is a little bit of luck. On this occasion Mawson's luck held.

He fully expected the sledge to follow him down into the crevasse, sending them both into freefall. But it didn't. It miraculously became lodged in the snow above him.

But Mawson was now hanging there, dangling in the void. Helpless. Above him, 14 feet of rope. Below him, a bottomless expanse of black.

His only way out was to haul his exhausted body up the rope.

Have you ever tried to climb up a thin rope unaided? It's hard, almost impossible work. But imagine what it's like in sub-zero temperatures, suffering from acute malnutrition, with the skin peeling away from your body and hands, with barely any strength left in your muscles. Plus, of course, being weighed down by heavy, wet clothing.

Shaking from fear, cold and loneliness, Mawson then embarked on the impossible. And he resolutely refused to die.

Mawson started hauling himself bit by bit up the rope, inching himself up towards the lip of the crevasse.

He was only one foot from the opening when there was a sickening crack. Then the lip of the crevasse broke away.

Mawson fell down back into the blackness once again. Once more he was dangling – at the mercy of the rope and the sledge.

He described this as his lowest moment – and his hardest battle. He considered ending it there. He could just loosen himself from the harness and fall to his death into the void. And end this suffering. Finally.

He found his fingers drifting towards the harness. He was almost looking forward to the peace that death would bring.

He wasn't just fighting a battle with his body. He was fighting it with his mind too.

But Mawson had more grit than most normal human beings, and he refused to give in to his despair. With a superhuman effort he struggled, again, inch by agonizing inch, up the rope.

This time he made it.

He fell unconscious on the side of the crevasse, spent. Finally he awoke, numb with cold.

'Never has anyone more miraculously escaped,' he later wrote.

Mawson had cheated death, but death was still on his tail.

His body continued to deteriorate. Festering sores broke out everywhere. Boils erupted across his face. His nails then started to fall out, and so did his hair. His beard now came away in great clumps from his face. The detached skin he had sandwiched on to the soles of his feet had shrivelled up and was rotting. He discarded the useless flaps of flesh, but now had to walk on the raw, oozing pads that were once his feet.

He then contracted scurvy. His joints ached as if on fire. Watery blood dribbled from his nose and wept from the ends of his fingers.

The ice was so bullet-hard and marble-smooth that he was forced to try to improvise some form of makeshift crampons from the meagre supplies he had on the sledge. When these failed, he simply crawled on his bleeding hands and knees, hauling the sledge behind him.

The weather didn't relent. Gale-force winds. Driving snow. And the dreaded cold. He was stuck in the heart of the blizzard. But still he kept going.

Finally, on 8 February, two months after Ninnis had fallen into the crevasse, he reached the expedition base camp.

The men back at base had long ago given Mawson and his men up for dead. When they saw a figure emerging from the snow, they ran towards him.

Three men had set out the previous November. But now, because of the state of Mawson's disintegrating body, they had no idea which one of the three was staggering towards them.

Mawson then had to stick out another long, dark winter in the Antarctic. He'd arrived back at base only hours after the ship

*Aurora*, which could have taken him back to civilization, had set sail. Killer timing.

He was, however, able to send a message back to his fiancée in Australia. A short message, but one so understated it could only have been written by one of those epic heroes of the age of Antarctic exploration.

There was no complaint or self-pity. No mention of the horrors he'd just been through.

'Deeply regret delay,' it read. 'Only just managed to reach hut.'

Now there's a quiet, humble, grit-filled hero.

# ERNEST SHACKLETON: 'THE MOST PIGHEADED, OBSTINATE BOY I EVER CAME ACROSS'

*'Men wanted for hazardous journey. Small wages, bitter cold, long months of complete darkness, constant danger, safe return doubtful. Honour and recognition in case of success.'*

ADVERTISEMENT PLACED IN THE TIMES

BY ERNEST SHACKLETON

S cott of the Antarctic was an awesomely brave guy. No question. And the men who accompanied him were pretty uncompromising too.

On Scott's first trip to the Antarctic, on board the ship *Discovery*, another young man was present who would join him in the ranks of the great explorers. Possibly the greatest. He too had gone to sea at a young age. One of his captains described him as 'the most pigheaded, obstinate boy I ever came across'.

He probably didn't mean it as a compliment, but it's worth remembering that where some people see pigheadedness and obstinacy, others see true grit.

This young man accompanied Scott on that first trek across Antarctica, braving the treacherous conditions that the polar region threw at them, and was part of the team that successfully reached further south than any man had previously journeyed. He deserves proper respect for that feat alone.

But this young man went further. And his epic adventures culminated in one of the most amazing rescues and survival escapes in history. His name was Ernest Shackleton, and he was one of the toughest and most inspirational leaders the world has ever known.

*

Captain Scott's *Discovery* expedition made Shackleton very ill. Hardly surprising. All three men who made the trek south suffered from frostbite, snow blindness and scurvy. But Shackleton suffered the most. When they got back to the *Discovery* he was sent home early. Some people say that he and Scott fell out over this, but nobody really knows the truth.

What is sure, however, is this: whereas many people would have been put off by the harshness of that expedition, Shackleton, like Scott, had been bitten by the Antarctic bug.

Back in Britain he tried to make a life for himself, first as a journalist, then as a businessman, and even as an MP. But he had the soul of an adventurer. These conventional professions were not for him.

Shackleton needed danger in his life. And he knew that if danger was what he wanted, then the Antarctic was the place to find it in abundance.

He headed back there in 1908, this time as leader of his own expedition aboard his own ship: *Nimrod*.

Even before they reached the Antarctic, Shackleton's crew faced difficulties. One of his men caught a metal hook in his eye. He was taken, bleeding and howling, to the ship's doctor, who declared that the eye had to be removed. And so it was: the patient was pinned down by two of his shipmates while the doctor gouged out the damaged eye with the help of only a lungful of chloroform.

Such were the realities those early Antarctic explorers had to endure.

The purpose of the *Nimrod* expedition was to be the first to reach the South Pole. But first, in order to keep the men on his expedition active, he ordered a small team to scale Mount Erebus.

If you've read the chapter on Sir John Franklin (see page 279), the name Erebus will be familiar. It was the name of one of his ships that got consumed by the Arctic ice. This Antarctic mountain was named after that ship, which was in turn named after a

Greek god of the Underworld. A huge, threatening, snow-clad volcano rising up out of the Antarctic ice, it suits its name. It's 12,500 feet high, and had never been climbed.

One of the men Shackleton sent up Erebus was Douglas Mawson. It took Shackleton's men five days to reach the summit, before practically sliding all the way back down. When they reached their base camp they were, according to one of the men, 'nearly dead'.

But they still had their journey south to consider. And they were all eager to follow their leader into the unknown.

Shackleton didn't reach the South Pole, but he and his men did beat the record of the *Discovery* expedition for the furthest south a man had ever trod. As Scott would find out for himself a few years later, their journey back to base – after seventy-three days of heading south – would prove almost unendurably harsh.

They marched on half rations, dragging their own sledges. Along with the usual Antarctic ailments, they were struck down with severe enteritis after eating spoiled pony meat. They suffered chronic dysentery – never fun in the frozen wastelands – and Shackleton himself was a physical wreck. He didn't let that slow him down, however – and the more his body deteriorated, the harder he marched. Near starvation, he even donated some of his rations to his flagging teammates.

He was showing himself to be a man who led from the front – always.

When Shackleton finally returned to Britain he received a knighthood and a hero's welcome. But it was not the *Nimrod* expedition – awesome though it was – that assured him a place in the history of exploration.

That accolade would come five years later, when he set sail for the Antarctic once more, this time in a ship named *Endurance*.

The name was truly apt for what lay ahead.

*

1914.

Captain Scott, by now, was dead. Amundsen had reached the South Pole. War was breaking out in Europe. But the Antarctic still called to Shackleton.

There was, in his opinion, only one more great Antarctic expedition to be completed: to cross the entire continent, from one edge to the other.

That, Shackleton decided, was the expedition with his name on it.

The *Endurance* set sail from Plymouth in August 1914. Its first destination was Buenos Aires, which it reached without any problems. From there it sailed to South Georgia, where Shackleton would prepare for his next battle with the Antarctic.

As they sailed south the omens were bad. They reached floating pack ice earlier than expected, and had to negotiate their way through half-frozen water as thick as setting concrete, which gave off great clouds of sinister frozen mist. Around them were holes, some as wide as 25 feet, where killer whales had smashed through the underside of the ice to find food.

Eventually, on 19 January 1915, *Endurance* became fully trapped by the thickening ice.

The men stayed on board for month . . . after month . . . after month. But the ship, strong though it was, was simply no match for the sheer, awesome power of the grinding ice. Little by little it began to break up. Giant oak timbers were steadily crushed and wrenched apart into matchsticks before the men's eyes.

On 27 October, it sank. Their way home, their ticket to freedom, was gone for ever. The men were totally alone, with no communications and no means of escape.

The men – twenty-eight of them – decamped on to the ice, along with three small rowing boats and the stores that they could rescue from the sinking *Endurance*. Their plan was to drag all this gear across the ice, towards open water. But it soon became clear that this was impossible for the exhausted, frozen men. So Shackleton made a different call. They would camp on the ice in the hope that it would drift north and take them towards safety.

It did drift north. Slowly. But they certainly weren't safe.

Provisions ran frighteningly low. They caught and killed seals to bolster their meagre supplies. They also had dogs with them. At first they kept them alive by feeding them seal meat. But as the seal meat grew scarce, they had to shoot the dogs, and eat them, in order to survive.

As the ice moved further from Antarctica, the seas grew warmer, and the ice started to break up. It was no longer safe for them to camp upon it. At one point, one of the men fell into the sea after the ice floe they were on split in half. He had to march around the remaining small floe all night, in soaking gear, in order to avoid freezing to death.

The men now had no choice but to climb into their boats and start to row.

They were at sea for five days before, utterly drenched and exhausted, they landed on a deserted stretch of barren rock called Elephant Island. It was the first time they'd stepped on to solid ground for sixteen months, and at first they were ecstatic to have reached land.

Their delight didn't last for long.

Elephant Island: population, zero. Temperature: sub-zero. It was as remote and windswept an outcrop as it is possible to imagine. A blip in the middle of the mighty and violent Southern Ocean. And many, many hundreds of miles from any civilization.

Shackleton's team had escaped the danger of the disintegrating ice, but their new home was harsh beyond belief. Living off the land was extremely difficult – they found a few seals and penguins, which they slaughtered for food and to provide fuel for their blubber stove, and they gathered whatever shellfish they could scavenge. But they were weak, and knew they couldn't survive long without help. No ships ever ventured into this area. The nearest place they could get help was at the whaling stations back on South Georgia.

That was 800 miles away.

But Shackleton wasn't going to let his men die on this bleak island.

He decided to go for broke.

Shackleton's decision was to take one of their little boats and a few of his strongest men and set sail in the vain hope of navigating and surviving his way across the coldest, most violent ocean on the entire planet – with the goal of reaching South Georgia.

It was a crazily ambitious plan, with almost no chance of success.

The rowing boat *James Caird* was the best of their small craft, but at only seven metres long and two metres wide it was no *Endurance*. They modified it to make it a little stronger, and made an improvised deck out of a sheet of canvas that would give them some scant protection from the Antarctic sea and storms. They would need fresh water, so they loaded 250 pounds of ice on to the boat that they could melt as they went along.

But as Shackleton and five of his crew prepared to leave the main party and set sail once more, they knew, deep down, that the little *James Caird* could not survive the harsh Southern Ocean for long. They packed only enough supplies for four weeks at sea. It was all they could carry. And with that they cast off the rock of

Elephant Island, wondering if they would ever see each other again.

The likelihood was not.

Make no mistake: the Southern Ocean is not for the faint-hearted, even in an ocean liner. You get waves 100 feet high. They either slam you back down into a trough with heart-stopping force, or they curl over and cover you completely. Shackleton's diary records many a terrifying moment:

> I called to the other men that the sky was clearing, and then a moment later I realized that what I had seen was not a rift in the clouds but the white crest of an enormous wave. During twenty-six years' experience of the ocean in all its moods I had not encountered a wave so gigantic. It was a mighty upheaval of the ocean, a thing quite apart from the big white-capped seas that had been our tireless enemies for many days. I shouted, 'For God's sake, hold on! It's got us.'

Somehow, the crew held on and survived these monster waves. But the ocean had other weaponry to throw at them.

It was so cold that the spray froze as it hit the hull and crashed over the boat, turning it into a lopsided, floating ice cube. The men continually had to hack the ice away to stop it capsizing the small craft.

Their only source of warmth was their wet sleeping bags. These were constantly drenched through, and often frozen – so much so that they had to throw two of them overboard.

Their skin – which had not been washed for months – was constantly cold, wet and raw from their sodden woollen clothes. The relentless salt water on that chafed skin worsened their weeping sores by the day.

Their exposed fingers became covered with massive blisters and frostbite.

They ate only the most frugal of rations, and had to draw on untold reserves of energy to battle with everything the Southern Ocean was throwing at them.

\*

Despite these unbelievable hardships, Shackleton and his men managed to navigate their tiny vessel to South Georgia – a feat of extraordinary and unsurpassed navigational skill in such a small boat, over so many hundreds of miles. Eventually, after fifteen days of hellish seafaring, the island loomed into view across the angry, dark sea. But their journey was still not over.

A storm with freezing hurricane-force ferocity blew up – it was strong enough, they later learned, to sink a massive whaling steamer ship in the vicinity. If the *James Caird* approached the island, it would be smashed to bits against the rocks in the huge swell.

But just to keep afloat in the open sea was a massive struggle in itself. The crew manned the oars and fought the sea for two days, before finally locating a small inlet on the southern part of the island where they could attempt to land.

Trouble was, the southern part of South Georgia was completely uninhabited.

The whaling stations were all to the north.

Between the whaling stations and Shackleton's men was an almost impossible 36-mile trek over snow- and ice-covered mountains and glaciers, reaching 4,500 feet high, which had never been crossed before.

Shackleton knew what he had to do.

He left the three weakest men behind, taking with him two of the most experienced mountaineers. Together they set out across the mountain range. To do or die. One final, monumental push.

It would be almost thirty years before anybody braved this range again. When they did, they expressed utter disbelief that Shackleton had managed it with nothing in the way of mountaineering equipment, no supplies and very little in the way of experience. But that's what makes Shackleton unique. 'Impossible' was not a word he believed in.

To battle up and over those mountains would have been epic at the best of times. To do it in the starved, frozen, injured and weakened condition they were in, was beyond belief.

When night fell, they allowed themselves a few moments to sit down and rest. They wrapped their arms round each other for warmth, and, almost instantly, Shackleton's two companions fell asleep out of sheer and utter exhaustion. But Shackleton himself knew that if he drifted off as well, then, more than likely, they all would die of exposure and cold. They would never wake up.

So, after only a few minutes, he roused his companions and forced them to keep marching.

He told them that they had slept for a few hours and it was now time to push on.

For thirty-six hours solid they continued over those windswept, frozen peaks until, finally, and almost beyond the limits of human endurance, they reached the Stromness whaling station.

The job was not yet finished. First Shackleton had to collect the three men he had left on the southern coast of South Georgia. He did this safely.

But then, of course, there were the twenty-two men still stranded on Elephant Island.

*

Life for the men left behind on Elephant Island had been almost unbearably harsh. When the food ran out, they were reduced to living off the occasional penguin they managed to catch. When the penguins stopped coming ashore, they had to dig up old seal bones and boil them with seaweed.

They started to joke, grimly, that they would have to eat the meat of the first of them to die. Deep down, they all knew that might soon become a very real possibility.

They drank teaspoons of methylated spirit to keep them warm. When one of them suffered frostbite on his toes, the ship's surgeons had to amputate them using only a little chloroform and their blubber stove for light.

Things were getting desperate. They could only pray that Shackleton had not abandoned them. That he and his party had somehow, miraculously, made it.

Shackleton tried three times to set sail to rescue the remainder of his men. Three times he was stopped by the ferocity of the unforgiving Southern Ocean and the Antarctic ice. But he never gave up. If the boats they had in South Georgia weren't up to the job, he'd just have to find one that was. He approached the Chilean government, who gave him the use of a navy tug called the *Yelcho*. And on 30 August, using this ship, he set sail for Elephant Island.

When he finally reached his stricken crew, he found that every one of the twenty-two men he had left there was still alive. Now, having risked his life and gone through hell in order to save them, their leader had returned.

His word was his bond.

*

Shackleton had left Britain in 1914 in the firm belief that the war would be over in six months. It wasn't, of course. His countrymen were dying in their thousands.

There is a cruel irony, though, to Shackleton's story. Within months of returning to Britain, a substantial number of the brave survivors of the *Endurance* expedition were killed on the front line. They had survived their Antarctic hell, only to die in the quagmire of the trenches.

Shackleton survived the Great War, but the Antarctic has a way of keeping you in its grasp. And, despite the dangers and hardships he had faced there before, he planned another expedition, with the goal of circumnavigating the Antarctic in 1921. He left England and arrived at South Georgia in 1922.

But Shackleton was to go no further. He suffered a massive, fatal heart attack, and remains buried there to this day.

Laid to rest in a desolate, lonely grave, surrounded by sea and the mountains, the place not only of his greatest achievements, but of one of the greatest survival escapes in the history of exploration.

# FURTHER READING

For those of you who've been moved by these stories and want to delve a little deeper, each of these books has been a huge source of inspiration to me. I hope they will be for you too.

Ash, William *Under the Wire* (Bantam Press, 2005)

Braddon, Russell *Nancy Wake: SOE's Greatest Heroine* (The History Press, 2009)

Callahan, Steven *Adrift: 76 Days Lost at Sea* (Mariner Books, 2002)

Harrer, Heinrich *The White Spider* (Harper Perennial, 2005)

Heyerdahl, Thor *In the Footsteps of Adam* (Little, Brown, 2000)

Heyerdahl, Thor *Kon-Tiki* (Simon and Schuster, 2013)

Howarth, David *We Die Alone* (Macmillan, 1955)

King, Dean *Skeletons on the Zahara* (William Heinemann, 2004)

Koepcke, Juliane *When I Fell from the Sky* (Nicholas Brealey Publishing, 2012)

Luttrell, Marcus with Robinson, Patrick *Lone Survivor* (Little, Brown, 2007)

Macpherson, Sir Tommy with Bath, Richard *Behind Enemy Lines: the Autobiography of Britain's Most Decorated Living War Hero* (Mainstream, 2010)

Moon, Chris *One Step Beyond* (Macmillan, 1999)

Parrado, Nando *Miracle in the Andes* (Orion, 2006)

Ralston, Aron *127 Hours: Between a Rock and a Hard Place* (Simon and Schuster, 2004)

Roberts, David *Alone on the Ice: the Greatest Survival Story in the History of Exploration* (W.W. Norton & Company, 2013)

Simpson, Joe *Touching the Void* (Vintage, 1997)

Urquhart, Alistair *The Forgotten Highlander* (Little, Brown, 2010)

Zamperini, Louis with Rensin, David *Devil at my Heels: a World War II Hero's Epic Saga of Torment, Survival and Forgiveness* (HarperCollins, 2009)

O Joy that seekest me through pain,
I cannot close my heart to thee;
I trace the rainbow through the rain,
And feel the promise is not vain,
That morn shall tearless be.

– GEORGE MATHESON

# PICTURE ACKNOWLEDGEMENTS

Every effort has been made to trace the copyright holders of photos reproduced in the book. Copyright holders not credited are invited to get in touch with the publishers.

6: survivors of the crash of Uruguayan Air Force Flight 571 in the Andes greeting their rescuers, 23 December 1972: SIPA/Rex Features.

20: Juliane Koepke revisits the scene of the crash of LANSA Flight 508 in 2000: © Werner Herzog Film.

34: John McDouall Stuart, engraving, 1865: Granger Collection/TopFoto.

48: James Riley, engraved frontispiece from his book, *An Authentic Narrative of the Loss of the American Brig Commerce, Wrecked on the Western Coast of Africa, in the Month of August, 1815...,* 1817.

62: Steven Callahan: courtesy Steven Callahan, author of *Adrift, Seventy-Six Days Lost at Sea.*

76: Thor Heyerdahl climbing the mast of *Kon-Tiki,* June 1947: Getty Images.

90: Jan Baalsrud, May 1954: Associated Newspapers/Rex Features.

106: Louis Zamperini climbing out of his bombardier hatch, January 1943: © Bettmann/Corbis.

120: Alistair Urquhart as a young soldier: Fotopress, Dundee.

132: Nancy Wake, June 1945: AP/Press Association Images.

146: Tommy Macpherson when with 11 Comando: © National Museums of Scotland.

160: Bill Ash, 1941: photo from *Under the Wire* courtesy Bill Ash.

174: Edward Whymper in climbing gear, mid-1860s: Getty Images.

186: George Mallory (left) and Andrew Irvine at base camp in Nepal preparing to climb the peak of Everest, June 1924: AP/Press Association Images.

198: Toni Kurz, shortly before the accident, July 1936 and hanging from a rope, 23 July 1936.

212: Pete Schoening climbing the Lighthouse Tower in the Cascade Mountains, Washington, 1949: Bob and Ira Spring Photographers.

224: Joe Simpson climbing in the Peak District, April 1989: Time & Life Pictures/Getty Images.

238: Chris Moon running the Badwater 135 ultra-marathon in Death Valley, 15 July 2013: Getty Images.

252: Marcus Luttrell, Afghanistan: US Navy Photo.

266: Aron Ralston revisits Canyonlands National Park, September 2010: Fox Searchlight/Everett/Rex Features.

280: Sir John Franklin, 1845: Scott Polar Research Institute, University of Cambridge.

292: Captain Robert Falcon Scott during the Depot Laying Journey to the Great Barrier, 1911: Popperfoto/Getty Images.

306: Roald Amundsen, *c.* 1911: Getty Images.

320: Douglas Mawson, on a later more successful expedition to Antarctica, claiming Proclamation Island for the Crown, January 1930: Popperfoto/Getty Images.

334: Ernest Shackleton, 1908: Getty Images.

# INDEX